Praise for *The Way of Boys*

"Parents are often overwhelmed when struggling with the behavior of growing boys. Dr. Anthony Rao provides the kind of customized wisdom that comes from decades of clinical practice and—most important—success for boys at home and at school. This book is an invaluable contribution for those families in need."

—Jerome Groopman, M.D.,
Racanati professor, Harvard Medical School;
author of *How Doctors Think*

"This book offers clear understanding of the various and varied ways boys grow and develop into healthy, well-adjusted adults. Many of the modern obstacles to this development—and the parental confusion they cause—fall away after one reads Dr. Rao's compassionate, specific, problem-solving book." —Michael Gurian,
author of *The Purpose of Boys*

"*The Way of Boys* is the ideal book for parents eager to understand what is going on in the minds and bodies of their young sons. It will allow them to fully understand normal boy development, in all its guts and glory, and show the way to the other side where a happy, healthy boy awaits." —Edward M. Hallowell, M.D.,
author of *The Childhood Roots of Adult Happiness*

"We are robbing boys of their normal developmental struggles. [Rao] presents his case with solid research, humor, and a strongly worded style that most educators need to hear. . . . Bravo, Rao."

—*Library Journal*

The Way *of* Boys

Protecting the Social and Emotional
Development of Young Boys

ANTHONY RAO, Ph.D.
and Michelle Seaton

HARPER

NEW YORK • LONDON • TORONTO • SYDNEY

HARPER

A hardcover edition of this book was published in 2009 by William Morrow, an imprint of HarperCollins Publishers.

HarperCollins books may be purchased for educational, business, or sales promotional use. For information please write: Special Markets Department, Harper-Collins Publishers, 10 East 53rd Street, New York, NY 10022.

FIRST HARPER PAPERBACK PUBLISHED 2010.

Designed by Renato Stanisic

The Library of Congress has catalogued the hardcover edition as follows:

Rao, Anthony.
  The way of boys : raising healthy boys in a challenging and complex world / Anthony Rao and Michelle Seaton. — 1st ed.
      p. cm.
  Includes bibliographical references and index.
  ISBN 978-0-06-170782-7
  1. Boys—United States—Life skills guides. 2. Boys—United States—Conduct of life. 3. Parenting—United States. 4. Child development—United States. I. Seaton, Michelle D. II. Title.
HQ775.R36 2009
649'.132—dc22   2009004900

ISBN 978-0-06-170783-4 (pbk.)

14 OV/RRD 10 9 8 7 6 5

In memory of my father, Sonny, who showed me how to be strong and kind
—A.R.

For my family
—M.S.

Contents

1 Your Problem Is Spelled B-O-Y 1
Faster Pace Equals Higher Demands; Other Contributing Factors;
He's Just a Boy

2 Little Girls Aren't Like This 17
The Machine; Systems Approach; Differing Responses to Stress

3 He Doesn't Have Any Friends 29
Almost Every Boy Is Normal; Social Skills at Play; What's His Style
of Play?; Action Leads to Talk; Encouraging Emotional Awareness; Why Is
He Playing Alone?; Socializing in School; Attachment and Separation;
Separation Anxiety

4 He's a Bully 49
Impulse Control; Practicing Boundaries at Home; Reading Social Cues;
Sharing and Turn Taking; Empathy; Boys Are Empathetic Late Bloomers;
What Are Appropriate Social Skills for Young Boys?; Bullying at School:
How to Deal with the Bullying Label; What Is a Bully?; Why Is He Doing
This?; Strategies for Containing Behavior at School; Setting Reminders;
Practicing Calm; Be Patient

5 He Won't Sit Still! 75
*Energy to Burn; Signs That He's Not Moving Enough; Activities
for Younger Boys; Activities for Older Boys; The Myth of Team Sports;
Shouldn't He Learn to Sit Still?; Practicing Sitting Still; Get Outside;
Causes of Movement*

6 He Runs the Household 93
*What's Wrong with Time-outs?; Take It Away; Detention: The New
Time-out; Time-Away Is Better Than Time-out; What if He Won't
Stay Put?; Wild Things; It's Not Just a Punishment; Diana's Story;
The Long View*

7 He Has to Win, or Else 107
*What Is Competition Good For?; Age-Appropriate Games; Keep It Fun;
How Boys Learn About Winning and Losing; The First Loss; Losing
Gracefully—or Not at All; The Battle Against Disappointment; Cheating
Is Developmental; What About Athletic Games?; Older Boys Who Struggle
with Competition*

8 He Wants to Be the Bad Guy 127
*What's Good About Being Bad?; Role Playing; Violent Toys; How Much
Is Too Much?; How to Join In; Rules for Joining In; How to Set Limits;
When He Crosses the Line; Why Consequences Work; He's Not Ready;
When He Obsesses; The Link Between Bad Guys and Fear; Bad
Boy Play Long Term*

9 He's Suddenly Fragile 147
*Growing Up Isn't Easy; He Wants to Be the Best; He Won't Leave My
Side; The Empathy Check; Where Have I Seen This Before?; I Hate
You; The Mini-Manipulator; Learning Self-Talk; An Anger Plan;
Give Him Headlines*

10 He Hates School 163
*Why School Isn't a Good Fit; Boosting His Behavior at School;
The Short Course in Behavioral Adjustment; Making Home More Like*

School; Relating to the Teacher; Practice Adult Empathy First; Making the Home–School Connection; Talking to Your Son; Take the Direct Approach at Home; Labels Aren't Always the Answer; Techniques for Home and Classroom; Keep the Relationship Positive; Problems Are Often Situational; The Pressure to Fix It; The End of Summer

11 The Teacher Thinks He Needs Testing 195
When Is Testing Helpful?; When Is Testing Not Useful?; When Testing Goes Awry; What's an IEP, Anyway?; Ignore Diagnostic Language; If They Say Your Son Needs Testing; Listen Even if You Don't Agree; Know Your Own Style; The Parent-Teacher Conference; Keep Track of What's Said; Updates from Home; Communication Breakdown; Intervention-Style Meetings; Practice Moderation; But I Don't Want Him Tested; Useful Accommodations; When to Refuse Accommodations; Changing Schools; Getting More Support and Help

12 He Has Already Been Labeled 223
The Criteria of a Symptom; Tracking His Behavior—Is It a Real Problem?; What Are the Tests?; Other Tests You May Encounter; What's the Rush?; What a Diagnosis Fails to Say; Get a Second Opinion; Medication; Sadness and Anxiety; What About Placebo Effects?

13 What Will He Be Like as a Grown Man? 243
Brett—the Boy in Charge; Kenny—Mr. Inflexible; Ben— the Worrier; Ronny—Mr. Meltdown; Some Final Thoughts

Acknowledgments 267
References 269
Index 281

The Way *of* Boys

Your Problem Is Spelled B-O-Y

Sandy stood in my office on the verge of tears. Her four-year-old son, Tommy, had recently been kicked out of preschool after slapping a teacher and throwing a toy, which hit another child in the face. Before Sandy could even hand me the packet of information containing the results of Tommy's testing and school materials, he had climbed aboard a swivel chair, reclined it, and stood on top of it like a surfer. He ignored her pleas to get down. Sandy apologized to me, and I could see that her days were filled with anxiety about what her son might do next and how others might perceive him. She was constantly vigilant and miserable and very worried about her son.

Sandy and I managed to engage Tommy with LEGOs, and then I listened to the details of her story. Sadly, it's one I've heard over and over again in my practice. After asking Sandy to withdraw her son from preschool, the director of that school told Sandy and her husband that Tommy wasn't developing normally. She told them that Tommy had trouble transitioning from one activity to another because he was either too engrossed or too bored. He would have tantrums and throw things or bother the other kids at craft time. The director referred them to a specialist who treats young children for developmental disorders. After a quick twenty-minute appointment in which Sandy completed one behavioral checklist, the doctor announced that Tommy had ADHD, or attention deficit/hyperactivity disorder. "He's going to struggle with this long term," the doctor said. "This is a lifelong issue. The earlier we treat it, the better." He handed Sandy a prescription for Ritalin.

"I don't want to give him pills," she said.

The doctor didn't seem to be listening. "I've had good luck with this in the past," he said. "Let's see how he does on it before we decide."

Sandy left that doctor's office in tears, feeling that she had no choice but to go along with his treatment plan.

Luckily, Sandy's next move was to reach out for some help, in this case a second opinion. Through word of mouth, she had heard that, over the past twenty years, first at Children's Hospital/Harvard Medical School and then in my own practice, Behavioral Solutions, I'd become known as a psychologist who treats young boys who are struggling, without relying solely on medication. I looked at Tommy's packet and was not surprised by anything I saw in it. The school reports and the specialist's checklist could justify a diagnosis of ADHD, but that isn't saying much. It's an easy diagnosis to hand out. Worse, in order to give that diagnosis, a clinician would have to ignore the other glaring possibility: there was absolutely nothing wrong with this boy. It was possible, and in my view probable, that Tommy was experiencing nothing more than a developmental glitch.

First of all, the fact that Tommy is having trouble in preschool is not surprising, nor is it an indication of a fundamental problem. There is an entire subset of boys who are not ready for circle time, for rigid transitions, for following complex directions or listening to a lot of talk until well past their sixth birthdays. The problem isn't the boys, it's our expectations of them.

Moreover, I told Sandy that in six months or so Tommy would be a completely different little boy from the one careening around my office. I told her that it was likely that the areas of his brain that control impulses were developing more slowly in him than in his peers. But I also told her that there was no evidence in the behavioral checklist that this would be a problem for him in the long run. My aim was to convince Sandy to stop worrying, to buy Tommy some time. In six months, he would likely be more settled, more able to concentrate, more verbal. Six months after that, he would be even further along. There was no pressing need to diagnose and medicate him so young. I knew in time he would settle down a bit more and change, even if he never takes a single pill. That's how fast a four-year-old's brain is developing. For the Tommys of the world who are struggling in preschool or day care, there are other techniques, behavioral methods for helping them learn to settle down when they have to and to keep them from hurting others when they play excitedly or act impulsively. In most cases, though, simply waiting a bit and giving a boy's brain a chance to catch up on its own is the best approach.

I wish this were the only example in my practice of very young boys sidelined by some kind of quick diagnosis or kicked out of preschool because of a transient behavioral problem or their quirky developmental path. But I meet boys like Tommy all the time. It's not just aggression or hyperactivity that is cited as a problem. I meet boys rushed into diagnoses with Asperger's syndrome because they line up their toys or don't make enough eye contact; other boys are tagged as antisocial loners because they haven't graduated to cooperative play at their third birthday; some get labeled with sensory processing issues or nonverbal learning disorder because they are not mature enough to stay on task during craft time, because they don't take turns readily or verbalize their needs, or because they move clumsily. While early intervention does help with certain diagnoses, such as speech impediments, prolonged language delay, and clear signs of autism, the truth is that the vast majority of young boys don't have a disorder. They aren't lagging in any permanent way. There is nothing wrong with them. They are just developing, sometimes unevenly, which is the way development takes place in many boys.

From the earliest days of my practice, I found myself getting many more referrals for boys than girls, and I soon learned that the vast majority of kids receiving psychiatric referrals are boys. But over the past ten years, I've noticed another trend that is alarming. Younger and younger boys are coming into my practice with what seems to me exaggerated and inappropriate diagnoses for disorders more commonly assigned to adults or teens. These very young boys are being labeled in alarming numbers as having ADHD, bipolar disorder, various learning disabilities, oppositional disorders, pathological anger, serious social skills deficits, and more. Their parents have read or been told that these disorders have a genetic basis and that they are best treated in a medical way, and that means drugs.

Yet when I work with these boys, I often find them to be in a developmental cul-de-sac that is causing them to seem different from their peers, when in reality they are just lagging a step or two behind. What is shocking to me about this quick culture of diagnosis is that no one is explaining to parents that there is no way to say with certainty that a three-, four-, or five-year old boy is going to struggle with aggression, extreme shyness, or a lack of impulse control for the rest of his life. No one is informing parents that most of these odd developmental pathways are quite normal and don't mean anything in the long term. The data are clear on this. Accurate long-term predictions for these disorders for kids under age five or six are very, very poor. These diagnostic labels mean nothing in the long term because boys, especially young ones, grow and change so fast.

Even when a boy doesn't have a diagnosis, even when he hasn't been kicked out of school or removed from day care, his parents are often struggling to shield their son from relatives and strangers who tell them that something's wrong with him because he has too many tantrums, because he doesn't make enough eye contact, because he doesn't share. More and more often, parents come into my office with a similar set of concerns. They have a boy with destructive, antisocial tendencies, or one who has failed to meet certain developmental milestones on time, or who seems nearly debilitated by anxiety or rage. These parents have been told by a chorus of voices—relatives, teachers, day care providers, and child health professionals—that their son needs an evaluation or some kind of medication.

I believe these fears signal a crisis in young boyhood, a bias against boys in terms of their behavior at home and in school. We know, for example, that boys receive the vast majority of special education services, in part because teachers report their behaviors as problematic.

While this has been true for older boys for quite a while, what we are seeing now are IEPs, or individual education programs, for three- and four-year-olds, most of whom are boys. Boys attending preschool under an IEP may be the lucky ones. Some don't make it that far. In 2005 researchers at Yale published a study that made headlines nationwide. The study examined preschool expulsion rates and found that children are three times as likely to be kicked out of preschool than at any other time during their academic careers. Less widely reported was the study's finding that boys were more than four and a half times more likely to be expelled than girls.

It's time we stop this madness.

I want to encourage parents, educators, pediatricians, psychiatrists, psychologists, and other developmental experts to reevaluate and radically alter how we deal with our youngest boys. The time between a boy's second and eighth birthdays is crucial to his long-term health in terms of cognitive, social, and emotional development. We must stop diagnosing and medicating every boy who doesn't quite fit in or who stumbles either at home or at school.

I'm not saying that medical intervention is never necessary. However, I am saying that, in most cases, we should just let boys be. We should stop robbing them of normal developmental struggles, which are necessary catalysts in the process of growing up. Children's challenges are actually their best source of strength; hovering adults can interfere unintentionally with their natural development. It is so tempting for us to label and focus on delays, disorders, and disabilities. In reality every child faces many thousands of developmental challenges over the course of those early years. That's what early development is: a constant battle to acquire new skills, to navigate challenging new situations, and to allow the brain opportunities to change and grow in the aftermath of failure.

Many years ago I was observing a group of twenty or so children playing at a preschool. I remember one little boy who moved between toys and play areas and engaged two or three girls in constant chatter, a real give-and-take. They moved as a group between blocks and cars and dress up. It was thirty or so minutes before I realized the boy was blind. The girls playing with him were also gently guiding him, not because they had been asked to, not because they were feeling sorry for him, but because they figured out that this was how to play with him. Their play, their movements around the room, didn't look any different from any other group of children. I remember thinking at the time how comfortable and easy it was for these young children to navigate around something we adults would consider a serious disability. I later learned these children had developed a way to play with one another all on their own. In short, they adapted without adult intervention. How many of us would have felt it necessary to rush in, teach, model, and even try to fix the situation for them? It was a clear example to me of how challenge is part of growing up and how development is not stymied by struggle but helped along by the hurdles we need to overcome.

We may well be robbing our youngest boys of this opportunity. Let's get back to Tommy. After a few sessions with me in which we worked on sitting skills, better eye contact, and better listening (facilitated with a sticker chart and small rewards), Sandy decided not to medicate her son. Instead, she learned about young boyhood development and learned to be the best behavioral coach she could be for her son. She worked with his teachers at preschool so that they provided him with a consistent, clear, and structured environment, which she continued at home. Within a month, he was no longer distracting the class as much, and within three months, he was thriving at school. Tommy is now a well-adjusted second grader who doesn't show any signs of ADHD. In fact, his teachers have remarked on how focused he is.

If Tommy's mother had never questioned his diagnosis or the prescription that came with it, she would have allowed that diagnostic label to mask a set of behaviors that may have been temporary and that may have signaled important new developments happening in his brain. Boys struggle hardest with behavior right before big breakthroughs in development. What's worse, sometimes medications seem to confirm that the diagnosis was right in the first place. They appear to change a child's behavior dramatically at home and school. A boy like Tommy might suddenly focus and be better behaved. Problem solved? No, it might not be the medicine at work, but rather that boy's developmental upheavals having gone through their natural course and resolving on their own. Further, medications such as stimulants improve a boy's ability to sit and follow directions, whether he has real ADHD or not. If you or I took these medications, they would do the same and improve our concentration and performance. That's not evidence of having a disorder. While these medications certainly have their usefulness, they shouldn't be the first and only option for boys like Tommy. There's plenty of time to track him, watch and gather more information, try other less invasive strategies, before pinning a diagnosis on him and medicating him.

To be fair, nobody knows for sure what would have happened with Tommy had he taken the prescription without any behavioral therapy, but I caution parents that we don't know in what way many of these medications affect mental and physical development in very young children in the long run. We do know that once medications stop, a child stumbles, often dramatically, as if you've kicked a crutch out from under him. Medications alone don't teach skills. Many boys I know who have to go off medications because of serious side effects have to start from scratch and learn better listening and self-control on their own. Every boy who is struggling can benefit from good structure at home and at school along with techniques, such as behavioral therapy and academic help. Medications should never be used alone without some form of behavioral or academic help. Had Tommy's problems at school continued after using behavioral techniques alone, I would consider the diagnosis of ADHD to be more accurate and refer him to an experienced physician who might add medication judiciously—but only after exhausting all other reasonable, nonmedical options.

This is a difficult thing to ask parents to do when the phone rings off the hook and a teacher is asking their son to leave the class. I work with moms and dads who come to me in real crisis over a boy's behavior at home and at school. When boys are engaging in what I call "the storm before the calm," that developmental moment just before we see a major leap, their behavior can really regress. Boys can fall apart. I tell these parents to stay calm, hold on, take a breath, and watch. Soon they will see progress that occurs on the behavioral front, signaling that the brain has reorganized itself. And when it does, the change they see in their son is often dramatic. A boy may have a series of terrible tantrums or outbursts just as he's getting ready to learn to read. He can forget his potty training entirely for a week or longer just before he learns to count to twenty. He can seem leagues behind his peers, even behind other boys, in terms of his verbal and social skills, then suddenly catch up. If he does get a little coaching from me, from his teachers, or from his parents, that work can seem to produce a wholly different boy. Yet it's not what causes a boy to improve. Coaching merely encourages and supports the brain to do what it's likely to do on its own.

In these moments parents often turn to me and say, "But we really thought he had a disorder. We really thought he had a medical condition. The testing proved it. His pediatrician said this is a common problem and treatable. How could we have been so wrong?" I can sense their fear. They want to know how they got to that point. How can so many parents and professionals be convinced that the problems young boys are having require medical intervention and long-term therapies?

Faster Pace Equals Higher Demands

I think several cultural influences are at work here, and they are worth looking at. We're rushing kids through their childhood, as the pace to keep up and compete with one another increases. The world is moving faster, and we all feel it. The stress of our high expectations trickles down, and our young boys often feel it the most. They are not always ready for longer days in school and the higher demands that go along with them. We're expecting too much from them, to sit, listen, and use social skills that won't be fully up and running until they reach the second grade. Even then, many boys have difficulties well into second and third grade. They are struggling to learn in larger classrooms. They are stuck indoors and not moving around, as they are hardwired to do. Nowadays, curriculums are geared more and more to tests and standards. Kids have more rote work, more lectures to listen to, and they are not allowed as much natural hands-on playful learning. Homework packets are arriving at home stuffed with one to two hours of work a night. The result? Greater numbers of boys aren't keeping up, are overloaded with stress, and are acting out in frustration. That gets them noticed, labeled, and diagnosed at alarming rates. More and more boys are being labeled with psychiatric and learning problems once reserved for only a few kids in real trouble. We've done a better job over the years making early education work for young girls, who historically were getting left behind and discouraged from learning. Now it is time for us to turn our attention to the unique developmental and learning needs of young boys and do the same for them.

What can we do? We should be hiring more male teachers for early grades. Research shows male teachers create a more boy-friendly learning environment. They rely less on language-only techniques and use more hands-on, real-life exploration for learning. Male teachers are also less likely to see active boy behavior negatively, or pathologically, and don't as often refer boys for evaluations. Along these lines, we need to increase physical movement and free play for all children, especially young boys, who are more sedentary than ever. We need to give boys more developmental breathing room, regardless of the pressures and forces trying to move all children ahead faster.

There is another trend we need to address. We need to stop medicalizing our problems and stop turning only to drugs to face our life struggles. The diagnostic criteria for many psychiatric disorders are getting broader and more inclusive of behaviors that a generation ago would have been considered odd or challenging but basically normal, such as social shyness, aggressive behavior, restlessness, bed-wetting, and slight delays in learning to read and write. The good news is that most boys do grow out of these problems, sometimes on their own, and sometimes with only a little help from their parents or a professional to guide their development. Yet studies show that psychiatric diagnoses related to many common childhood issues, along with the use of pills, are on the rise among younger and younger children.

The trend to seek medical causes and cures for what ails us is pervasive. The *Archives of General Psychiatry* reports that about half of all

Americans would meet the criteria for some form of "mental disorder" at some point in their lives. With such loose criteria, is it any wonder that diagnoses of mental disorders are on the rise among children? Consider one example, bipolar disorder, which increased by more than 4,000 percent in children and adolescents over a recent eight-year period, again, mostly among boys.

While no doubt beneficial for the few children who may be in need of such help, psychiatric diagnoses and pills have become a first, only, and one-size-fits-all approach. We need to take responsibility as adults and not push problems onto our youngest children. A diagnosis of a mental disorder says clearly to these children, "You have the problem. There's something wrong in your brain." No solid evidence exists to make those statements conclusively in very young children. Fortunately, there are established, research-proven behavioral therapies and other nonmedical treatments that can be as effective as, and last longer than, pills in treating a range of challenging childhood problems.

Other Contributing Factors

Schools and other institutions play a role in overdiagnosing young boys. Given the budgetary squeezes in most educational systems, parents can't get special education services or insurance coverage for therapy unless their children have a diagnosis or an IEP. This can encourage practitioners, teachers, and parents to give or accept a diagnosis in a borderline case. Once diagnosed, medications usually follow.

The professional standard is supposed to be different: to entertain all likely diagnoses and causes, then prescribe only the most reasonable and least invasive therapies first. More serious medical treatments can follow in time, but they should be applied cautiously in non-life-threatening situations. This is often referred to as the first rule of medicine: first, do no harm. That means proceed with caution. For the reasons I've listed above, this no longer seems to be the case. Young boys are commonly diagnosed and placed on medications within a single fifteen- to twenty-minute appointment.

I began my practice more than twenty years ago, when the diagnosis of children with disorders comparable to ADHD, bipolar disorder, or Asperger's syndrome was rare, no more than 1 to 3 percent of the population, depending on which problem we're talking about. At that time, these diagnoses were reserved for cases in which the children's behavior was dysfunctional enough to prevent them from engaging in school despite good efforts to help them improve and for those few children who were unable to handle reasonable routines at home despite good parenting and home management skills. Further, it was considered out of bounds to use these diagnoses on very young children unless absolutely necessary. Now I see these diagnoses applied to kids whose symptoms are much more mild and at drastically younger ages. Recently, for example, a five-year-old boy came to me with an ADHD diagnosis because his teacher reported that he was having trouble staying on task in kindergarten, because he was yelling indoors, and because he was "grabby" and excitable in class. I meet other kids all the time, tagged as mildly autistic, or "Aspergery," because they speak with a flat intonation, are shy, or prefer not to play with their classmates. I meet kids whose parents want them tested for bipolar disorder because they're groggy in the first hour after a nap or because they sometimes become suddenly hyper when asked to calm down during dinner or at bedtime.

This troubling trend in the use of medical jargon and loosely defined psychiatric symptoms to describe bothersome behaviors of children is growing, and in most cases, the children being labeled as dysfunctional are young boys. Drug companies encourage parents to self-diagnose and ask for medications during visits with pediatricians, as in the "Ask your doctor" and "Talk to your doctor about . . ." commercials we've seen so many times on television. In my office, I usually have to stop parents as soon as they ask me to diagnose and label a boy's behavior in our first meeting. I like to draw a pie chart that illustrates how many young children have a psychiatric disorder. If we were to put all young children together on one chart, we would find that only about 1 to 2 percent have a chronic, severe mental illness. Other real psychological problems do exist, but they come and go depending on problems that challenge families and children. These include feeling depressed after a loss, a divorce, or stress after moving or entering a new school. Pointing to this pie chart, I say to parents, "Look, this is fantastic news. It means that your son is unlikely to have a serious condition for the long haul." Also, I point out that the brain almost always sorts itself out and adapts. On hearing this, many parents are willing to consider that their boy has a set of troublesome behaviors that are temporary and that will likely diminish with some guidance. This guidance can come in the form of short-term therapy, tutoring, other help at home or school, or perhaps trying out a new activity that builds social skills. The parents might even allow a problem to resolve on its own, taking a hands-off, wait-and-see approach.

In most cases, the parents I see have never heard about this possibility, the possibility that nothing is wrong with their son long term. No one had said to them that boys develop differently from girls, or that a girl's brain tends to seize on those skills most prized in a typical preschool setting. Girls use more words; they cooperate with others; they use social skills effectively. A boy's brain, by contrast, is working on other tasks that are equally important but not always valued as highly in schools, such as learning through touching and exploration, developing motor skills, and engaging in spatial tasks. Boys are also engaging in normal aggression, and they have a healthy interest in challenging rules to test the limits of their power. No one mentioned that if parents better understood the way a boy's brain develops, they would have a better sense of how to deal with their sons at home. No one said that a rather significant subset of children will struggle in their development at some point, because that's what development is: it's a struggle to learn. No one said that new research is suggesting what many of us have long suspected: that ADHD (the most common disorder diagnosed in boys) is temporary in most children and that their minds will catch up. No one brought up the fact that a growing body of research suggests that even the best doctors make mistakes in diagnosing patients (as often as 20 percent of the time), which means that a diagnosis is not irrefutable proof of a medical condition. Few suggested to parents that they get a second opinion, which dramatically decreases the error rate in misdiagnosing very young children.

I don't mean to suggest that I'm pitting myself against these diagnoses, or against any physician or other child expert who makes such a diagnosis to describe a boy's behavior. Any parent dealing with a crisis at home and at school with a boy's behavior should consider all available information and resources. I just like to point out to parents that this includes the possibility that nothing is wrong and that the earlier they look for a problem, or diagnosis, the less accurate it will be. Parents need to understand that in our rush to medicate, fix problems, and use magic pills, we rely on a bias that something is wrong with boys and that somehow we are harming them by not getting them into treatment and therapy quickly.

I am often the first person to say to a mother that her son's odd behavior or troubles at school are in fact keys to understanding the unique and successful young man he will become. For example, the boy who prefers to line up and count objects instead of socialize at school may be a future engineer. I am often the first person to tell a father that his struggling son is not destined for failure as an adult. If parents can manage crises properly and can encourage their sons' development to move ahead, boys will likely be stronger and more capable because of their developmental struggles.

Let's remember that young boys are unique, that they are being lost in our narrow definition of boyhood and exceedingly high expectations, and that they can be reclaimed and best nurtured when we use the right methods and adopt the right attitude. I want to tell you to remember that your own boy's struggle is really his greatest source of strength. Lost underneath our need to diagnose and intervene is a boy trying to become himself. A bossy boy is learning to lead. A shy boy is learning to observe the world closely. A tinkerer is learning to fix. A daydreamer is learning to create. All boys have special skills and special struggles, and often the two are linked.

He's Just a Boy

A friend of mine went to get an eye exam. As she was leaving the office, the doctor asked about her kids. She highlighted her son's odd behavior, his reluctance to speak, his seeming inability to make eye contact, his need to tear up the house, and his fits of frustration and rage. "He doesn't listen," she said. "Nothing we say or do matters to him. He's like Frankenstein, only shorter." The doctor chuckled. "Mine were like that, too," he said. She couldn't believe it. "Yep," he said. "Your problem is spelled B-O-Y."

What a great response! These behaviors really are a normal part of boyhood, and for many boys they last in some form or another past their sixth or seventh birthday. Yet these are the same behaviors that typically cause young boys to be diagnosed with developmental delays and disorders. As parents, teachers, and caregivers, we are ever vigilant to the signs of a developmental problem. As a result, boys as young as two are expected to hit their developmental milestones on time, or else face a battery of tests, screenings, and mounting anxiety from the adults in their lives. However, in most cases, it's not the boy who has the problem; it's the people in his life who have a problem dealing with him. Young boys don't come to my office and say, "Dr. Rao, my problem is that I can't sit still in class." Nor do they worry about why they love to stack blocks instead of listening to a story. They aren't hurting or in any distress. These boys are resilient, the younger ones thankfully oblivious to the sea of adult anxiety around them. They don't believe they have a problem. The grown boys I know sometimes look back with anger and on more than one occasion have said to me, "It was my teachers, my parents, and you professional types who had the problem!" Point taken, I tell them. I myself have fallen into this trap on occasion and have had to work hard to resist offering too much help when it's unnecessary. I've had to resist drawing conclusions from exciting new brain-imaging studies that are, at best, simple snapshots that don't tell us very much about how the miraculous brain actually works. I have to be careful not to get pulled into the tidal wave of studies funded by pharmaceutical companies, knowing that sometimes the data are slanted to make a product more sellable. I have to resist my own anxiety that by doing nothing and waiting, or by intervening cautiously, I might be missing something big.

When parents come to my office with a folder of test results, I read the information, then file it away. During our sessions it's of no use to us, because we're not going to focus on problems and reasons for those problems. We're going to focus on solutions. That means understanding how a boy's development directs his behavior. It also means focusing on teaching him how to behave in more positive ways. In some sessions I deal with teaching boys how to better sit still, because this is a skill that doesn't come naturally. In some sessions I teach parents how to deal with a boy's rages without taking them personally and feeling that their son hates them. This is something all parents of boys should understand. Troublesome behaviors can be shaped and improved upon with the right tools.

Parents who treat these boys as wonderful people-in-training and who view parenting as an opportunity to coach and support their sons through the rough spots of childhood do much better. They can even deal better with their sons' egregious behavior because they can detach and focus on solutions. Before parents can do this, they need to understand how boys are built, how they are wired.

CHAPTER 2

Little Girls Aren't Like This

Over the years I have worked with a few boys who were born with an extra Y chromosome. While girls have an XX pairing of chromosomes, and boys typically have an XY pairing, these boys had an XYY pairing, which is rare. These boys are sometimes called "super males" because they can be taller than average, more active, and more aggressive early on. They may also face more learning challenges, although most of them also have normal IQs. Basically, they are a lot like all young boys, just a little more so. Most men who have this disorder don't know it, and would have no reason to know it.

In Ian's case, the behavioral problems that his parents noted and his hyperactivity were also exacerbated by the fact that he has two brothers. When Ian had his first appointment with me, he was six years old. His brothers, who were four and eight, would follow him around the house either fighting him or egging him on.

Their mother, Karen, reported that the level of noise, activity, and general destruction created by Ian and echoed by the other two boys was too much to take. Why go to bed at night when you can wrestle and fight and tease each other? Why eat your food when you can throw it instead? She complained about being "the only girl in the house." She also marveled at the way her husband dealt with this situation. He could ignore the projectiles, the shouting, and the hitting. He would stay calm until the boys had crossed some line; then he would yell, and they would stop. It was like magic. After a while, though, the chaos would begin to build again. In meeting with the family, we all quickly discovered that Ian's behavior wasn't the main problem; rather, the entire dynamic in the household had to be managed. The boys were like particles in an accelerator bouncing off each other and creating much more destruction than three individual children would. In explaining to Karen how she was going to survive the next decade of motherhood, I had to resort to that sports cliché that coaches use to describe star players on an opposing team: you can't control them; you can only hope to contain them. Karen was so relieved. It wasn't Ian's extra Y chromosome that was ruling the household. Instead, it was the combined Y chromosomes in all her children.

I often thought about how different Karen's life would have been if she'd had three girls or children of both genders. Beyond the genetic factors, boys are socialized far differently than girls are all their lives. If Karen had even one girl, her household would function in an entirely different way. Some parents don't want to believe that boys and girls are different. But they are, especially at this young age, primarily because boys are building skills in a different order than girls. Language and social skills develop later in boys because their early focus is on developing spatial and tactile abilities. That's not to say that these differences are profound. Every toddler's mind is hungry for information. Each child has a unique style for snatching up and storing information, yet there are certain differences that do fall along gender lines. My first task with Karen was to explain how brain development was driving her sons' behaviors.

The Machine

Think of a very young child's brain as a complex machine that revs up slowly and unevenly. Certain areas of the brain will heat up quickly in some toddlers, making some tools more available to one child and less available to another. In girls, the hot spots tend to be those areas of the brain that develop language and encourage eye contact. A girl's stronger preference for eye contact, for looking at human faces, shows up in infancy. Studies have tracked the amount of time babies spent looking at faces. Even at one day old, boys spent far less time looking at faces than girls did; in fact, boys preferred looking at a mechanical mobile. As babies mature, this preference continues. At the age of one year, girls are still making far more eye contact than boys. They literally get more "face time" than boys. From this, girls are able to notice and understand the nuances of facial expressions. They begin to intuit the meaning of smiles, frowns, raised eyebrows, and hundreds of subtle facial expressions. They figure out what they are feeling and match that to what they're seeing in others' faces. They attach labels to emotions and begin to sense what they are feeling more quickly and more accurately. Your two-year-old daughter can turn to you and say, "Mommy, I'm happy at you," or "Mommy, you mad at me," and mean it. Your son might be as old as four or five before he understands that the tidal wave of feeling inside him has a name, or that using words might be a useful tool, a shorthand, for explaining himself to others. When he does, he's likely to use it as a blunt instrument. He'll say, "I hate you." What he means, actually, is, "I'm mad because I can't get my way."

The trouble for boys comes when making a lot of eye contact and using feeling words become social norms in a preschool classroom. Lots of parents come to me after teachers have said that their son isn't making any eye contact and isn't talking in terms of his feelings. They wonder if he's what they call "Aspergery." Boys who tend to be shy or who hang back at first in social situations can easily get tagged as being on the borderline for Asperger's syndrome. I have to remind parents in this situation that boys in general don't make much eye contact and that some flat out hate it. Because they don't have a genetic predisposition to study faces in the way girls do, many boys avoid it. When adults stare at them, boys often get upset. Eye contact feels hostile to them. You know that when you give your son that stern look for some misdeed, he is going to yell, "Stop it!" He means it, too. The fact that he doesn't turn his face to you seeking approval, as would a girl, is not evidence of a problem. He is looking at you, just not for very long. If your son knows you are in the room with him, if he glances in your direction when you say his name or tell him dinner's ready, then he's fine.

One mom complained to me that she could never get her son to talk about his time at preschool, but when his dad came home from work, the little guy opened right up and chatted away. She couldn't figure it out. What was she doing wrong? Why wouldn't he talk to her? I told her to try talking to him while he colored or played with his cars. While his hands tinker, his mind is roaming around, sometime collating the events of the day, sometimes not. Because many boys don't easily make eye contact, or they may interpret direct eye contact as confrontational, the best way to begin a dialogue with your son is to sit next to him. Rather than starting any conversation by saying his name with the expectation that he's going to look up at you, you might consider asking him questions while his hands are busy doing something else. These questions will feel more casual to him. Don't press or insist on a certain level of detail. Be happy with whatever he says. Let him set the pace of the discussion. This mother tried it at home and had great success. (She has since confided that the technique works well on her husband, too.)

On average, girls also talk earlier than boys do. Studies have noted that by age two, the average boy already lags behind the average girl in verbal skills and vocabulary. Boys who have fewer words have fewer tools for expressing themselves in fantasy play and in negotiation with other children or adults. They are also less ready to learn to read and write, which is why so many boys struggle with literacy concepts presented in kindergarten. Some researchers have postulated that if reading readiness were delayed to even the first-grade level, many language-based learning disabilities would virtually disappear.

From a parenting position, it seems that young girls are easier to deal with than boys. Girls talk more; they seek more interpersonal connection, more parental approval. They seek to nurture and to engage in the social scene. As girls get into early grade school, these needs can work against them. When they want connection but find themselves excluded at school or in social groups, when they encounter the disapproval of others, deserved or not, they can crumble, while young boys seem to remain more resilient if only because they're a bit less plugged in and responsive to social information.

For example, I remember watching three kindergartners, two girls and a boy, doing a literacy exercise in school with a teacher's aide. They were playing bingo as a way of learning their letters. One girl at the table began to say "Yay" out loud every time she found the right letter on her card. The other girl at the table countered every "Yay" with "Stop saying that." This escalated rapidly, with the one girl saying "Yay" louder and pointedly looking at the other girl when she said it, and the second girl becoming more insistent and distressed. The boy at this table was all giggles over this. To him, the whole thing was a game, and he wanted some part in it. Quickly, he chose to join the "Yay" faction, which sent the girl, who wanted silence, over the edge. She cried; she quit the game; she went to tell the teacher. At this point, the boy turned back to the teacher's aide and waited for the next letter to be called, but the girl remaining at the table turned to watch the teacher, to see what she would do. For the two girls, this was a drama about interpersonal control, one that would play out over several rounds. For the boy, it was just a momentary game.

If girls excel at talking and nurturing, what are boys good at?

In a boy's brain, the hot spots tend to concern physical activity, spatial awareness, and categorizing information. Studies have shown that boys move more than girls do. They run; they jump; they spin. As babies, they may roll more, try to crawl and walk and travel more. Many moms remember clearly how their young sons would drag themselves across the floor before they could even crawl to get at something interesting, or how they would pull themselves up in their cribs and stand for hours. One mom told me that her son learned to walk at nine months, and before he was even a year old he had given her the scare of her life by climbing the fire escape. Any grandmother can tell you that a three-year-old boy has a motor turned on inside him that causes him to run from the moment his eyelids flutter open in the morning until he drops off to sleep at night. In a school or day care setting, boys are no different. When told to sit, they fidget, squirm, reach, nudge, crab walk, and roll around.

Boys also do consistently better on tests for spatial skills, such as being able to describe how an object would look when rotated, or understanding a map, or copying a three-dimensional LEGO model. They have innate tactile sense, wanting to touch and move and manipulate the world around them. This need to grab first and ask questions later can be disruptive in the home and classroom. How many parents have said to me, "I had to tell him not to lick the bathroom floor!" I have to hold back the urge to say, "Porcelain tiles, right? Cold and bumpy. Of course he licked them!"

Systems Approach

Boys also have a talent for categorizing everything. Simon Baron-Cohen, director of the Autism Research Centre at Cambridge University, summarizes the mind's broad gender differences in this way: "Males on average have a stronger drive to systemize, and females to empathize." This is a great guide to parents. Preschool boys search their world for systems. What are the variables that bring punishment? What are the variables that bring mom's attention? They want to know how everything comes apart. How does it work? How does this feel? How does it taste? How does it smell? How is it like other things I have touched or tasted before? A toddler boy is looking at everything—including the family—as a system to be explored. He wants to break it down, examine it, and thereby control it. Boys drive their parents crazy by counting, sorting, and ordering. Is butter a wet thing or a dry thing? Is Darth Vader the boss of all the bad guys? Is Jupiter bigger than Mars? Am I older than Sam? Am I older than George? Am I older than you? Over and over again. Your son will ask the same questions every day for a month, just to see if you give the same answers. Parents want to see some sort of obsession or compulsion in this, but it's just the scientist in your boy at work.

A preschool girl will more likely see the emotion emanating from others around her. She wants to understand your emotions, then learn to use them in more sophisticated ways to get what she needs or wants. When moms and dads complain about their preschool daughters, they say, "She's such a drama queen; she's so manipulative." Well, you. That's the way her brain is built right now. (And believe me, she needs all the practice she can get before she faces the shark-infested social scene in middle school.) Your son, by contrast, is trying to figure out new ways to break the remote. When he finally figures out ways to control your emotions, his biggest thrill will come from pushing your buttons and making you mad. Your rage will become a spectator sport for him.

One mother I know complained about her four-year-old son who had just figured out that adults have emotional buttons that can be pushed. The day before, when she was trying to get him to put his coat and boots on so they could go to the store, he resisted. Then he started chanting, "Mommy is a poopy butt." She was so taken aback that she yelled, "Stop it!" She said he got the purest look of joy on his face when he figured out that he'd made her mad enough to yell. He kept saying it in quiet moments for the rest of the day to see if she'd yell again. "I want the stoic silence back," she said to me. "What's he going to be like as a teenager?" I told her not to worry about that now. The good news is that the social part of his brain is waking up. With boys, everything is a weapon at first, or a tool, even the emotions of others. As a parent, the trick is to control your own emotions first.

If we consider the positive side of this, we see that boys love figuring things out. To the extent that you can present any rule or any idea as a set system, or a code, your son will be better positioned to understand it. That means that discipline needs to be absolutely consistent. If you think you are taking a toy away every time he hits his sister, but in reality you're doing it every time except when you're on the phone, he'll find that loophole. That's his job. Later on, when he wants to learn to read, he's going to learn that as a system, a code to break.

When he wants to make friends, he's going to learn mostly by trial and error. Over time, he'll learn that some behaviors have good results and others fall flat. A boy will get better at socializing, not by reading others and empathizing, but by testing out a system over time that gets him what he wants. This also means he is going to make colossal social mistakes, embarrassing mistakes. He will go through phases where he's thought of as the bully, the nudge, the shy guy. He is going to learn every wrong way first, and you have to let him do that, and explain only the relationship between an action and its result. "You hit your friend Conner. Now he's mad." That's all a preschool boy needs to know. Just telling him to play nice or think of other's feelings isn't going to work, but you can reinforce the idea that making friends is a series of steps to try to practice. Also remember that other boys are pretty socially forgiving—or forgetful, whatever you want to call it—and can tolerate a lot of blunders.

Even complex skills such as baking can be presented as a system. Many preschool boys love to help bake something. Think about it: measuring, counting units, cracking eggs (here, breaking is a good thing!), and especially mixing two things to watch them become something else are all part of an endlessly fascinating process. If you make some kind of dough that your son can play with and manipulate, even better.

Having a brain that likes to categorize things leads naturally to competition. Boys want to know who is fastest, who is tallest, who is first. One mom told me that every time they get in the car, her four-year-old son demands to know which car is first. He insists on being told what car is at the front of the road. When she says, "There is no front," this news confuses him. It makes him angry. In his mind, there must be a winner.

Differing Responses to Stress

Girls and boys in their toddler and preschool years react differently to the stresses they encounter. For both groups, the first big test is going to preschool or day care, where they spend lots of time with other children and have to interact with them in a space that is likely more crowded than their home environment.

Studies have examined how children react to crowded environments, such as the classroom, where they have to deal with lots of other children and may feel that they have less personal space and less access to toys they prefer. What researchers have noticed is that girls tend to use more social skills in these environments. They talk more and share more. When things seem rough, they engage with each other, using their words, making eye contact, and using other social skills to their advantage. Boys, by contrast, shut down and get aggressive when things get crowded. They grab and hit to get what they want. They compete, and they use hands-on methods for getting toys or crayons rather than talking or sharing. One can imagine them becoming overwhelmed and anxious when other kids crowd their space. There are more faces to read, more words to process, more body movements and noises to distract them.

JoAnn, a young mother of a sweet two-and-a-half-year-old boy named Declan, came to see me because her son had started biting at day care. This little boy radiated sunshine and warmth all the time, to the extent that other, slightly older kids in the neighborhood always crowded around him, wanting to play with him and talk to him. He seemed to relish this attention, and his mother put him in day care thinking that things would be fine. Things were fine for about ten months, and then Declan began to bite kids at school. This usually happened when he was playing quietly and another child attempted to join in or take the toy away. JoAnn was in a panic, concerned that he would regress and become antisocial. She confronted the day care teacher, wanting to know what she was going to do to help shape Declan's behavior. The day care teacher told JoAnn that the center's policy is to remove him from the area whenever he bites, tell him it's wrong, and find him something else to do. JoAnn asked me if this makes sense. Removal and distraction are the way most day care centers handle discipline, and the method often works well. When she didn't seem convinced, I told her, "Look, he's not going to be biting in college." Good day care providers know these behaviors are transient.

Next, I asked JoAnn for more details. I asked her what the room looked like, and she said it was one fairly small open classroom with about fifteen kids. She told me that in a couple of months, Declan would be old enough to move into the day care center's preschool room, which would have a few more kids, all of whom would be older than he is.

Then she began to describe the new room he would be joining in a month or so. Although larger, this room had been divided into distinct play areas. There was a little reading area, a play area, and a crafts area. All had dividers around them, so that a child sitting in a chair or playing on the floor would feel protected and safe in a small, quieter personal space. This is ideal for many boys because they focus better without as much stimulation. I told her that this new space might be the solution to her problem and to Declan's behavioral issues at school.

Once you understand how a boy's brain works, you can begin to look at early school experiences from his perspective. You can look at a preschool or day care room and see right away if your son can be made comfortable there. In the new room JoAnn described, Declan would be able to take a favorite toy into an area by himself where he is less likely to be encroached upon. Given that Declan is already very comfortable with older kids, he would probably do better in his new room where he could watch and follow the routines of others. I told JoAnn that if she liked the center, if she liked the teachers, and if she could just hang on until her son made the transition to a new room, she would probably find him more settled there.

Of course, not all boys fit this model. Some excel at social skills— some like people and love talking and making eye contact—but these boys are less typical. The majority of boys need a little extra space in which to move. They are very tactile and need toys that they can take apart and put back together over and over. They need to explore the world as little scientists looking for variables and reactions, trying to figure out how things work, what's inside, and testing everything to see how it reacts. They need to do and see first, while the talking and the listening will come later.

In the chapters that follow, I will explain more about every aspect of young boy development, about how a boy's style of thinking affects his behavior. Before I turn to that, I want to stress again that brain development is uneven and that a behavioral setback often signals a cognitive breakthrough. Your son is driving you craziest when he's about to figure something out. Quite often boys are the most disorganized in their thinking and behavior just before a major advancement. For example, younger toddlers might have trouble separating from their moms or become fussy eaters before a big language breakthrough. Older boys may shut down emotionally or engage in long tantrums for a week or two, exhausting their parents. Then one day they sit down for forty minutes straight and practice writing numbers and letters, while their parents look on in disbelief.

One boy I worked with recently who was five had a terrible time getting it together in preschool. He gave his parents flack every day, not wanting to get out of bed, not wanting to get dressed or go to school. His parents were in tatters, trying to argue with him. After a month's struggle, though, he suddenly got up and went to school and started writing letters and whole words. He now can't get enough of school.

This pattern is normal, and I tell parents to look beyond the crisis for the leap that will surely follow it. A boy's development takes time. Rather than worrying about a boy's struggles, parents should spend time imagining the healthy young man he is becoming.

CHAPTER 3

He Doesn't Have Any Friends

Quiet-spoken Marla called me to make her first appointment after what she termed a disastrous parent–teacher conference at her son's preschool. The well-meaning teacher went on and on about how her son, Eric, was "a loner" because he had no friends and didn't seem to be engaging any of the other kids in play. "He walks in, picks out a toy, and sits in the corner by himself with it," she told Marla. "We're very concerned." The teacher said that by now, at age three, Eric should be engaging in cooperative play. He should be making up pretend scenarios with friends. He should be engaging in the give-and-take of play. This is crucial, said the teacher, to his social development long term. Marla, who shares Eric's sandy hair and green eyes—as well as his temperament—was shocked and a little embarrassed. She asked the teacher if Eric was making a disturbance in class, hitting the other kids, or refusing to do crafts and activities. The teacher shook her head. "He does what we ask him to do," she said, "but he doesn't look at us or anything. He doesn't talk to us." The teacher also said that Eric lurked around other kids who were playing together, sitting just far enough away from them to avoid joining in, but close enough to overhear what they were doing. No amount of coaxing would get Eric into the group. When urged to join in, he would turn away. And at music time, when all the other kids were singing and dancing along, Eric would just watch.

Marla confesses that she was always shy in school and was slow to make friends. She envies her husband, who is chatty with neighbors and expansive at parties. She asks me if Eric will struggle to make friends his whole life as she did. Her question to me is a fair one, given the grave tone of this meeting. I reply with a question of my own: is it that Eric can't socialize, or is it that he prefers not to? This is an important distinction that few of us adults consider.

Questions about social issues are common in my practice. Parents are highly concerned about whether their sons are maturing with the right mix of social skills to achieve success and happiness later in life. Some parents complain that their sons are bullies or show-offs (which I'll address in the next chapter), that they can't share and take turns, that they claim that everyone hates them. Moms tell me all the time they envision their young sons still hitting others or refusing to share twenty years from now, or perhaps sitting alone and friendless. They ask me: "What's he going to be like when he grows up?" They envision their adult sons hitting other kids in a dorm room or cubicle or being the loner at work.

This concern is definitely something that has increased over the past two decades. Standards to achieve and fit in at school and day care are at an all-time high. Parents have been told that boys have to be social high achievers early in life in order to be successful later. From that, many people assume that their children have to be socially adept early on to be considered normal. Quirky kids need not apply to day care, preschool, and playgroups anymore. Boys who are on the shy or aggressive side temperamentally or who are having a temporary developmental glitch are more likely to be evaluated for disorders such as Asperger's and autism, ADHD, even bipolar disorder. Parents are understandably worried about these trends.

Almost Every Boy Is Normal

The first thing I tell most parents is that their sons are probably doing just fine socially, if we're talking about the parameters of normal behavior. What's that? Well, first, let's get rid of all the judgmental terms thrown out by well-meaning folks who want to place everyone into some sort of behavioral category. Blanket terms such as *Aspergery, ADHDish, loner, bully, troublemaker, shy guy, contrarian, aggressor*—none of these words can offer you a shred of information about your son. I tell parents it's okay to turn to anyone who offers one of these unhelpful labels and say, "What do you mean by that? What are you noticing? What are the specific behaviors?" Only when you hear about specific behaviors that are bothering someone else can you either take action to change these behaviors or make the decision to let your boy muddle through on his own. Developmental challenges are healthy, and that includes social challenges of every sort. They are often a child's greatest opportunity for growth. Don't let others diagnose your son's developmental challenges, especially based on a few behaviors or incidents.

I also think it's useful to lay out for any parent or teacher the real parameters for social success. The skills your son needs to build his social awareness are pretty complex. Let's break them down and look at each one. Once we see each of the subcomponents, we can work with them. Then you'll also appreciate that socializing isn't as simple as it seems. Social awareness and socialization are behaviors that can take years to develop.

Language. A boy needs to understand what's said to him (often called receptive language), and he needs to speak, to make himself understood (we call this expressive language). The general rule with kids is that they understand far more than they communicate. With boys, this disparity can be pretty extreme. One mom I know was encouraged to have her three-year-old son tested because he was very shy at school. As sometimes happens, she was further encouraged to have him sit through comprehensive testing, covering everything from emotional adjustment to academic readiness. On one such exam, the tester asked him to name a letter that was written on a card. The boy looked away as though he hadn't seen it. Then the tester put a bunch of letters on a magnetic board and said to him, "Which one is the *G*?" After scanning the board, the boy pointed to the correct letter. In fact, when he was allowed to respond without using words, he was able to identify more than half the alphabet by sight. He didn't have a deficit. He was just shy and preferred not to speak to a stranger.

Listening and watching. A boy needs to be able to pay attention to verbal and nonverbal cues of the person who is speaking to him. These include tone of voice and facial expression, even body language. In addition, he needs to understand that these can convey information about what's being said. This is not to say that he has to make constant eye contact or that he has to always respond in predictable ways to the people around him. Few boys, as we've seen, make steady eye contact with anyone. They may glance at faces and then away, but they can remember and quickly process what they see. Often boys will exhibit how socially observant they are in unexpected ways. For example, many moms complain to me that their sons smile or giggle when they are being punished, even as young as age three or four. These moms want to know if this is evidence of a social problem. Is he a little sociopath? I reassure them that, no, he's not a sociopath. Then I have to add, "Sorry, you've got yourself a smart one here. Not only does he understand your anger, he's trying to provoke it."

Referencing. Sometimes watching and listening aren't enough. In complex and confusing social situations, boys have to look at others and see how they perceive the social situation. This instructs them on what they should do and how to behave. For example, a toddler will look to his mother's face at a family gathering to see if the person reaching for him is a friend. Mom's face will show tension if it's not okay. As kids get older, they turn to a wider group of people to figure out what's going on around them. This group might include babysitters, grandparents, older siblings, and teachers. By the time your son is in first grade, he will be looking more and more to his peers to read what's going on around him socially.

This social referencing is no different from the way you read

social cues in your life. For example, you can walk into a room,
perhaps at a party or a meeting at work, and know immediately
if the atmosphere is friendly or tense. Even at very young ages,
boys can read your face and gestures, even things you don't
want to communicate. If you are with your son, let's say at the
grocery store, and you run into someone you don't like, your son
might start to act out, tugging at you or shouting or running off.
It's possible that he's referencing your tension in that moment.
Tugging at you and running off may not seem like evidence of a
social skill, but it is. Some boys gain this type of social skill earlier
and more easily than others. Boys who don't make a lot of eye
contact or who are shy, inattentive, or aggressive sometimes lag in
this skill. It is also harder to use social referencing in early school
situations when there's a lot of activity in the room.

Social Skills at Play

We've all heard the statement that "play is the child's work." Play is
the means through which most of a child's growth and emotional development accrue. Armed with the above skills, very young kids practice and learn how to socialize mainly through play. Kids start out
by playing alone. We call that solitary play. Even when playing alone
they begin to learn basic social skills. How? By listening and watching
others around them, by picking up on social patterns of people in the
room with them.

After a while, sometime before they turn three, kids start playing
near each other. They might be doing the exact same thing, each
playing with clay or coloring a piece of paper or building a tower, but
they aren't spending much time looking at each other or talking to
each other. We call that parallel play. At this point, they are picking
up on another child's social behaviors and skills by having a buddy
next to them.

Sometime after their third birthday, and later for many boys, kids
move into a new, more advanced style of play, called cooperative play.
That's when they acknowledge other kids, talking to them and including them in their play. "Let's play robots," says one little boy, while the

other says, "You be the bad guy, and I'll be the good guy." Outgoing kids and highly verbal kids are going to take to this kind of play earlier, while less verbal kids and shy kids will wait to try this out until they are older, sometimes years older. The fact that your son isn't engaging in parallel play by the time he turns three or even four isn't, in and of itself, a sign of a serious social problem or disorder, such as Asperger's or autism. It's not a deficit of skill necessarily, but more likely a preference. His social style will evolve in the next few years. It can change dramatically as his development continues.

Some parents ask me why their boys are shy, why they are so socially reticent. I tell them that not everyone can be the same. Every group, every social situation, such as a classroom or working environment, needs a range of social types. I also like to remind parents that their shy son is modeling important behavior for the super social kids who can't slow down and put the brakes on their gabby, grabby style. He's doing something right, I tell them. There are times when we all need to be able to pull back, watch, and block out the social stimulation around us.

In addition, there are different styles of play that can be defined as either pretend or nonpretend. Fantasy play involves make-believe and makes heavy use of imaginary skills. It is often considered the hallmark of healthy young child play. But let's not sell nonfantasy play short. Nonfantasy play is moving dirt, moving cars, building things, climbing, swinging on swings, running. It features doing real things over imagining. It should be no surprise that many boys, particularly the more physical boys, prefer doing over imagining.

Which is better, fantasy or nonfantasy play? It's a question I hear a lot.

Some boys favor concrete activities, such as lining up toys, sitting for hours at the beach moving sand and digging holes. Perhaps they like to pour water from one container to another, or they take their toys apart to see what's inside. One boy I know used to be obsessed with balancing toys on top of each other. He would become enraged when he couldn't get a toy to balance on top of a ball.

Other boys are fascinated almost exclusively with fantasy play.

They need to engage in detailed scenarios with killer robots and volcanoes erupting and sharks in spaceships. At the beach, where most kids would dig and build, they seem hopelessly lost and bored without their toys or props that facilitate their wild play fantasies.

Both of these rather extreme styles of play are healthy and normal. Each reflects a preference for how a boy's brain may be hardwired. The nonfantasy player likes to see the details of things, processes pieces of information around him, observes small differences between things, and organizes them rigidly. The fantasy player sees the world more fluidly. He wants to manipulate objects and ideas in his head. He uses the things around him as vehicles to explore and express his inner thinking or imagination.

Maybe one will become an engineer or scientist, and the other a creative ad exec or writer. What scares parents the most is the way each type of boy excludes others and doesn't easily engage in social cooperative play. Almost all boys eventually open up to include other types of play and bring others in socially.

What's His Style of Play?

Marla tells me that her son can't name the kids he spends his days with at day care. His teacher also reports that he spends most of his time stacking blocks and playing with Duplos. When Marla asks him what he did that day or even what he ate for lunch, he says, "Nuffing," or "I don't know." Sometimes he ignores her questions altogether and stares out the window on the drive home.

Clearly Eric's style of play is solitary and heavily nonpretend. Marla accepts that he will be slow to warm up to joining other kids, but she is also frustrated that Eric won't talk with her about what happened at school. I tell her that many, if not most, boys don't like to talk. Judging them on their social skills based on how much they chat at age three or four—or really at any age—is a serious mistake. It's misleading. I, myself, deal with boys all day who have problems that have to be talked through, such as extreme phobias, compulsive behaviors, and difficulty completing schoolwork because of learning disabilities. I need to talk to these boys, and I need to hear what they have to say about their experiences. Still, I tell moms that if they could listen in on these sessions, they would be surprised by how little is being said. (Dads, on the other hand, might be surprised by how much is being said.)

There are two issues here concerning Eric. One is that, because of his style of play, his teacher is afraid that he's not practicing the social skills he should be developing. The second issue is that Marla wants to have a more solid exchange of ideas with her son. Moms like to talk and listen. For them, talk is the cornerstone of any healthy relationship and the major mode by which they parent. The good news is that there are ways moms can encourage their sons to open up to them.

Action Leads to Talk

Marla wanted to facilitate conversation with Eric, to get him to tell her things in his own time rather than grilling him at the end of every pre-school day. I remind her that many boys just aren't comfortable in a formal face-to-face conversation, particularly at this young age. Some boys never get used to this type of conversation, as I've discovered in my practice. That doesn't mean they don't feel they need to talk about themselves or their problems or their feelings. Sometimes they do need to talk, but they don't know how. In other cases, they are just not that interested in chatting.

In my office, I use simple, repetitive activities to set up a dialogue with a boy who has something on his mind but no real way to start talking. Throwing, rolling, or tossing a ball will give him something to do during the silences, of which there are many. Some boys like to do simple puzzles or color a picture or build something with LEGOs or blocks. My role is to sit next to a boy and watch or hand him a piece now and then. I don't make much eye contact or expect it. Still, we are so-cializing. We are making or finishing something together, and the talk will emerge from that. Remember that engaging with boys does not come just from exchanging ideas and emotions. It comes from work-ing on something together, and seeing what it is together. Socializing is about having your friend help you and see what you've accomplished. Sometimes, it's about using your friend, and his skills, to get what you want. This is the start of teamwork and cooperative play in boys.

When boys get older, and when they are adults, they will still use these activities as the primary means by which they socialize with others. The question is: how can a mom, who is hungry for details about her son's inner life, encourage some sharing? Here are some ideas.

1. *Repetition*. I know several moms who have had great luck with rudimentary basketball. Many, many office cubicles feature a tiny hoop over a trash can. Lots of men like to try to hit the trash can with a wad of paper. Boys love this, too. Moms can try a variation of this. Some moms I know have taken paper grocery bags and sat down next to their sons to take turns lobbing Ping-Pong balls (or some other type of ball; something light or made of foam works best) into the bag. But it doesn't have to be a ball. One mom I know used foam blocks; another used stuffed animals to toss into a laundry basket. You can throw playing cards into a hat. It's a simple, repetitive task with clear and instant feedback, and boys love it. (Moms love it, too, secretly. This is their chance to play with their sons and become a fun mom.)

2. *Cooperation*. Build something together. I don't mean bringing home a LEGO toy or other model so that your son can sit and watch you parse over the directions and get frustrated while trying to put the little pieces together. I'm talking about asking him what he wants to build. When he answers, watch his imagination drive the drama. You can make suggestions: "Should there be a moat around this castle? Great. What would that look like?" Or you can just let him go. Often, unrelated talk will emerge from this. Ask, "Are there sharks in the moat?" and he might respond by saying that Joey threw food at lunchtime today, or he might ask if you can live without a brain. Follow his conversational thread. I caution moms to allow for long silences during this play, while their son wanders in his thoughts.

3. *Parallel play*. Childhood development books argue that children should graduate from parallel play, the kind where two kids sit next to each other and work on separate tasks, by the time

they're three. Many boys don't give this up right on time. The truth is, many of them enjoy parallel play, or some form of it, forever. Try sitting next to your son and color while he colors, or build a tower next to the one he's building. Being near him while not pressuring him to talk is a great way to get him to talk.

When moms and dads give this approach a try, sitting next to their son while he does something and giving him gentle guidance or asking him questions—very occasionally—about what he's doing, the results stagger them. A few drops of discussion ("This is a shark eating the people") become a stream of description, a whole story ("And then the robot comes and captures them"), which becomes a tide of questions ("Which planet is orange? How many sharks are there in the whole world? Are robots real? Can we build one?").

The key is to resist the urge to talk too much, to process it for your son, or to ask too many questions. Stick to the basics: "It looks great," or "Need another piece?" His task is to complete his tower or drawing or puzzle and not to process the experience. He will open up in his own way, at his own pace. In the meantime, you're playing with him and spending time with him on his terms. Even if he doesn't show it with words, he loves this quiet one-on-one time.

Encouraging Emotional Awareness

Eric's preschool teacher fears that he's not developing social awareness as he should because he doesn't talk to the other kids or join in their play. Marla is still worrying that he might have Asperger's syndrome or something in the autism spectrum disorders because he's not engaging emotionally with other kids at school. She asks me what she can do at home to help Eric become more emotionally aware, if that's possible. I tell her that I doubt he has a disorder, based on what I've seen in our meetings in the office, but that I will keep an eye on it.

As we talk, I discover that Marla's husband, Dave, tried to use the bedtime stories he would read to Eric to help him connect with the characters. Dave would stop in the middle of a story and say to Eric, "What do you think Curious George is feeling now?" Eric refused to answer at first, maybe not understanding that he should say something, or that there was any point to saying something. Then Dave would give him choices: "Do you think George is happy or scared?" Eric would answer sometimes, and sometimes he would punch the page and yell, "Read!" He just wanted the story. At lunchtime, Marla would ask him about movies or shows he had watched. He loved *Finding Nemo* at the time. He loved to watch a bit of the movie every night. So she asked, "What happened after Nemo and Dori met the shark?" She told me that Eric thought for a moment, then he pointed with his hand and said, "He chase them." It was a huge moment for Marla. Eric had reached into his memory and reconstructed part of a story that he knew, and he was clearly excited about that moment. Within a few weeks, Eric was asking questions himself about stories and about the world at large. When pressed about what happened at school, he could recount simple anecdotes.

To be fair, these results might have been coincidental. It's possible that Eric's brain was ready to make this leap to a new social and emotional awareness and to put language to feelings and recount cause and effect in stories. But practice is the basis of all developmental change. Eric's practice at having small conversations with his parents during story time or during the day in his play likely helped encourage this developmental change. At the very least, it gave him a chance to practice an emerging skill of matching language to emotion.

Why Is He Playing Alone?

Moms especially often ask me why their sons don't play with others. Isn't that a problem? A lot of parenting books say that cooperative play, meaning playing with others, should start at around age three. Having read this, most parents and teachers assume that by age three young boys will stop ignoring each other in the sandbox and start engaging each other. While it's true that boys do transition from parallel play to cooperative play, they don't all do it at this age or by this age. Many boys make this transition much later, and in very different ways. Also, parents and teachers sometimes fail to recognize "cooperative" play as it occurs. Boys who are fighting over a toy are engaging each other, after all. Throwing sand at another kid is engaging him in play, although not the kind many moms like to see.

Further, cooperative play in boys may not look the same as it does in girls. The first thing I like to ask moms to do is to think about what socialization looks like in more grown-up boys and even men. How do men generally socialize with their buddies? They sit, side by side, play cards, play video games, attend a ballgame, watch a movie, and don't communicate much with words except to show their knowledge or highlight "cool" things. I tend to act this way myself with my friends, even though I talk for a living. When boys are sitting side by side, doing similar things while not talking much, they are socializing. They are connecting emotionally, and this type of play is highly meaningful for boys, even though it's not the way many girls or women would socialize. Many father-and-son bonding events and outings are nonverbal. They make trips to sporting events and museums. They play cards, checkers, or catch. They watch TV. They fish for long, quiet hours. The common theme is boys have a pal with them, someone who shares the event, not someone who wants to talk it through or share emotions about the event. Yet this is real socializing. There's nothing wrong with this style of play, either in boys or in grown men.

Socializing in School

Working and playing with other kids at school may look different for boys than many adults think it should. When Marla asked for more details from Eric's preschool teacher about what contact he does have with other kids, she got complaints. She learned that Eric sometimes gets in trouble for sneaking up behind other kids and taking the crayons out of their hands while they are coloring. Other times, he and another boy get in trouble for hiding a favorite toy from someone.

Wait a second, I tell her. That's socializing. It's not a tea party. It's not a chatty exchange of ideas and emotions, but it is a form of socialization. Egging another kid on to get him in trouble or taking a crayon away from someone to watch her get upset isn't the sort of thing that is going to make him the star of the office social scene when he's forty, but his techniques will probably have evolved a bit by then. Eric is working with other kids in school to get what he wants, to get a reaction out of his peers. To do that, he has to make eye contact, suggest some sort of rudimentary plan, and get a cohort to go along with him. While I sympathize with his teacher, I disagree with her assessment. Eric is not a loner; he's shy but also more of a contrarian, a guy who stirs things up—but quietly. He can play with others; he can communicate his needs and take social cues. When he's ready, he'll open up to more and more of the children at school. In the meantime, he'll learn (through their annoyance) why it's not okay to bother other kids as the sole method of getting their attention.

The other behavior reported by this teacher is the one mentioned earlier, Eric's habit of lurking at the margins of a group and watching them. Many shy kids do this. They don't feel confident to jump into an activity without knowing the social rules, so they hang outside and eavesdrop on the group. Watching others socialize is actually a great way for kids to practice socializing. Many times the kids inside the group who are happily playing together don't realize that they are being watched, or they don't seem to care. I've found that parents and teachers are the most upset by this arrangement and feel that they need to facilitate one big open group in which all the kids are playing and no one is outside watching. If I could advise adults on this, I would suggest minimal intervention, if any.

Boys in particular learn by doing. If Marla saw Eric doing this at a party or playgroup, and she waded in to introduce him to the other kids and to encourage them to invite him into their play, she would be teaching him (and them) that Eric needs help saying hello. By leaving him alone, she's giving him the chance to try various methods of inserting himself into the group. He might start by bothering them or by stealing toys from them. At that point, he can find out what does and doesn't work. Or he'll lurk until lurking gets dull, then ask to join in. Remember that three- and four-year-olds don't expect much from each other. Kids can tolerate a lot of strange behavior from other kids.

If it seems intolerable to let your son lurk outside a group, I would suggest saying to the kids playing in a circle, "Eric is going to sit next to you while you play. Is that okay?" Generally, the kids will say yes, and you can then leave the situation. Most times, one of them will enlarge the circle to let the newcomer in, allowing him to sit among them until he wants to join in.

Attachment and Separation

These are the other important components of social development. It takes a boy some time to feel secure enough to move from his mother's side to explore new social relationships. A healthy attachment allows for positive separation. Some boys can separate very early and easily—they speed off from their moms as soon as they eye something of interest. They are often more active, physical, and fearless. They check back with their moms for brief hugs or nose wipes, then move out again to explore. Other boys are completely different but no less healthy or normal, just different. These shyer boys may hover close by their moms and are tentative in their approach to playing with other children.

Handling these two types of boys requires different approaches, as you can imagine. The first needs consistent rules put in place about when it's okay to leave your side and to return when called. That means getting down to your son's level, insisting on eye contact from him, and stating the few rules clearly. (For example: "Don't go where I can't see you; don't run into the street; hold my hand in the parking lot.") Then ask him to repeat the two or three most important rules you've just stated.

Boys who seem to have no separation issues need to repeat and agree to these rules before they go into a socially stimulating place or situation, such as a shopping mall or a birthday party with lots of kids. Otherwise they can get carried away, because they get pulled into and love the stimulation.

One seven-year-old boy that I worked with would bolt across a street without looking, ignoring traffic and his mom's pleas to stop. His mom and I worked together with him to teach him to wait at stoplights. We coached him at cross streets and repeated the practice of waiting at a light over and over, with his mom on one side of the street and me on the other. We taught him how to look at the light and wait until he got the signal to cross. And we talked to him about paying attention to the fact that other people are walking, too, and that he had to pay attention to them. I also pointed out to him when other people were breaking the rules and jaywalking. At the end of the practice session, we went to get ice cream to create a reward for getting it right and making it into a fun learning exercise.

You want to give kids like this a place to explore, a park or a playground where they can run around without having their moms or dads in lockstep behind them. These boys need to range a bit and explore on their own terms, in safe places.

What's interesting is that the shyer type of boy doesn't need as much parental guidance. On the surface, I know that may sound wrong. I tell moms they don't need to spend inordinate amounts of time coaxing, luring, and overencouraging a shy kid. It accidentally gives him attention, which is a very powerful social reward, for not going out to play with others. You make a huge deal of it—and accidentally communicate the message there may be something wrong with him. At the same time, the attention is a powerful incentive to stay by your side. See it from his point of view: why socialize with kids when you can socialize with your mom? The shyer type of boy is trickier to manage in groups of children and prefers more one-to-one, less stimulating activities. He tends not to do as well in organized team sports, generally speaking, such as T-ball and Peewee League sports. But never say never. Try everything and be flexible.

Not all shy boys shun activity. Some are very shy only around other kids, while at home they can be forceful and energetic. At two years old, Terri's son, Patrick, smiles constantly and loves to grab his mother's face to give her kisses. At preschool or outside the house, though, he shuts down. He won't talk to adults or other kids. Outside the house, he seems fearful and stands behind his mom. Yet he is a "madman" when he's at home. Terri tells me that Patrick can scale the front door to undo the dead bolt so he can open it up and run outside, into the street. I tell her that he may be doing this for attention. He knows he can draw her attention, even the negative kind, by running outside and watching her panic while she looks for him. But he also wants to explore. He's stimulus driven, meaning he responds to stimulation, and any distraction will do. With kids like Patrick, you have to watch them carefully, and you can't leave them alone in a room with anything you don't want broken. They may continue to be thrill seekers at ten or fifteen, but they can channel this urge into activities such as skateboarding, snowboarding, and paintball, which are edgy but have rules and competitions and use safety equipment.

Boys like Patrick are wild and social among family members and in environments in which they feel most comfortable. Terri may feel that she has the worst of both worlds—a little guy who needs a ton of supervision and interaction from her at home, yet can't readily burn off steam at a playground or on a playdate with other kids. I tell moms in this situation to be patient. Their sons will develop socially and have successful playdates, although they will probably be highly energetic affairs with giggling and shouting and sound effects instead of talk. In the meantime, if the boys can frequently visit a large playground area where they can roam without their moms in tow, they can release some of this wild energy.

Separation Anxiety

Some boys have a hard time detaching from their mom or dad. One mom came to me after having taken her son, Kyle, who was two and a half, to day care for the first time. He went to visit, and she said he played quietly. Even though he didn't acknowledge the other kids or her, it made her think that things would go well on his first day of school. Unfortunately, that wasn't the case. Kyle clawed at her when she tried to leave the room and shrieked, "Mommy, Mommy!" She became upset, particularly when the day care provider snapped at her, saying, "Just go." She told me she was a wreck afterward. She went home to her empty house to get ready for work. "This is what I thought I wanted, the chance to go back to work," she recalled. "Yet what I really wanted was for Kyle to be happy. I kept thinking: what have I done?" She called the school to check on Kyle, and the day care teacher said he was just fine. She wasn't convinced. "I asked if I could come and get him right then," she told me, but the day care teacher was adamant. She said, "If he doesn't make it to lunch, he'll never make it through a day here. He has to get through this, and he'll be fine."

I had to tell this mother that the teacher was right: Kyle needed to get through this phase of separation. If she kept calling and giving him the message, "Mommy will be there soon," it would be an unneeded rescue and too stimulating for him. He needed a chunk of time in this new environment on his own to get used to it. It looks worse than it is.

Remember that your son has to separate from you. It's a natural process and a part of life to say good-bye to people and trust that you will see them again. Your son will need this skill in school, and if you are a working parent, he needs to begin to learn it now. Also, keep in mind that your son will seem to be at his worst in front of you. He can show you his most awful behavior because you are the one who takes care of him. He trusts you enough to let it all out.

Separation anxiety is normal. It starts somewhere around eight months, when a boy's mind is developed enough for him to know that you exist when he can't see you. At such times he can conjure up an image of you in his mind. Developmental experts call this the start of "object permanence." It's among a child's first sophisticated cognitive tools. Then he can really miss you, and he gets scared. That's normal. Separation anxiety can go on for a few years and taper slowly, then pop back temporarily during life changes and stresses. I see it more often in boys than girls (but I also have more boys in my practice). Some will have it all the way through first grade.

Sometimes a boy who seems to have moved beyond this phase may suddenly seem to regress. He will cling to you again as you leave the day care center as if it's his first day. Don't panic. That's normal. These regressions are transient and may signal that a major cognitive leap is on its way. Sometimes boys are a little bit more vulnerable and disorganized while their skills are upgrading.

Remember that your son is an explorer, and deep down he wants to leave your side and investigate the world without you. He might do this in intervals of a week or two, of wanting to be with you but also wanting to be out in the world, trying new things. The cues you give him are incredibly important. You want to stay calm and relaxed and in control while reinforcing all his successes to leave you. Let him know that it's okay, that he's going to be safe: "I'm fine. You'll be fine when you go off to day care. *Look at me, I'm okay.*" You have to put on your poker face. You have to behave confidently. It's okay to push your son off a little bit each time. When he comes back to touch base with you, he is refueling with love and security. He may need less reassurance each time. Be prepared for that, so that you don't give him more direction than he needs.

If separation anxiety seems particularly strong or unusual, it might have nothing to do with your son's development. Check yourself first; you may be behaving differently, or something else may be going on at home to confuse him. You might have a different work schedule, or something as simple as daylight savings time might throw him off a bit.

Some moms struggle with their own separation anxiety long after those first few years at day care. One mom I know took her son to a town recreation center for a day camp, which was offered a few hours each day for a week in July. The camp counselors were high school students. Her son, who was six at the time, was going to learn to do science experiments, and he was really looking forward to the camp. But when they walked in the door on the first day, she said that he just shut down. He looked spooked, and he grabbed onto her shirt and stood next to her, frozen and unable to move. He watched the other boys and girls in the room. This mom got scared, too, thinking that her son wouldn't be okay at camp, that he wouldn't make friends or fit in. She leaned down and gave him a pep talk, hoping to bolster him. Then she said the camp director, a nice woman with a clipboard, walked over. The woman said to her, "Are you okay?" The mom was pretty taken aback by this. She said, "What?" And the woman said, "Do you need anything?" The mom said, "No. It's just that it's his first day." The woman smiled and said to her, "It's going to be fine. We've got it from here."

I love this story. It really gave this mom a reality check about the messages—the social referencing—she was giving to her son. By leaning down and talking him through it, she was saying to him, "You need a mommy to get you through this," when in reality, he needed to freeze up a bit, get his bearings, then dive in to the new situation, using his own style. By leaving him alone (but in the capable hands of the camp staff), this mom was going to give him a different message: "You're a big boy, and you're going to get through this and have a great time." It's important for parents to remember that being afraid, or a bit lonely, or lost for a few minutes is not fatal. Momentary confusion or fear may be an important confidence-building experience for a young boy, showing him that he can go into new situations and be just fine.

CHAPTER 4

He's a Bully

J oseph is six years old, yet he could easily pass for a third grader. He has the angular face of a much older boy and is tall and stocky. Joseph's father is also very tall and seemed to grow up faster than his peers, just as Joseph is doing now. He favors sports and athletic figures that are popular with older boys. He wears T-shirts touting famous skateboarders and snowboarders rather than Sponge Bob or Scooby-Doo. In public, people are constantly overestimating Joseph's age, which causes them to have higher expectations of him.

Joseph also has a very strong personality. He moves in on the things he wants. He touches or grabs interesting objects without asking. He refuses to make eye contact with adults or with kids his own age. His parents have to pin his shoulders and demand eye contact. "Look at me; look me in the eye," his mom says to him several times during our first session. His lack of eye contact makes him miss important nonverbal social cues. That, coupled with his physical size, makes him seem like a self-absorbed giant stomping around his dominion.

In our second meeting, he came into my office with his mother, Joyce, and almost knocked me over on his way to a basket of toys. Many young kids won't explore my office without asking permission, or at least checking to see if anyone is watching them. Most are aware of the basic rule that you don't touch someone else's belongings. They are especially wary of adults. Not Joseph. His mother is horrified as he overturns the basket of toys and paws through them. "Joseph Edward!" she shouts. "Is that how we behave?"

Joseph ignores her and makes a beeline for my shelves. He's smart; he knows that adults put the good stuff out of reach. When he can't reach the toys he sees, he wiggles his way behind my desk to grab some trinkets I have placed on my bookshelves. They serve as a test. I'm looking at Joseph's behavioral style. How does he navigate a new environment? How does he behave around a new authority figure, especially when he sees something enticing, something he wants? Can he suppress his desire to touch and take? Does he read the invisible boundaries and barriers we adults have set?

Joseph behaves as though there are no boundaries. He seems to travel in a kind of social oblivion, much as a toddler does. Either he has no idea that these boundaries exist, or he ignores them. I'm betting the latter. Joseph is tall enough to grab at my collection of fossils, sand dollars, gemstones, arrowheads, sharks' teeth, and a desiccated puffer fish with sharp, thorny skin.

Again, Joyce appears horrified and embarrassed. She calls to him, using all three of his names. She continues to shout at him to put the toys back, to get down off the chair he has climbed to reach them. "I'm so sorry," she says to me. "Is it okay if he does that? It isn't okay, is it?"

I note how many questions Joyce places in her commands. Despite her loud voice, she doesn't sound in control. She sounds frustrated and weak. She must feel completely overwhelmed by her ever-growing son. What will she do in a couple of years (yes, that soon) when he is bigger than she is? Joseph will not magically acquire common sense or an awareness of social boundaries. He needs help noticing and respecting boundaries, and she needs help setting them. Although Joyce's main concern in making appointments with me is to deal with his troubles at school, where he has had some run-ins with his classmates, I'm going to talk to her first about dealing with his bossiness at home and lack of social awareness with adults.

I remind Joyce that at Joseph's age, boys are building upon rudimentary skills. In the next couple of years they are careening toward

much more complicated social situations, and while they make progress, they are continually being challenged as social expectations climb.
I often think of it as running up a downward moving escalator. You do
make progress, but it's slow and very frustrating. Boys also will make
social gains in wildly uneven ways. Just because a boy like Joseph has
missed a few steps and gets overly aggressive doesn't mean he's a bad
kid, or that he's destined to be a bully. In reality, he just needs guidance
and direction over the next few months in order to build some basic
skills that counter his assertive, grab-at-the-world temperament. These
basic skills are controlling impulses, being aware of boundaries, reading
social cues, and learning to share and take turns.

Impulse Control

The first skill for Joseph to practice is impulse control. Before his
mother can stop him, Joseph has grabbed one of the arrowheads from
the shelf. He brandishes it like a knife and makes stabbing motions in
the air. Then he looks to a higher shelf, where he sees other objects
that I keep out of reach.

Without asking or even looking at me or at his mother, he climbs
the leather chair next to the bookshelves to get a model of the human
brain that sits on the top shelf. He's still holding the sharp arrowhead
in his palm. I've been asked by many moms to move this chair, but I
keep it here intentionally. It invites dangerous climbing behavior, and
it allows me to test a boy's ability to follow my office rules not to climb
and grab. (In my twenty years of experience working with children,
I can never recall a single girl climbing that chair to grab something
out of reach.) At this point, I wait a little longer to see what his mom
will do. She yells again at Joseph: "We do not go on chairs." Then she
interjects a question: "We don't go on chairs, do we? Please ask Dr.
Rao nicely. Say, 'Can I have that?' Okay?"

I walk over to stand next to Joseph. On the chair, he's a bit taller
than I am. With a firm and measured voice, I ask him to look at me. I
don't use his name. It's been so worn out by now that he doesn't hear
it. "Look at me," I say. When he does, I say, "Good. Is there something
you want here?" He points to the top shelf.

"That," he says. I have already noticed that he doesn't have a good vocabulary. I'm pretty sure that language started late for him. Formulating sentences takes longer for him and is more frustrating than it is for highly verbal kids. That's part of the reason why he grabs first and asks questions later. He needs practice with this.

"What?" I say. "Use your words."
He points again. "That thing."
"What is it? What is it called?" I'm going to insist on some language from him. He looks at me like I'm an idiot.
"That brain thing," he says and rolls his eyes.
"Good," I say. It's important to praise his compliance. "First, give me the arrowhead." He does. "Great. Now, down from the chair." It's not a question. He wants to disobey or to ignore me, but he can't because I have the model of the brain, which he wants. He gets down from the chair, and I give him another task. I hand him the arrowhead and ask him to put it back where he found it. I reward him with another "Good," and reinforce the rules of the office.
"Tell me the rules that we all know about furniture. Your mom has told them to you many times." He smiles at this. He has heard her, but she has allowed him to ignore her.
"No standing on them," he says.
"Good. Excellent," I say. "Now, you sit back over here on this chair for thirty seconds. Count them if you want. Then I'll reach up and get that model for you. Those are the rules. It's your choice." I hand him a small clock with a sweeping second hand. I have deliberately seated him on the chair next to the bookshelves. This is a small test. He could try to climb and take the model, but I've given him an alternative. He can delay or control that impulse and get what he wants. This first delay is a very short period, something I'm sure he can manage. I tell moms that impulsive, grabby boys should be asked to practice this delay at home several times a day. When he grabs something, you take it away for thirty seconds at first, then up to a couple of minutes.

* * *

Believe it or not, this is how to foster social awareness among boys with stronger, more aggressive personalities. Stop them in the act and pause. This allows them to reflect and to gain control over strong impulses. Then teach them a socially appropriate alternative, such as waiting their turn or asking for something first.

Joseph does sit in the chair for thirty seconds, but it's not easy for him to last that long. He sighs dramatically several times, announces his boredom, and calls the clock "stupid." Joyce, for her part, looks extremely anxious during this time. She rises up out of her own chair more than once as if to rush over and hold him in the chair in an effort to make him succeed. I suspect that Joseph is going to give his mother a hard time when she tries this exercise at home. He might slam doors, kick walls, or throw things. He might even cry and say, "You hate me." Other boys shout, "I hate you!" Boys at this age are trying out rudimentary manipulations. They seem to have a sixth sense about what noises and statements will make their parents cave in. It's important to ignore all of this blowback. The task is to wait for thirty seconds. If the boy can't, he gets no toy.

At the end of the thirty seconds, I move over to the bookshelves, and Joseph is right behind me. I point at the model and give the ground rules. For this, I want to be sure he's making eye contact with me. Many boys avoid eye contact when they're very young because it's uncomfortable, but they need to learn to look at adults in order to absorb social cues and take responsibility for their actions. Boys of every age (even grown-ups) sometimes refuse to make eye contact in order to screen out what's being said to them. Then later, they can claim they didn't hear you. I know of one basketball coach who says he never puts a player into a game— even a star player—unless that player makes direct eye contact with him during a sideline huddle. "If a player is not looking at me, he's not listening to me," he says, and he's right, even though he's coaching grown men.

I bring down the model. Joseph shouts, "Cool!" and throws his arms up to take it. Before he can grab it, I say to Joseph, "Look up at me first. Watch me while I talk." When he does, I give him the rules.

He can touch it and take it apart, but he has to be gentle with it. And he has to leave it on the table where I've set it down so that the pieces don't get lost. It's not a long list of rules, but they are rules I can easily enforce. Then I ask him to say the rules back to me. Making him say them out loud means that he has to take responsibility for them. We're making a social contract, something he's going to need to learn to do over and over again at school and in life.

Practicing these things at home will have an enormous impact on life at school. In Joseph's new world, he has to state what he wants in words. No grunting or pointing is allowed. Yes, this will be frustrating for him. It will work his brain and make him cranky in the first couple of weeks. If he defaults to grabbing, he has to sit through a delay of thirty seconds at first, then longer, up to two minutes. If he fails to wait, the toy or privilege is taken away. Finally, he is going to be given simple instructions about behavior before he enters a new social situation. For this he has to make a lot of eye contact and repeat what's said to him. Mom will get down on his level, and insist on eye contact. She'll then state the rules and make him repeat them. ("We're going into the grocery store now. You hang on to the cart. No grabbing cans off the shelves. If you want something, ask first.") Making him repeat her words will give him more practice with language. It will also teach him to take responsibility for following rules. Slowly, we're chipping away at his bullying habits.

Practicing Boundaries at Home

A young boy can look like a bully when he unintentionally plows through boundaries to get at what he wants, reaching over others, grabbing at things, running past others, and knocking into other kids waiting in line. One trick I offer parents is to have their son practice being aware of boundaries in their own home. We set up areas where he can and can't go, what things he can and can't touch. With rambunctious boys, moms and dads sometimes surrender all the real estate in the house to their children, just because fighting those battles all day is exhausting. But many boys really respond to these boundaries. Saying to a boy, "That's Mommy's office. You can't go in there," or even telling him that he can't come into your bedroom, is okay, as long as you're consistent. In many homes children are not welcome to come into their parents' bedroom unless invited. When they have a question at night or first thing in the morning, they stand on the threshold of the room. What's great about that is you've allowed your son to practice the same impulse control he'll need out in the world while he's still at home. At school, he's not going to be able to grab things off someone else's desk or take things away from the teacher. He's not going to own all the real estate in every room he enters. Adding these boundaries to the home will help him practice impulse control. It will recalibrate his expectations for all social situations if he has to think about, and rehearse, these things on a daily basis at home.

Some moms are reticent about setting these sorts of boundaries with their kids. They like the romantic idea of the kids bounding into bed with them in the morning and having the toys and stuffed animals in every room, and that's fine. Eventually, you will want to push back a bit and take back your private life as an adult, and take back your relationship with your spouse. Before your kids enter their teens, they will also want some separation along these lines.

In addition to keeping him out of certain areas of your home, it's okay to tell your son that his toys can't be in every room. No toys are allowed in the bathroom, for example, or no toys in the living room. These seem to be reasonable rules. If he ignores this, remove the toys immediately and hold onto them for a day or so, until he gets the message. Tell him that his toys have to be corralled in one room at the end of each day. Again, we're starting to make him aware that there are rules for behavior in the home and in the world. With daily rehearsal, he will begin to go into other situations and scan the environment around him, looking for those rules. I tell Joyce that Joseph is going to need a lot of practice at this in their home, but this practice will pay dividends almost immediately. His next step, getting better at reading social cues, will be more challenging to learn. By first practicing greater awareness of his physical space, being aware of his belongings and how his actions can disrupt others around him, we are building a good foundation to learn what comes next.

Reading Social Cues

Some boys get tagged as bullies-in-training when in fact they're simply missing social cues. I know of one boy who seems to have little or no social awareness at all. He's the opposite of a shy boy. He is almost six, and when he sees a friend from school at his neighborhood playground, he runs and tackles the other boy. He will hug the other boy and kiss or touch his face and stand way too close. This mortifies his mother, who is working hard with him to set boundaries, as she puts it. She says it's especially hard at the swimming pool, just before his lesson, because he's in the water, and she's not. He'll tackle the other kids in the water. So she calls to him from the side of the pool, and he comes to her, and she makes good eye contact and explains to him that other kids don't like that. To me, she complains that he's fine as long as she's watching him, but as soon as she starts chatting with another mother, he goes after one of the other kids.

That's no coincidence. Here is a boy who seems to have no idea what appropriate social behavior is, yet he knows when his mom is watching and when she's not. I call that reverse referencing. Rather than looking to his mom for approval before deciding how to act, he's looking to see if she's watching him before doing something he knows she'd dislike.

Here's a boy who has been identified with nonverbal learning disorders and sensory processing disorders, who has his mother trained to watch him constantly and has figured out how to escape discipline. Smart little guy. No doubt he has some real issues. He fails to take in social cues that would stop him from barreling through other kids. Still, we need to understand that he isn't totally socially clueless. There is some element of choice going on here. He's more aware socially than his diagnosis would let on. I see this in nearly every boy I've met. Don't let these types of diagnoses make you think that you can't train a boy away from these behaviors.

He may have a disposition to be strong or impulsive, but pull him out immediately. Cut the swim lesson short. Reward him for every five minutes that he doesn't rough up another kid. Overpractice getting in the pool and getting out. Do it over and over again until he gets it right.

When considering how to temper a boy's naturally aggressive social behavior, I caution moms to consider their son's environment. What are his immediate influences? I worked with one little boy, named Archie, who was six years old at the time. His mother told me that he struggled to get through playdates and had earned himself a reputation as the neighborhood bully. He was a kind of hockey goon, especially with younger or shyer kids. He threw elbows, pushed kids in the face, and grabbed toys away from them. He threw body blocks, initiated games of keep away, and had learned at least one swear word. With such a vast array of antisocial habits, it's no surprise that he was not invited to many neighborhood parties and picnics. When I met Archie, he was sporting a Mohawk and carrying the latest portable electronic game. This signaled to me that there are older boys in his life whom he strives to emulate. I suspected that many of the habits he used on other kids had been used successfully on him first. His mother told me that Archie spends his after school hours with his cousins, who are between three and five years older than he is. They tolerate Archie's presence in their games only under duress from their mom. It's probably safe to assume that this group of boys gets very little supervision, unless they're breaking something.

In social terms, Archie has a twofold problem. First, he's got a very strong personality. He has always been louder and more active than the other boys his age in the neighborhood. His second problem is that he's been tossed into an environment that's too sophisticated for him. For a couple of hours every day he has to deal with boys who are bigger, smarter, and stronger than he is. That means he needs to be even more aggressive to keep pace, and he has to ape their type of teasing and wrestling. When he is instead surrounded by kids his own age, he has no idea what the parameters of good behavior are.

Boys who need some help reading social cues can improve if they have a chance to practice. Step one: initiate rules and take away playtime right away if they are violated. Examples are "No touching other kids" and "Ask before you reach." These simple rules you can practice at home. Withhold something your son wants if he grabs for it. Make him wait. Make him use his words to state what he wants without grabbing or pushing. Step two: prompt him again before any social encounter. Get down on his eye level and go over the rules again while he watches your face. No touching. No pushing. No grabbing. Use your words. Make him repeat these rules. Step three: during the play-date, remove him if he violates any of these rules. Put him on the sidelines for a few minutes. Over time, he will improve. He might show noticeable improvement right away.

In Archie's case, his mother also needs to consider how much she wants his older cousins to influence his behavior. It's clear to me that he's learning social habits that aren't useful to him in his peer group and are going to cause ongoing problems for him at school. I cautioned his mom to rethink Archie's after school time. Either she needs to limit his exposure to these cousins, or she needs to provide more supervision for these playtimes.

Sharing and Turn Taking

This is a fundamental social concept based on reciprocity and fairness. If I have something, so should you. Very young kids don't understand this concept fully. Think of your two- or three-year-old toddler trying to grab a piece of fruit or candy out of your hand. He's thinking, "You have that; so should I." This is a fundamental me-only application of fairness. Or consider when your son sees someone at the grocery store with a balloon. He's going to turn to you and ask, "Where's my balloon?" The harder part is when there is one resource and your son has it, and he must give it up to someone else. When it's someone else's turn to go on the swing or down the slide or to hold a puppy, he has to give up the experience he's having or anticipating. That's hard for him. He also has to trust that he will get another turn.

Many boys get stuck in this toddler mode of grabbing, pushing, and taking objects away from others. Is it because they don't have any character? Are they bullying? Not at all. It's because boys are driven heavily by sensation. They crave direct experience with the world. What they need is practice in controlling that impulse to grab. They need lots of practice in giving up a resource in order to get it back. I tell parents to remember that there are plenty of grown-ups in the world who haven't learned how to do this and don't know how to share or to control their impulses. Just because your son needs to be taught this skill doesn't mean there's anything wrong with him. But don't ignore this. He has to learn to wait turns, to give things up to get them again, and to tolerate watching while others have what he doesn't have at that moment.

I tell parents to add what I call a staged errand to their routine a couple of times a week. Take your son to a place where you have to wait in line. This can be at a bakery or coffee shop, the dry cleaners, or the post office. Tell him what you're up to. You're waiting in line for something, and at the end, if he's good, he can have a reward. The key is to choose an errand that is not crucial to complete that day. Keep the option of leaving immediately if he can't wait with patience. If he does wait, give him a reward. This could be a cookie at the bakery or the return of a toy that has been taken away. It doesn't have to be a big reward. The point is to treat these errands as practice for him, a learning opportunity about delaying gratification.

Empathy

Moms especially often see this skill as the hallmark of healthy social development. They frequently ask me about their sons' apparent lack of empathy when playing with others. I tell moms not to expect much when boys are young. Even boys at age six or seven don't show much empathy. Empathy is difficult to explain or teach. Being able to feel or imagine what others might be feeling is pretty sophisticated stuff.

A young boy's need to compete, to win, to be the best will likely eclipse any feelings of empathy that are growing inside him. But these feelings are probably in there, even if you don't see them much.

Empathy is a social skill that allows you to appreciate what someone else may be feeling. ("I won't take a toy away from you because if someone did that to me, I wouldn't like it.") Obviously, this is an essential ingredient in later positive social behavior.

But we're talking about much later. Even when boys are six to eight years old and are getting into board games such as checkers, Battleship, Connect 4, and organized sports games like Wiffle ball, 4-square, and shooting baskets, they will display empathy only on a limited scale. These games have set rules, which means that everyone needs to take a turn in order for the game to work. If a boy doesn't allow others to take turns, they get angry, they quit, and the game stops. That's how boys learn to share and take turns. "If I cheat and take two turns and throw a tantrum, you'll walk away": that's the extent of their thinking. I'm sorry to say this, but boys generally don't take turns or share because they want to be nice. For many young boys, it's about keeping a playmate in the game so they can try and beat him.

Boys have to weigh their own need to be best and in control against the real possibility of presiding over an empty game board. Don't expect overt sharing and empathy in your very young son. It's there, emerging very slowly, but at such early ages it is often hidden beneath the more important developmental tasks at hand—to explore the world, move about, and express power. Young boys tagged as bullies are often late in the empathy game. Be patient, but be firm with your son. Remove him immediately or take away toys when he's acting mean with others. Don't lecture. He's heard it a million times over. He knows what he's supposed to do. What he needs is more practice on holding back, pausing, and thinking a little more outside himself.

Boys Are Empathetic Late Bloomers

I once worked with a boy named Matthew, who never shared. He sought out much older and much younger playmates, "victims," I called them. They became human puppets for him to pose and do as he said. They'd be playing simple physical games of tag, climbing, who could run the fastest, who threw the best, and so on. Always, he set the rules. Always, he decided the outcome, and always in his favor. His mother first began to worry about this when he was five, and it was still an issue when he was eight. His CEO dad fought with Matthew about this, warning him he had to play fair with other boys, telling him that everyone was equal. What's interesting is that this dad is in a job in which he can't play fair himself. He has to be tough, directive, and use workers to achieve specific goals that he sets. Sound familiar? I also found that when this father was playing with Matthew at home, he was accidentally modeling his CEO behavior. Playing with Dad was about doing everything Dad's way or not at all. Matthew's mother said to me, "Nobody in the neighborhood will play with Matthew except the ones who are really little. Is he a bully?"

"Wait," I cautioned. "Don't assume this is all bad." She was pretty confused. But the truth is that this is the way social groups work. Some lead, and most follow. I told her that Matthew will adapt, because he'll have to. When kids get angry and walk away, he'll be alone. He will learn it's less fun to play alone, and he'll be more apt to share more and give in to get friends to stick around. The truth is that Matthew is bossy and direct, as some boys are. (Some men, too.) He leads because he wants to set things up for his own successes. It's true that this appears completely selfish and self-centered, particularly when compared to the seemingly sensitive boys who share and take turns easily. Remember that shy boys sometimes share and capitulate in order to avoid conflict, or because they are afraid to be left alone on the playground. They are often attracted to boys like Matthew who take over. This dynamic will change in time. The shyer, more compliant boys may get sick of giving in after a while and learn to become more assertive. At that point, Matthew will have to mellow out a bit. I tell moms of these assertive boys that their boys are just taking a different path to social awareness. Forcing compliance on them doesn't work.

Kids aren't fully able to empathize, or take another person's emotional viewpoint, until around eight years old, and for many it happens later. The best way to gently introduce some of this is to reinforce the connection between a boy's bossy actions and the outcome. Do this in a calm, objective way, not as a lecture. Say, for instance, "Matthew, I know you're mad that Ben left and won't play with you. When you don't give him a turn, he leaves." Then ask a question: "What could you do to get him to play longer next time?"

Lengthy moral lessons don't work. Your son will just tune you out. Instead, stating a fact and asking a question will put the burden on him to think of a different way to behave.

What Are Appropriate Social Skills for Young Boys?

Recently, I helped a mom think through this very question. Suki's son, Evan, is three, and she's been taking him to a playgroup as well as the park to help him make friends and socialize. Evan is very active and doesn't like to play cooperatively with other boys. In the sandbox, he's the one who grabs trucks away from other kids or throws sand at them when they move in on what he considers his territory. At playgroup, he pushes kids out of the way to get what he wants and hoards toys. Also, he has become fascinated with the younger sister of one of the boys at playgroup, and he plays too roughly with her. Once he knocked her down, and a couple of times he tried to touch her face, which made the little girl's mother angry.

Naturally, Suki would love to sit casually in the park and chat with other moms while Evan runs about and plays nicely with the other children, but Evan's not ready for that yet. Suki has noticed that there are boys Evan's age at playgroup who play well with the other kids and ask to take turns. These are the ones who run to their mothers to report Evan's bad behavior. Suki asks me if there's something wrong with Evan. When is he going to play like the other kids? I try to reassure Suki that social skills vary widely in young boys and that Evan will develop these in time as his development proceeds and new opportunities to learn come his way.

Often those reassurances calm parents, but I noticed that Suki was very stressed when talking about Evan's social adventures in the park and playgroup. She tells me that she's getting odd looks from the other mothers at the playground, and that one friend invited her to an informal playdate at a mutual friend's house and then called back to withdraw the invitation. Suki suspects this is because Evan had a problem with one of the other kids at the playground the week before.

I tell all parents that the playground is not a performance; it is a dress rehearsal. The same is true for playdates and even birthday parties at this age. Think of these experiences as a time for trial-and-error learning. Here your son can get the cobwebs out and make his mistakes. You have to understand that he's new at all this. You can't expect too much beyond where he is now. By making mistakes, and by learning from them, he will grow and mature.

The trouble with trying to encourage a boy's social skills at this age is that playdates and playground time are also public social experiences for the adults. Parents are judging other parents based on their children's behavior. The first task is to separate the two.

You can't go to the playground feeling as if you're on the spot. That will communicate the message to your son that you're not confident and in charge. And it communicates to the other adults that you aren't a confident parent. You go in and set the tone that this is the way your boy is, and that's that. Some days are good, and some days he struggles, but you're dealing with it as a parent and not as a person worried about the judgment of others.

I gave Suki something concrete to focus on. Between appointments, I instructed her to keep a journal to record notes about her outings to the park. I asked her to write down what happened. Specifically, she was to note how many kids there were, the noise level at the park, and on which toys or in which areas of the park her son spent his time. Then she was to briefly describe what went wrong and what went well. I emphasize to moms that when they are noting their son's behavior in this way, they should be sure to note the positives as well. If they focus only on what is going wrong in their boy's behavior, they end up with a distorted and negative view of his real social abilities.

From Suki's notes, we learned something interesting. Turns out Evan had his hardest time entering into play areas and when it was time to leave. When arriving at the playground or playdate, he used aggressive tactics to stake out his space in the room or the playground. Also, when it was time to leave, he had trouble shifting gears to end the playdate. That frequently caused a meltdown and a fight with her. So, essentially, he made a bad first and last impression. People have a tendency to remember first and last impressions. A bully is born!

Still, the middle wasn't always so terrible. Evan was more successful playing with younger or much older boys and passive kids who let him lead. He wasn't great at sharing his toys, but he's three. A lot of kids aren't young diplomats at this age. I assured Suki that this wasn't an unusual profile for an only child, one who also has a strong assertive temperament.

Once we went through her notes, I announced, "Great! Now we know his baseline." A baseline is a starting point, the level at which he's behaving currently. We now know what is reasonable to expect from his social skills. We also know with whom he plays most successfully and least successfully. We have a place to start training him to develop better social skills.

We came up with a basic plan, one that will work for most kids. I encouraged Suki to bring Evan to the park as often as she could, even every day if she wanted to. Be sure, I said, to bring him around the same time, a time when he's not hungry or tired. Then I instructed her to prime him for the experience. That is, she should squat down to make eye contact with him. Using a nice but serious voice, she could give him one or two simple instructions for this social experience: "No touching any other child at all. No touching. If you do, we'll leave immediately. Promise?" She makes him repeat these instructions. No touching. Promise.

Every day she did this before entering the park, and his hitting decreased dramatically to just a single incident later in the week. True to her word, Suki removed him, screaming and kicking, immediately from the park. No second chances, no long debates or promises, no lectures about why it didn't go well. I further coached her to keep the playtime relatively short to increase Evan's success rate. Leave kids to play too long, and things usually fall apart at some point. Based on Suki's journal, we knew Evan was good for about twenty minutes.

At playgroup, where there was a girl whose face he liked to touch, Suki went through this same routine all over again. Learning is often like this. Young boys may become better behaved in one place, only to need work generalizing that behavior to other situations or groups of kids. Suki said to Evan, "No touching little Emma." He learned to back off from Emma and on his own give space to the other kids based on this instruction. That showed he was starting to generalize the "no touching" idea by himself. That's progress!

Suki began to relax. She gained a system to teach her son better and better behavior, while not feeling she had to change him completely. She began to focus on what she needed to do rather than on what others thought she needed to do. Evan continued to try to lead all the time. He always wanted to decide the game, the rules, and who got which toy. That's his nature. He would never turn into the quiet, compliant, wait-your-turn kind of kid. Suki began to see that maybe it was a good thing, actually, as long as Evan could control his powerful personality.

Bullying at School: How to Deal with the Bullying Label

A lot has been written about how to help kids in school who are being bullied by others. Relatively little has been discussed about how to help kids who have been labeled as bullies at school. Many of the kids I work with have strong personalities, and after a couple of problems at school their parents are called in for a meeting at which the teacher or school administrator uses the *B* word to describe a boy's behavior. What they're really describing might be a discipline problem in the classroom that involves several kids, or it might be a situation in which an overwhelmed teacher wants some support from parents, and using this charged word is the best way to get everyone's attention.

Back to Joseph. He's struggling more at school since being labeled as a bully. It doesn't help that he's the biggest boy in first grade, and he's also one of the youngest and least socially and emotionally mature. Many boys like him go through a progression in which they are first thought of by teachers as troublemakers, then the teacher describes this behavior as "bullying." Before long, these boys have been labeled as a bully at school and perhaps at home.

At one of our meetings, Joyce arrives very upset. She is clutching a small note, which she hands to me, and says, "On the bus, he was sitting next to a little girl, who told him to move to a different seat. He took his baseball cap off and hit her in the face with it. It left a mark. This note says that he could get kicked off the bus permanently."

Like a budding defense lawyer, Joseph bursts out, "She was bothering me!" Then he tears up and turns toward the wall, his chin on his chest.

His mother continues: "Last week he and another boy were arguing over a book at circle time, and Joseph took the bin of books and threw it across the floor. He's constantly bossing the other kids. His teacher says he's a bully in the classroom."

There are a number of things going on here. One is that Joseph knows he's in trouble, big trouble, at school. While he might not know what the word *bully* means, he knows it's a lightning rod for all the adults in his life. The other is that Joyce is afraid the school is right and that she's failed to shape her son's character in some fundamental way. Many moms like Joyce fear that their rambunctious boys will never soften into polite, well-mannered young men. I have to tell them that this may be only the beginning, that in terms of hard edges and bad attitude and boundary pushing, well, it's going to get worse before it gets better. Their sons will improve, but it will take some time. They'll need to stay calm in the meantime.

I've worked with many young boys who have been identified at school as bullies, boys as young as three and four years old, because they have hit or bitten another child, grabbed toys away from someone, teased another child, or are naturally bossy. None of these behaviors in isolation, or in one or two incidents, is enough to call a young child a bully. Many kids engage in these behaviors at some time or another; many of them experiment with teasing and bossing and grabbing and hitting. They are negative but expedient social tools, and the truth is that in the short run, they work. Boys who tend to be shy and hold back do these things less often. Boys who have stronger personalities do them more often. But these experiments in bad behavior have nothing to do with real bullying.

Other boys get labeled as bullies because they lag in their development of emotional control and can become easily overwhelmed. Parents tell me that their boys' anger comes on like a summer storm. These boys seem okay for a while until they blow up. I tell moms especially that boys and men alike tend to sit on their emotions until they can't control them any longer. Boys have even less control than grown men. They give no real sign that they are losing control of their anger until it's already gone.

In Joseph's case we have to add his physical size to the mix. Because he's so tall and so big, the teachers on the playground are going to expect more of him. They will treat him like a much older boy, even though he's one of the youngest members of the first grade. Also, boys of his size are always being told not to "pick on" smaller kids. Listen to that message. Joseph has to be more gentle, more mature, and more in control than anyone else on the playground who may want to tease him or take a shot at him. Some kids who are two years older than he is, and therefore much more verbal and savvy about how playground antics work, can taunt and tease him, knowing that when he strikes, he'll be the one sent to the principal's office. I'm not suggesting we pity Joseph. This is his lot in life. He's big, he'll always be big, he's immature, and he will grow up emotionally at his own pace. What we can do is give him skills to help him cope with a situation that will likely follow him throughout his school years.

What Is a Bully?

Joyce is not quite convinced, and I understand why. The bully label is powerful. When teachers use it, it gets serious traction, and it sticks. Still, I try to help parents understand why their sons can't really be bullies at this young age. It helps to allay fears before we talk about the techniques that will help their boys get along better in the classroom or at the playground. Otherwise there are so many overlapping behaviors (scuffles, pushing, and bossiness) that can be confused with bullying.

A bully is a boy (or girl) with deep-seated insecurity and low self-esteem. A bully is often a very hurt and neglected child who tries to steal a few confidence points by taking the wrong, if easy, approach of knocking around someone smaller and weaker. Bullies select their targets carefully and use intimidation through words and fists. They challenge other kids in order to get a quick self-esteem fix. They use this technique, brute physical force and angry words, because they have been taught to. Many bullies have been victims themselves, often at home, of parents or much older siblings. They come from home environments that are not nurturing, and in some cases, they don't feel safe. They've learned that there is only one power dynamic in the world, and that's domination.

That doesn't describe Joseph. In fact, it doesn't describe any of the boys I have seen in my practice. The boys I see tend to have problems with managing their impulses and emotions or with taking social cues. They don't have strategies for managing their own behavior yet, but they are ready to learn. Joseph is a great example. He's not seeking out younger kids and picking on them or using intimidation. Rather, the incidents come from disputes in the moment. Joseph gets into scuffles at school because he believes he's right about something important. In his mind, he's trying to protect himself or his belongings. His frustration is sudden, not calculated. The trouble is that he overreacts and expresses himself inappropriately. Although it's not bullying, it's a style of behavior that needs to be upgraded.

Joseph's teacher is pressuring Joyce to have him evaluated for ADHD. She hints that he might also suffer from "oppositional disorder" because he often defies the rules she sets in the classroom and sometimes deliberately annoys the other kids in class by taking paper away from them, for example, when they're trying to write or read. The clinical definition for oppositional disorder is pretty broad, but it tends to describe those who oppose authority figures and are defiant, negative, and hostile toward those in charge. These people are often touchy; they rebel against all rules, and they spend a lot of energy stirring up trouble. In almost every case, including this one, I believe we should make a serious attempt to modify a boy's behavior before looking for a diagnosis to attach to it, and to him. I'm not blaming the teacher for making these suggestions, though. Intelligent people like to find solutions for problems. They often look at behavior as a puzzle, one they can solve if they find the right label for it. Yet, with young boys, the labels aren't very good at describing what's really going on. They certainly don't describe the temporary nature of these problems.

Why Is He Doing This?

Almost every parent faced with a teacher's charge about a boy's bullying or violent behavior in his early school years responds with these questions: (1) "What did I do wrong?" (the answer in almost every case is nothing) and (2) "Shouldn't he know better?"

This seems so reasonable. "Other kids understand that hitting is wrong. Why doesn't my boy understand? Shouldn't a boy know by age six that hitting is wrong?" Yes, he should, but my bet is that he does know that already. A lot of boys this age know that what they're doing is wrong, but they just can't stop themselves. There is a huge difference between knowing how to behave when you're calm and knowing how to behave when your emotions are boiling over, even for adults. For young boys, rage can overtake them and then disappear in a couple of heartbeats.

Also, a boy who is still developing language skills is at a further disadvantage. If a classmate grabs something from him or says something mean, he doesn't have a little voice inside coaching him to ask for what he wants or to stand up for himself. When someone encroaches on him or frustrates him, he can't put the words together quickly enough to say, "Stop it." He probably can't even say, "No." He can't find his voice because he has had very little practice using it. That's a skills deficit. He can't talk his way through his emotions. He probably doesn't even know what they are. When his brain develops more fully, and when his language skills strengthen, his behavior will change. Aggression is normal, and it won't go away. What a boy has to learn is how to suppress that aggression when he needs to. Eventually he will learn how to channel aggression into other outlets.

Finally, many parents fail to realize that even adults need constant reinforcement of society's most basic rules. I ask parents to imagine what life in their town would be like without the presence of law enforcement, parking and no-parking signs, and traffic signals—even for one day. Try to imagine what a single major league game (in any sport) would be like without the presence of referees or umpires. Many of us can't wait in line at the deli without heeding the written reminder to "please take a ticket." We need thousands of reminders each day to do what's expected of us, so let's be fair to our preschool and grade school boys. Most of them don't have signs around them saying, "Don't grab; please ask your friend to share." The schools won't give them these signs, but we can.

Strategies for Containing Behavior at School

Joseph's mother is already working on helping him respect personal boundaries at home. He's learning to make eye contact; he's learning to use his words more often; he's learning that when he grabs, he's going to lose the thing he wants; he's learning to sit for thirty seconds or more. All of these skills will help him in school.

We need to build on these skills by setting up similar expectations for him, and similar skills to practice, at school. He has to know that he has very clear, firm rules for his behavior when he's away from home. Removing the gray zone for him will actually be a relief for him. A boy like Joseph with a strong personality actually responds well to firm rules. We have to get both of his parents involved in order to do this, and we have to get rid of the bully label. These are the priorities.

Setting Reminders

Many teachers are willing to help with this kind of behavioral training. In Joseph's case, we can set up a graduated scale of reminders for him in the classroom, although I wouldn't want to burden his teacher with a whole litany of reminders. Teachers at the kindergarten and first-grade level already work very hard. They are teaching core skills, including reading, on which an entire academic career will rest, and they are dealing with jiggly, impatient, rambunctious kids all day. Still, if Joseph's mom can identify one skill she'd like him to practice that week, she might ask the teacher to help by giving him a key phrase a couple of times an hour.

One excellent teacher I know of does this automatically with kids who have certain predictable issues. For example, a few students each year struggle with personal space. They pick at other kids' hair and clothing, for example, and hug too aggressively. They also favor slow-motion pushing; that is, they lean against other kids to move them out of the way. It may not look like pushing to an adult who's watching, but it's a definite body block. If a behavior like this occurs, this sly teacher will quietly say the offending child's name and add, "In your box, please." She has already explained that personal space is like an invisible box, that we all have our own space, and that we stay inside our boxes. At the beginning of the school year, she says, "In your box, please" several times an hour, but by the end, she hardly needs to say it at all.

If Joyce is willing to sit down with Joseph and explain the concept he has to work on, for example, asking for something instead of grabbing, or saying "Stop" instead of pushing if he doesn't like what's going on around him, his teacher might be willing to reinforce this behavior several times a day. At the start of every activity, she might say, "Joseph, ask first." Then, if he does grab, she can say it again: "Ask first." Perhaps Joseph can earn points that get him something special at school, or when he returns home, if he can listen and stop his impulse to grab or be too physically aggressive. If at all possible, Joyce, Joseph's teacher, and all the adults who work with Joseph should use the same language and prompts. One last important thing that I would encourage Joseph's teacher to do is to help Joseph earn a new image at school. The bully label is hard to shed. Joseph's teacher could enlist his help in carrying out tasks for her, running errands, and doing other high-status chores that communicate to the other students that she values, likes, and trusts him. She also could pair Joseph with another boy or girl who needs help with something. We need to help boys who've been tagged as bullies to be seen in a new way, or else many times these labels keep boys like Joseph stuck in the bullying rut. If the class thinks of Joseph as a bully, even if he's been working to change his aggressive behavior, they may not give him a chance to change. Soon, Joseph will give up trying to improve because it's not getting him anywhere. That will cause him to give in to others' expectations of him. We call this a self-fulfilling prophecy, and it's how expectations of us can accidentally drive us toward the very behaviors we don't want to show.

Practicing Calm

The other thing many boys need practice with is lengthening the time between the incident that triggers their anger and their response to it. Anger in boys at this age really is like a lightning flash. It can arrive and be gone again instantly.

I know of another teacher who uses "flower breathing," which works great with some boys. In this technique, the child is instructed to take a deep breath through his nose, as if he were sniffing a flower. He then lets the breath out through his mouth. The teacher tells the child to do this whenever he's frustrated or angry or upset. At first, this type of controlled breathing is a distraction, a chance for the child to begin to control his emotions. So, when a child in her classroom gets upset, this teacher uses the prompt "flower breath." The kids now have something to do, something other than throwing a toy or hitting.

One boy I know did well clasping his hands together in his lap whenever he felt angry. That method could work well with Joseph. Physically strong boys who have lots of energy can channel their powerful feelings into a simple act. Literally flexing their muscles gives them the feeling that they're doing something, and they are. They're just not hitting anyone or breaking anything. Teaching boys like Joseph to do this when they're at home and then slowly use it at school will take time and a lot of practice. They'll need to be shown how to do this when they're angry at home and praised for doing it whenever they get upset. Eventually this behavioral technique will become part of these boys' bag of tricks for getting through the day. When boys get older, they can use their imaginations. When their feelings get out of control, they can use specific imagery, such as hitting a home run or thinking of their favorite toy or place to play, to convert those negative feelings into positive ones. They can learn to ask for help from adults when they feel their emotions careening out of control. I wouldn't introduce this idea to most boys under age six. They might need to be seven or eight years old, even older, to be able to use their thoughts to control their feelings.

Be Patient

The final piece of advice I would give to Joyce or any parent working with a boy who is struggling behaviorally is to be patient. Calming yourself, using your words appropriately, when your son is upset models for your son good self-control. Kids, after all, watch and learn from us, more so than when we lecture or yell. Remember that, for many young boys, controlling the impulse to grab and shove is not an instinctual skill. It has to be taught and practiced. We need to start with only one or two skills, and rehearse them over and over, before they can get nailed down and it's time to move on to other skills.

Many parents expect their sons to learn faster than can be expected, given their developmental level. They are fooled by their sons' strength, physical confidence, size, or cleverness in other areas. They assume that their boys can learn new self-control skills at the same fast clip as, say, their athletic or mathematical abilities. They use themselves as a comparison, or older children, or children who aren't struggling with these behaviors. That's a mistake. Never be fooled by bright kids. They still need time to decipher, decode, process, store, and rehearse in order to learn a new skill. With your guidance and patience, your boy can learn, too.

CHAPTER 5

He Won't Sit Still!

David is an energetic six-year-old who has gone through more babysitters than anyone in the neighborhood. He is an unusually handsome boy with dark eyes, black hair shaved in a buzz cut, and a dimpled smirk. He is always running, always yelling. He scales furniture and swings from the banister. If he sees something interesting—a knife, a piece of raw meat, or a pan on a hot stove—he will grab it rather than asking what it is. His curiosity and physical energy seem endless to his parents and teachers. Two years ago, he watched his grandfather, who was visiting from Brazil, climb a ladder onto the roof of the house and then surprised everyone by climbing it himself—all the way up onto the roof. To say that his mother is always tense would be a profound understatement. She has grown accustomed to monitoring his every move and even shouts a preemptive "no" whenever he takes a step toward anything dangerous or toward anything he knows he's not supposed to touch.

David had already been diagnosed with ADHD at age five. While this diagnosis could apply, a label doesn't deal with how to help him cope with the behavioral demands of kindergarten, which require him to sit still and listen. David is often in trouble at school because he jumps around and wheels his arms and invades the space of other kids. In addition, an ADHD diagnosis can't help his mother enforce common-sense rules about how to remain safe. At home, David likes to turn the radio up loud so he can jump and spin around in dancelike spasms. He has already been to the emergency room once with a cut forehead. He was doing cartwheels in the living room and landed on the glass coffee table. The ER doctor who gave David his stitches hinted that he might need to file a report with the Department of Social Services.

David's mother feels that she's being held hostage by his frenetic behavior, and she's very concerned about his situation at school. She's afraid he'll fall behind if he can't sit still. Lots of parents tell me they think their three-, four-, or five-year-old son has ADHD because he fidgets. He moves constantly and can't control himself; therefore, medication might help calm him down, they say. Right? Wrong. Boys at this age fidget and run around and scream and get crazy because it releases healthy energy and helps them calm down. For a boy this age, the only way out of the extreme ants-in-your-pants feeling that builds up in them is to plow through it, mow it down with activity. That activity, those crazy dance moves, the jumping in place, the wiggling, all of it clears his mind and gets him ready to focus. Physical activity works better than medication—faster, too—and parents had better be ready to encourage fidgeting and jumping and, yes, throwing if they want sanity in their homes. This is all healthy and normal. When your son is older, he can go outside and shoot baskets for forty minutes or play catch with someone or hit a tennis ball against a wall before he has to come in and do homework. Right now, your little guy doesn't have those skills. He doesn't have the freedom to do that. He has to handle pent-up energy however he can.

Boys like David, who have been tagged with ADHD, crave lots of movement. In fact, adding movement to David's day, and lots of it, may have a profound impact on his behavior. Some kids with an ADHD diagnosis who struggle in school and who are allowed to do their homework standing up, leaning on a counter, or sitting on a large exercise ball on which they have to maintain balance see their fidgetiness diminish rapidly.

Some parents say that they've had great luck telling their boys to balance on those big fitness balls while doing homework. The fitness balls engage the brain with low-level stimulation because they require the boys to constantly readjust their balance in order to stay seated. This stimulation is like playing music in the background. In fact, many of these boys will do better listening to music while they do their homework in high school and college.

By engaging the brain in this way, boys who struggle with attentional problems can focus on their homework. I think you should use anything along these lines that works, but you should be careful about how you use it. One solution isn't going to work all the time. I know of one mother who had her son use a fitness ball at the dinner table for the same reason. It was the only way she thought she could get her son to sit still and concentrate on eating his food without fidgeting and wreaking havoc at the dinner table. The problem is that he's now almost eleven years old, and he refuses to eat at the table without this fitness ball. Obviously, he doesn't need it at school; he'd be laughed out of the cafeteria if he tried to roll a fitness ball in there. But he's got his parents completely on the ropes about this. If you do start using a crutch of some sort to get your son to behave, you have to have a plan for weaning him, and sooner rather than later.

There are many other strategies available for helping easily distractible boys to focus. Taking activity breaks, a few minutes here and there, to let off steam can significantly help boys maintain focus when asked to do so. Some experts have proposed that the symptoms of ADHD can be treated with regular exercise. John Ratey, a noted Harvard psychiatrist and the coauthor of *Driven to Distraction,* believes exercise benefits our brains, elevating chemicals that improve focus and self-control, decrease fidgetiness, and sharpen our ability to learn. Further, Ratey speculates that if children could get enough rigorous exercise, they might not need any drugs to treat ADHD. We can see why the average school day with its six hours of enforced sitting and listening just doesn't work for most boys.

Energy to Burn

The first question is how to burn off a boy's excess energy. A generation or more ago, children were sent outside to play and expected to stay outside and find something to do pretty much all day long, weather permitting or not. The parents of many of the little guys I see have fond memories of playing outside for whole afternoons or whole days. If they lived in a suburban setting, they used communal back-yards to play spy games, touch football, or tag, or made up games with whatever was available, such as kick the can. If they lived in an urban area, they walked to a park or playground with older kids, or they just played on the block, where other kids would congregate after lunch and dinner.

One dad recalled for me an elaborate game of bouncing a ball on the steps of his front stoop. Unlike suburban kids, he had no backyard, nor did any of the other kids in the neighborhood. No matter. They found a game that could test their skills at throwing and catching. In this game, which they called baseball, the person holding the ball was the batter, while the other person was the fielder. Each step had its own value. If the batter threw the ball and hit the top step, it was a home run. If he hit the bottom step, it was a strike. There were different rules for games with two kids or three kids, different games that could include older or younger kids. And this dad remembers them all.

These days many boys don't spend much unsupervised time out-side. Parents feel that they need to keep an eye on their boys, and they do. The trouble is that parents don't have eight to ten hours a day to supervise their children's play. Preschoolers wind up getting all their physical activity in short bursts of supervised time at a playground or during athletic lessons that generally last forty minutes to an hour. This is not enough time to burn off all the physical and emotional energy generated by a little boy. The result of all this pent-up energy can be a kind of hyperactivity seized on as the primary symptom of an attention deficit disorder.

Know that boys who have been tagged with ADHD crave a lot of physical activity. They need to run around. At the very least, they need space in which to move. A few parents have told me that they bought a mini trampoline (including all the safety gear and accesso-ries) for their ADHD boys, and they say that these boys go out in the backyard and just jump for hours. Afterward, they seem calmer, more alert, and more responsive to their parents. This is just one example of how providing a physical outlet can make a big difference.

Signs That He's Not Moving Enough

Are you after your son every two minutes to slow down? Is he touching and moving all the objects in a room? Is his fidgeting so loud and distracting that you find yourself telling him to just stop doing that? Is he melting down, crying over nothing? Maybe he's not getting enough activity in his day.

One of the first things I say to parents of boys who are having trouble paying attention and sitting still at school, or who are tearing through the house at home, is that they've got to get more activity into their son's daily routine. Parents sometimes hear this and think, "Okay, I'll sign him up for Little League or soccer." That's not what I'm talking about. The kind of movement that will help a young boy calm down is much more primitive than organized sports. Also, it has to start much earlier in a boy's development than most organized sports will allow.

Let's first break down movement into its most basic components. Don't think "sports" or highly organized "activities" just yet for boys ages two to four. Think big, gross motor movements. A young boy needs ways to release energy and rehearse moving his legs and arms—walking, running, jumping, rolling, tumbling, and kicking for the large muscles of his lower body; twisting, throwing, tossing (catching comes later on), and other big arm movements for his upper body. Boys at this age should be encouraged to freely move in a fun and playful way, maybe with a ball or some other simple, safe object, such as a foam bat or Frisbee. They will need space and room to explore. They should be moving about and playing on a grassy area or on safe playground equipment, or in a spacious carpeted basement or playroom, but no matter, they should be free to move in the way their body was designed.

I know of one mom who found her son hanging onto the towel rack in their bathroom. He was holding onto it and lifting his legs up, so that he would dangle from the rack. She got a little upset with him because he was about to rip the towel rack from the wall. Her solution was to buy a fitness bar that she could install in a doorway in a temporary way, the kind that older boys would use to do chin-ups. She was a little sheepish when she described this to me, but her son loves it. "Does he try to do chin-ups?" I asked. She shook her head. "He just, you know, hangs there for a while," she said. "He does it every day. He says it feels good." It probably does feel good for him to work those muscles and to defy gravity, if only for a few minutes.

Activities for Younger Boys

I know of one mother of two boys, ages three and five, who takes them outside nearly every single day, regardless of the weather. True, if the temperature is below zero, they stay in, but if it's merely raining or snowing, out they go, all of them together. In rain, they stomp puddles and don't care if their clothes get wet. On one recent outing, her oldest boy dove headlong into a particularly deep puddle as if sliding into second base. His mother just laughed at him, and they kept going on around the block. "Well, we knew he couldn't get any wetter," she said to me afterward. The only potential problem was that one of the neighborhood kids saw all this out the window, and he turned to his parents, wanting to know if he could do the same thing. In winter, they march in the snow and make forts, or if it's a bit windy, they just run around the yard for a few laps.

Another mom I know times her son while he runs. Really. She tells him to run to the fence in their yard and back, and she counts out loud for him while he does it. He loves to run and, at age four, already prides himself on being fast, so she times him. Back and forth he goes four, five, six times, and when he's winded, she knows he's ready to come back inside for a few minutes of quiet play.

One thing parents need to do to give boys a chance to expend energy is to develop a sense of humor about strange behavior. Many young boys bounce on the couch, crab walk across the floor, spin around in one place, hop in place, and do other odd things seemingly for no reason. I remember one appointment I had with a boy, who liked to give himself little physical challenges to alleviate his own

boredom. One day he walked into my office and had a funny kind
of limp. I realized that he was walking while holding an empty juice
box between his knees. I asked his mother when this started, and she
told me that he'd picked the juice box up in the parking lot outside my
office. Understand that my office is on the third floor. He walked up
two flights of stairs and down the hall and into my office, where he
waddled over to the trash can, dropped the juice box in with his knees,
and skipped over to me to collect his high five. Then he was ready to
sit down and talk.

My advice is that as long as what your son is doing is not dangerous, or dangerously annoying to you, let him do it. Burning off energy
by children is like adults' attempt to burn off unwanted calories. Every
little bit helps.

Dancing is a wonderful activity at even the youngest ages. Some
preschool television shows already encourage dance breaks so that kids
aren't sitting like couch potatoes during an entire hour of television (it's
the least they can do). You can encourage dancing in your own way.
Boys often like loud, banging music, so start with that. Put some on,
show your son some moves, and see if he joins in. One boy I've worked
with likes to do what he calls "karate dancing." His mother says it's
basically a bunch of martial arts moves that he's cobbled together and
mixed with manic dance moves. As long as he's happy and a bit winded
at the end and not breaking furniture, it sounds fine to me. It may be
best to designate a safe dancing area in your house or yard, someplace
where you can clearly mark boundaries with blue painter's tape or pillows, so your son doesn't hurt himself if he gets carried away.

Singing is as natural and universal as dance. It also involves chest
movement, breathing, and vocal and facial controls, and it has great
emotional release qualities. Long before teenaged boys pick up guitars
and drum sets to pull together their garage bands, boys should be encouraged to sing. Give them a toy microphone, designate an area as
"the stage," and let them perform songs for you along with dancing.

Mini trampolines are a fantastic way for children to release energy.
Be sure the one you choose is approved for young children and meets
safety guidelines. It should have padding, built in or at low ground

levels, and have safety netting. Often, when a child is acting up or frustrated, it can be good to redirect him to an activity such as this, rather than argue or spend countless hours coaxing him to be better behaved. Acting up can just be a sign that he needs to let off some steam.

Activities for Older Boys

A six-year-old named Brian arrived in my office after having been diagnosed with mild Asperger's syndrome and ADHD. His mother, Ellen, was seeking some guidance for helping Brian get along better in groups. His social skills, even when compared with other boys his age, were underdeveloped. Ellen told me that Brian was not very coordinated or athletic. "Frankly, neither are we!" she said, and laughed. "We're more the bookworm types. My husband hates sports. I played some field hockey in high school, but back then anyone who could carry a stick was allowed to join the team." She told me that they signed Brian up for T-ball recently. "Most of the kids in our town go," she said, "and it's sort of a good way to start making friends and all that. But it wasn't great. Many of the other kids, especially the boys, seemed to already know what to do with the ball and bat. It was obvious to us they'd been practicing. We hadn't had much luck playing catch with him in the yard, and he couldn't hit anything—but, well, it's worth a try, don't you think?"

I admired Ellen's willingness to try new things. I said, "That's the model to adopt. Keep it going. Be willing to experiment. T-ball, soccer: who knows until you try, right? But the main point is to try. Most things may not be successful at first. So what? Don't make a big deal of it, and move onto something else. It's not a bad model for life in general. You know, sometimes you can go back to activities like T-ball—even Little League or soccer—once some new development in coordination and skills comes along."

I talked with her about alternatives to team sports. I told her that in kid-friendly martial arts, for example, there is much less stimulation. Kids like Brian are often overwhelmed by all the running around and loud voices at T-ball. Imagine it: kids screaming, parents screaming, coaches screaming. Even if these are cries of encouragement, it's a lot of noise hitting a young boy's brain all at once. While listening to that, he has to know how to process the ongoing game and figure out what to do when the ball shows up, rolling or flying his way. He has to know how to grab it and then where to send it. And if he doesn't, then everyone knows he has messed up. When you break down the demands of many team sports, you realize how complicated they truly can be. Sustained eye contact, quickly reading and reacting to your teammates, shifting bodies and voices, fast reaction times: all of these are essential.

Ellen was open to the idea of martial arts. In particular, she liked that Brian could work in small groups and watch one instructor to model his or her behavior, step by step, then rehearse the movements. Given the fact that Brian enjoys repetitive behaviors, the movements would not bore him. He might even enjoy practicing at home too, and wouldn't need to have other kids around to practice. We then discussed how martial arts might have benefits later in life. I told her that the discipline also teaches older boys how to move confidently and handle themselves.

I think practicing martial arts is perfect for older boys who aren't able to get much out of organized activities. They learn how to use their voices in positive but assertive ways, and they have to listen to directions and follow rules. More aggressive boys learn they can't let their inclinations run wild. Shyer boys learn how to assert themselves and feel strong and competent. These boys are taught how to respect their peers (bowing, respecting the personal physical space of others, and using only appropriate language/physical contact). They learn that there is order to social groups and that only one person, the martial arts master, is in charge. They also stay in great physical shape and develop a healthy sense of power.

The older boys I know who have stuck with martial arts training seem to be good at managing their aggression and also good at avoiding bullies. They don't take the verbal bait when other kids taunt them—and all kids do this to one another at some point. They seem to be in fewer fights, if any. Those are great possible long-term benefits, but I remind parents that the immediate goal of any activity is to get their sons as much opportunity for healthy physical movement as they can. If a boy gets all that energy out of his system, he'll be less active, and perhaps more focused, when he needs to sit and listen at school. It should also help him sleep better.

One caution, I tell Ellen, is to really check out a program before she signs up. Many are not regulated, and some are becoming more about "mixed martial arts," which is code for children fighting. This is unacceptable for very young boys. Unfortunately, this is a growing trend, as Ultimate Fighting has gained popularity among adults and in the media.

As boys get older, they will be able to learn new activities that are more structured. When you sign up your son for athletic activities and lessons, be sure he's getting lots of activity relative to the instruction that's being provided. Standing around listening to a coach or waiting for your turn on a ball field is not an athletic activity. If you do choose a sport for your son, be sure that the lessons involve movement. Sometimes the worst sports are the ones parents love most. I'm going to pick on T-ball for a moment. I've seen T-ball games at my local park where there are twenty-five boys ages four to six, all in uniforms or matching T-shirts, with the parents and grandparents on the sidelines taking pictures. It seems very sweet, very traditional. Yet, when I look out on the field, the kids are just standing around. The outfielders are staring off into space. The infielders are kicking at the dirt. The pitcher is an adult. And the rest of the boys are all in line waiting to bat.

Standing in line is not an athletic activity. What's worse, the boys themselves are bored and restless. I know that the coaches are going to have trouble keeping them focused. Soon the parents will be calling out to their kids: "Pay attention! Watch for the ball! What are you doing out there?" This is no way to create a love of baseball or any team sport. Also, it does virtually nothing to teach the important skills boys could be learning at this age, such as body control, balance, coordination, and self-discipline. Contrast this scene with any class at a martial arts studio, where the kids spend much of their time doing ritualized movements called forms, or in swim lessons that teach graceful body movements to glide through the pool. In these classes, kids are moving all the time. Soccer is also a popular activity that burns a lot of energy. Of primary importance is making certain these programs have lots of physical activity during the lesson or game. When parents ask for recommendations about getting their boys moving after school, I try to help them think beyond traditional team sports.

Swimming is a great activity. Although for older kids it can be a highly competitive team sport, early on it's a great way to keep boys moving all their muscles and working on their body control and co-ordination. Get lessons and arrange as much pool time as you can, daily if possible. Almost every town has a community pool. There are group lessons for very young kids, parent–child groups, and free swim time activities for older children. Swimming is one of the best physical activities we know of health-wise. It is something your son can do for his entire life, and you won't have to worry as much about his safety when he's around water.

Some communities offer rudimentary gymnastics classes in which boys have their own classes taught by men. In these classes boys can build upper body strength and learn the simplest skills for doing floor exercises and tumbling, working on the parallel bars, practicing the movements of the pommel horse, and even jumping on a trampoline or swinging into a foam pit. These can be great activities to build strength and confidence. Don't worry about whether your son is a budding gymnast. The point is for him to keep moving, try new things, and have fun.

Older boys can revisit dance in a more structured way. Some boys really love to dance. I know a seven-year-old who watched ballroom dancing one day on TV and was fascinated by the music and the twirl-ing and the lifting. He then asked his parents if he could take lessons. His father, a stonemason and a black belt martial arts expert, loves the idea of his son taking up ballroom dancing. "Why not?" he told me recently. "It's great for his coordination. I love the idea that he has to move to music; it's very creative. Besides," he added with a smile, "he won't be shy or left out at his sixth-grade dance someday!"

Although this dad thought it was a great idea, he got some flack from his own parents, who thought it was just wrong for a boy to dance. I was impressed with this boy's dad, though, who viewed ballroom dancing as a discipline, which it surely is, something to learn in stages while you develop your body and self-control. He's since noticed that dancing has helped his son improve in other sports as well.

The Myth of Team Sports

Many parents still say to me, "But don't boys need to learn to be part of a team? Won't the other kids ostracize them if they can't keep up in sports? What about staying healthy later in life—they should be in sports now!" I know that there is a real push to "give" boys athletic experience so that they'll fit in later in school and in life. But the truth is you can't make your son excel in team sports, and you can't make him love playing on a team. Very few boys do both of these things throughout their middle school years, and even fewer continue past high school regardless of the amount of time and money their parents spend on lessons and team fees and equipment.

Team sports in most communities have become too competitive. It used to be that only high school varsity sports had competitive tryouts, pressure tactics by coaches, and a strict hierarchy within the team of skilled versus less skilled players. Now that culture has filtered down to some club teams and town recreation teams on which very young boys and girls play. These players are introduced early to the concept of traveling teams and skilled positions. Some of them are exposed to attitudes by coaches and other players that are patently damaging.

Many boys have told me about harsh criticism by coaches, putdowns by fellow players, the stress of parents watching at team sporting events, and other negative team sports experiences. As boys get older, past the age of ten, consider the fact that you have to be better and better to "make it." Most towns and league teams have become progressively more competitive and selective. The days of pickup stickball games that include kids of all abilities and ages are all but over. Today, youth team sports are big, organized, and highly specialized. Certainly, by middle school, you have to be into these sports seriously to make a team and feel competent. It's becoming the norm for many children to go to summer sports camps that specialize in narrow skills development (batting, hitting, throwing, skating, and so on). This is fine if you're one of the few kids who can tolerate all this and can keep up. Most boys, statistically speaking, cannot. Think of how small the opportunity is for a boy to succeed and to feel competent in team sports. Only a few kids score most of the points over a season. Only a few positions get the opportunity to show success.

If you can find a team for your son that offers a positive, healthy type of environment in which everyone learns and everyone gets a turn, that's great. But why not expand his repertoire of skills and activities as well? Give your son both opportunities, to participate in team sports and in some individual sports and activities in which he can improve his skills at his own rate.

Parents often ask me, "Doesn't our son need to deal with competition? Isn't a Peewee league, like T-ball or youth soccer, a good thing for him?" Yes, I tell them, but only a little competition is good, and only in small groups. Research has shown that most of us won't try very hard to compete in larger groups. We pull back when we figure that there's little chance to succeed. Kids are the same way when they are put into highly competitive sports in which lots of other kids are vying for the attention of a few coaches. In these settings, boys won't give it their all. This doesn't happen only in team sports. Many parents have told me that their sons have lost interest in a swim team experience or martial arts class when there were just too many kids vying for the attention and praise of a single coach or instructor. When choosing a sport or team activity, think of a smaller sized team that has a low level of competition. Teams that emphasize fun and building basic motor skills are best.

To this, parents say, "But he loves to compete. He competes over everything. He loves to win. Why aren't sports a natural fit for him?" That's absolutely true. But let's remember that although a boy this age has an immediate need to win, he has no real ability to understand how team sports work. Ideas such as team loyalty, or team standings or playoffs or even working with another player to create an outcome— these concepts are completely alien to boys at this age, and they should be. The only thing a boy can really comprehend is what he's doing moment to moment and how the adults around him are responding. Even when boys seem to understand team concepts, they are more likely imitating our talk in order to please us.

My final argument against team sports as the sole method of expressing athleticism is to consider the fact that most people don't maintain a lifetime of physical fitness through team sports. It isn't easy to organize a team to play basketball or football in order to stay in shape as we get older. The real athletic activities that truly keep us healthy throughout adulthood are those that work our cardiovascular system and keep our muscles strong and flexible. These include working out, swimming, biking, running, and walking, or simple, individual sports such as tennis and racquetball, or martial arts and yoga. For most boys, once they grow up, the only reason they'll need to understand a neutral zone trap in hockey or a double play in baseball is because they're watching team sports on TV.

Shouldn't He Learn to Sit Still?

Once you've given your son an opportunity to burn off excess energy, then you can focus on teaching him when and how to sit still. He should learn to do this because he will need to do it more and more as he gets older.

One mom I've worked with is in a nearly constant battle with her husband over this very issue. At every meal Tanya's son, Spence, likes to lean back in his chair. He spends a lot of time tipping the chair and holding onto the table, practicing tilting and balancing, or not. The chair goes crashing to the ground at least once a week, while Spence jumps out of it, thrilled by his escape. Tanya's husband has had enough. He yells at Spence, who will stop for a few seconds or minutes, but then pushes his chair back again. "It's as though he doesn't know he's doing it," Tanya told me. Her view is that Spence is not hurting anyone but himself, and she wants to let it go. Her husband's view is that Spence is going to break the chair or crack his skull eventually. Plus, it's driving him crazy. He wants Spence to follow the rules at the dinner table. And he's got a point.

As much as I'm in favor of boys being allowed to fidget and run around and burn off the energy they need to, I also know that boys need to learn self-discipline. One of the reasons I advocate so much movement in a boy's life is because it helps ready him for practicing the other important skills he's going to need: sitting still and paying attention. You can't play whenever you want, or move about, jump, or sing just because you have the impulse. Maturity is, in large part, an exercise in holding back what we want to touch, want to say, and want to do because the situation just isn't appropriate. For many young boys, asking them to sit on the impulse to jump and scream is like asking them to hold their breath while being tickled. They can do it for a second or two, but the impulses inside their heads are just too urgent. Still, they need to learn how to control these impulses and get better and better at it through practice. Let's start with sitting still.

Practicing Sitting Still

Yes, sitting still is a skill, and it must be practiced as such. You cannot expect your young son to sit still 100 percent of the time when asked, but you can expect him to do better and better over time. With boys ages three to five, you need to start slowly. First, set up a time of day or a specific activity during which your son can practice his sitting skills. Lots of parents choose the dreaded dinner hour. That's fine if you've got the patience and the time to devote to this. If you've got three other kids running around and a baby to manage, and the phone is ringing and you're trying to cook, however, this is not the best time to help your son practice sitting quietly. Find a time when you can pay attention to him and encourage him while he tries out this skill.

Tell him he will get a special reward, something specific, such as a small cookie or a penny out of a jar. (At this age, rewards need to be small, because you'll be using many of them.) Set a timer where he can see it. An egg timer, something he can hold and focus on, is very helpful. I've kept one of these in my office to show parents how to do this exercise. It really helps boys to feel that the time they have to conquer is real, something they can hold. If your son can sit for a full minute, and by that I mean he stays in his seat and is calm, give him the reward and praise him. Try this exercise again right away. On the next night, or at his next opportunity to sit still, offer a similar reward, but increase the time by a minute. If he does a little better, give the reward and lots of praise. Keep increasing the time by small intervals. Some kids may tolerate just thirty-second increases.

Remember that you shouldn't expect perfection. There will be times your son doesn't earn any reward. If there isn't a good sitting episode one night, don't make a big deal of it. Tell him there's always tomorrow and move on. You may want to keep a notebook of his successes over a period of a few weeks and should see gradual increases in his ability to sit still. A temporary setback is normal. He might have a couple of bad nights with tantrums at the dinner table, along with peas and carrots on the floor. If that happens, remove him immediately from the table (see page 101 on Time-Away). Remember, if he's learned to sit for several minutes despite these occasional setbacks, he will quickly bounce back to his previous ability level. He has already learned the skill. It's inside him, like balancing on a bicycle. You won't have to retrain him.

Remember, though, that transferring a skill such as sitting still to a new situation isn't automatic. We as adults can do it easily, but young boys typically can't. You have to use the same training strategy in every new situation. The good news is your son can easily link his previous learning to new situations. That is, he should learn to sit more quickly in new situations once he's done it really well at home, for example, at the dinner table. But not all situations are equal. Sitting in church or synagogue or at a children's library or a birthday party may be a lot tougher—or easier—depending on who's there and what's going on. The point is to practice this skill by using small immediate rewards for graded improvements, just as you did at home.

Get Outside

A brief plug here for the great outdoors. We're a society that spends too much time indoors, with longer school days, higher homework demands, more electronic gadgets, and greater fears that the world out there is dangerous or uncomfortable. I think we need to give boys greater freedom to move about and explore their backyards and neighborhoods, to camp, hike, bike, and discover spaces outside their home. Reductions in stress and general improvements in psychological well-being have been associated with being outdoors, enjoying natural light, experiencing natural sounds and sensations such as the wind and a myriad of sights and textures that television or computers can't duplicate. When we are so disconnected from the natural environment we were designed to experience, many of us feel empty and a bit depressed. For young boys, being stuck indoors increases their stress level and lowers their frustration tolerance. We were designed to move about and explore, and boys in particular have a very high drive for this.

Studies have shown that among children diagnosed with ADHD, symptoms decrease significantly when they are in more natural settings. Giving your son as little as twenty minutes of outdoor play can yield a few hours of improved concentration afterward that is as good as, or may even exceed, the improvements given by stimulant medication. The important factor seems to be nature itself. Whatever the cause, this "green advantage" has been noted to help all people improve emotional control and decrease aggression. Young boys who are by nature a bit more aggressive and active absolutely need more time each day playing outdoors in parks and other recreation areas.

Causes of Movement

Parents sometimes ask me what causes all this agitation and fidgeting. Why is the activity level of boys so high? He grabs; he pushes; he chews his clothes; he flaps his arms; he jumps in place. Isn't this proof of some brain-based disorder? No. Curiosity and creativity are what is driving most of these movements. Think of all the explorers, surveyors, archaeologists, and scientists of every type who have had the insatiable need to wander the world around them and who probably drove their parents mad with their pent-up need to do something all the time. This is pure boy energy at work. Sure, this energy is sloppy at these early ages, and annoying, too. It's probably difficult to imagine a young Jacques Cousteau or Neil Armstrong fidgeting during dinner every night, but I'll bet they did.

CHAPTER 6

He Runs the Household

The first thing Megan says to me after I ask about her three-year-old son's behavior at home is this: "Time-outs don't work." She's frustrated and embattled, and she feels betrayed by all the parenting books that tell her to position a chair in the corner of a room and make her son sit in it for a prescribed length of time (usually one minute per year of age) to reflect on whatever he's done wrong. The theory sounds great, except that Megan's son, like so many boys his age, won't sit in the chair. He just gets down and runs off. He won't stay in one spot for any length of time.

Boys are driven by their internal engine, their brain, to wander, investigate, grab, and take apart the world around them. They are so driven that they may shrug off disapproval from their parents. Sometimes they seem impervious to shame and often ignore nonverbal social cues in their quest to get at things. As a result, most tactics for maintaining order and discipline in the home just don't work. Boys tune them out, and that keeps parents in a one-down position, forced to threaten and beg their sons to acknowledge household rules. The worst of it is that the traditional trump card of discipline, the time-out, is ineffective with most boys.

Megan didn't know this when once, in a heroic, or perhaps exhausting, attempt to impose time-outs, she sat Ryan on a chair and then physically restrained him for three minutes. This was worse, because Ryan considered this to be a kind of wrestling match. While Megan got angrier and more frustrated, Ryan wiggled and laughed. This was no punishment; for him it was a game in which he had his mother's full attention. Megan is doubly furious because her best friend has adopted a daughter exactly Ryan's age, a beautiful little girl named Polly. When Polly refuses to eat her food or get into the car seat or put down some object she's not supposed to have, her parents just count. "They count to three," says Megan, "and it works. I've seen it." Megan's friend often implies that the reason her daughter is so compliant is her own superior intuitive parenting. I can't resist asking what happens after Polly's parents count to three. "No one knows," says Megan. "They've never gotten to three."

This story doesn't surprise me at all. Polly sounds like a girl who is highly tuned in and socially aware of others around her. She studies the faces of her mom and dad, looking for signs of approval and disapproval. In general, girls in this age group tend to be more aware of the emotions of others, and they are developing an understanding of social rules as a kind of game, one they can excel at and like to play. They aren't any more compliant than boys, but they understand disapproval, and they hate it. With many girls, and only some boys, parents have good luck wielding disappointment and shame in order to coerce compliance.

Many boys just don't work this way. The youngest ones don't yet understand the complexities of social structures in the world. Sharing, waiting your turn, saying hello to someone when you first see them, chatting while you play: it's all like gibberish to them compared with the strong internal need to experience the world hands on, study it, manipulate it, and reconstruct it. As one mom said to me, "It's like the fog in that part of his brain hasn't lifted. He's just not seeing socially yet." Exactly. These boys are busy doing other things, such as building spatial awareness and testing physical boundaries. That's why your son is tearing the house apart. At three, four, and even five years old, Mom's rules are just speed bumps. Repeated shaming and yelling doesn't work with these strong-willed and fearless guys. Lectures don't work. And here's the big one: time-outs don't work for many such boys.

What's Wrong with Time-outs?

Putting your child in one spot as a punishment assumes several things. First, it assumes that your child is physically capable of sitting still. Most boys at this age are not. Studies have mapped the movements of toddlers in a room. Researchers have put a dot on a map for every movement a child makes. When they connect the dots, they find that toddlers are all over the place. Boys in particular are far more active than girls at this age, but almost all children bounce from one place to another. Not until they are older can most of them sit still for minutes at a time and focus on one activity. There's no point in telling your son to sit and stay in one spot before he can physically do it.

Second, a time-out assumes that your child feels your disapproval and wants to avoid it. At age three or even four, many boys aren't there yet. Sensing the emotions of others is a kind of listening. The little boy who is careening through the house, hungry for things to touch and take apart, isn't listening to your words or watching your nonverbal cues. His strong emotions are ringing so loudly in his own head that he doesn't notice yours. To the extent that he can sense your anger, he might see it as something to play with or test. For him to register your anger, it usually has to be off the charts, and no one likes to be that kind of parent.

Third, a time-out is a kind of social ritual in which the parent imposes a symbolic punishment, a loss of privilege. The punishment isn't such a big deal if you think about it. It represents a loss of contact with his social group and the potential to miss out on being in the action for only a few minutes. And if the child adheres to it, no matter how much he doesn't want to, he does so in order to earn back the privilege of being in the family's social inner circle. In the end everybody starts over.

The problem is that not every child is ready to take part in this ritual. Parents say to me, "If we can't get our son to do a time-out now, how will we ever have control in our house?" They're right. Teaching this social ritual now is crucial. You will never be able to ground your son later, or take away his bike, his scooter, his cell phone, or the car keys, if you don't start teaching the ritual now. The trick is to teach when he's ready to learn.

Take It Away

Long before little boys are ready for a version of a time-out that will actually work for them (which I'll discuss in a bit), they need discipline that's going to help shape their behavior. Boys need immediate consequences for their actions. Two-, three-, and four-year-olds don't listen much to words. They understand language, of course, but language is the last resort for most of them. Think about it. Instead of asking, they grab. Instead of saying no, they push or hit. When you want to communicate with them, you need to use the same order. Give the consequence first, then give the rule. People hate hearing this, but it works. You don't have to get angry—and please don't yell—but you do have to act immediately. When your son does something wrong, you have to take something away right away. No exceptions.

I once watched a preschool teacher working with a couple of giggly three-year-old boys who were blowing bubbles in their cups of juice and spilling the juice down their shirts. She reached over and took the cups away and said, "When you do that, I take it away." She set the cups on a high shelf. The little boys watched wide-eyed while the cups traveled away. They reached for them. They cried out for them. She said, "Nope. Cups are for drinking." And that was it. No yelling, no lectures, just a tangible result. No more cups for today. There was no dead air between their act and the consequence, not one or two or fifty reminders stretching out the link between inappropriate behavior and its negative consequence. This is the key strategy. Making the time between the action and its consequence as short as possible heightens your son's sense of control over his environment. He thinks: if I do X, I get Y. Every time. When adults are consistent, then the universe is clear to a little boy. The rules are known. He knows he affects what happens next, and in this way, he decides his own fate. He brings on his own consequences.

Some parents focus on a favorite toy or object, putting the beloved toy in a time-out—the stuffed bear he likes or his blanket. One mother took away her son's baseball cap. This little boy loved to wear his cap and insisted on wearing it even to nap time. When he hit his little sister or threw a toy at his mom, she just reached over and took the hat. When her son grabbed his now bare head and yelled, "No! Please," that's when she'd say, "No hitting. When you hit, I take it away." That's perfect because there is no lecture. Your son feels the consequence first and then hears the rule.

The consequence can be removing a favorite toy or the toy he's playing with at that moment. Instead of putting your son in a time-out, put the object in a time-out, somewhere he can see it but can't touch it. If he's breaking a toy or hitting someone with it, that toy goes into a time-out. On some days, you'll need a big space for all the toys that go into a time-out. That's okay. You are showing your son the ritual. Bad behavior leads to a loss of something. Return the object when he complies. Give a fresh start, but if he does the negative behavior again, remove the object for a longer period of time.

Consistency is key. Yet consistency is the hardest part for most parents. For example, punishment will often cause an emotional firestorm in your son, even violent outbursts. Some parents, particularly those who were raised by a harsh disciplinarian or those who were raised in quiet homes where no one yelled, shrink from this. Parents sometimes yearn for a Hallmark discipline moment in which they explain everything, and the child nods tearfully, and everyone learns and grows and hugs. Instead, you've got a three- or four-year-old boy who is hitting you and screaming, "I hate you," while his favorite teddy bear sits on top of the refrigerator. This doesn't feel like progress, but it is. The trick is to do it swiftly, without emotion. In fact, walk away if you can.

Sometimes you may say to yourself, "I can't deal with this right now. I'm too tired. He's been acting out all day. It's almost bedtime anyway. It's just a broken vase; I'll clean it up and tell him I'm mad." I think of this as discipline fatigue. Unfortunately, parents who are hesitant to punish or who cannot stand the tantrum that follows are laying the foundation for chaos in their own homes. There are classic mistakes that all parents make at one point or another in dealing with their young boys, often due to exhaustion or frustration. These include:

Excessive warnings with no actual punishment. "I've told you and told you not to throw your toys. If you keep doing that, you are going to your room, and I mean it."

Explaining the rules and the reasons behind the rules rather than giving immediate and appropriate consequences to actions. "It makes Mommy really sad when you scream like this. The reason we're leaving the playground right now, honey, is because it's lunchtime. Don't you want to eat lunch?"

Asking rhetorical questions instead of dealing with the behavior. "Can't you see I'm on the phone? Why do you always do this? Do you think I like cleaning up your messes?"

Avoiding punishments or cutting them short in an effort to "make up" or apologize for being angry. "Are you okay? Can you see why Mommy was so mad at you?"

Dissolving into rage and name calling. "You're a bad boy. Get away from me; I can't even look at you."

These are all weak responses. It's important to remember that this kind of parenting demonstrates your inability to control the situation through action. If you are using any of these, chances are good that you are using several of them on a rotating basis, which weakens your parenting skills even more. In many households, Mom uses one set of techniques, while Dad uses another. This is how parents end up fighting each other instead of helping their children mature.

Detention: The New Time-out

Making your disapproval tangible is going to give you immediate leverage on your son's behavior in the short term. Parents think of this as a magic bullet. Enjoy it while it lasts. As boys mature, so does their ability to challenge authority. Sooner or later, and certainly sometime between the ages of four and six, your son is going to raise the stakes at every conflict. Yes, that does mean that he's going to misbehave on purpose (while laughing at you). Then he will watch to see how you respond. When the punishment comes, he's going to refuse it, or fight you physically, or have a nuclear tantrum until he has brought the household to a grinding halt. Why? Because he wants to see what will happen next.

Here's what should happen next: you send him to his room. Tell him to go to his room, or take him by the arm and guide him to his room, or carry him there. Shut the door and keep it shut and let him rage by himself. Most parents ask how long they should leave their son alone. The answer is you should leave him there until he's done crying and raging. That's a time-out.

For some reason, most parents have been told that children should be sent to a time-out for a set period of time. They think the time-out should last one minute for every year of age. In this system, a four-year-old gets four minutes, a five-year-old five minutes, and so on. This seems to make sense logically, particularly to parents who want to do everything just right, but it doesn't make any sense emotionally. Your son is not a turkey; he's not going to be done "cooking" after a certain number of minutes. A five-year-old might need just a couple of minutes to calm down, or he might need six or seven minutes. He might need to be alone for fifteen minutes to get control of himself before returning to his toys or a meal.

It's important not to wind him up again by talking to him, interrupting his tantrum with such questions as "Are you okay now?" This is like throwing gasoline on a fire. You can expect to reignite the conflict and drag it out.

Time-Away Is Better Than Time-out

You may be wondering how the system of giving time-outs could have become standard if there are so many boys for which it doesn't work. I wondered that, too, and when I researched it, I found some surprising information. The time-out as it was described decades ago would have been perfect for boys. In fact, it was created to help one particular non-verbal autistic boy, and it did so in a way that stunned his doctors.

The time-out was first proposed in the early 1960s by behavioral psychologist Arthur Staats. It was later developed and researched by Montrose Wolf, Staats's graduate assistant. Wolf was asked to work with Dickie, a three-year-old autistic boy who was living in a psychiatric hospital and whose tantrums were so violent that he was hurting himself. Wolf's theory was that adult attention was the cornerstone of controlling a child's behavior. He felt that by paying attention to bad behaviors, adults were inadvertently rewarding and encouraging them. Wolf believed that the more the hospital staff attempted to punish and restrain Dickie, the more they were encouraging his tantrums and misbehavior, while doing nothing to encourage him to speak or function socially.

Wolf's solution was to remove Dickie immediately from the common area whenever a tantrum began. Dickie was put in his own room without a lecture or even a single remark, and there he stayed for at least ten minutes or until he had stopped his tantrum. This system worked so well that soon Dickie was going whole days without a tantrum. By removing attention from his bad behaviors, the staff was able to focus attention on him when he behaved well and attempted to socialize and communicate. They had completely turned around the dynamic.

This system of removing a child from a situation, using social isolation instead of a physical punishment, had never been studied before by child experts. Wolf decided to coin a term for this. He knew that when behaviorists worked with pigeons, and the pigeons made a mistake or did something that the researchers didn't want to encourage, they erased the behavior by turning out the lights for a few minutes. The temporary darkness disoriented the birds and made them forget what they had done just prior to the lights going out. This method was called a "time-out," and that's what Wolf called Dickie's time in his room.

Interestingly, the staff at the hospital where Dickie lived disagreed with this strategy, even though it worked. Their complaint was that it wasn't a punishment. Dickie liked going to his room and would often just sit there humming to himself or staring off into space until the time-out ended. Wolf concluded that Dickie responded best to time alone in his room, where he could decompress. In his study, Wolf maintained that these techniques would work with any severely disabled child and would be better than punishments, especially physical violence.

Decades later, the term *time-out* is used by parents almost universally, yet in practice, the time-out varies widely from what Wolf intended. Most parents have their sons sit in a chair or in a corner, which is not far enough away from parental attention. This situation sets up a dynamic in which you have to constantly police your son's whereabouts. Is he staying in the corner? Is it three minutes or four minutes yet? And he can still affect what's going on in the room. He can cry and scream and disrupt a conversation. He can call out to you. He can complain. All of this leads to more parental attention, more reinforcement of his bad behavior, not less. Boys need real time alone, and some of them need much more than a few minutes' break. An alternative to the time-out is what I call Time-Away.

In a Time-Away, you send your son to his room with the door closed, and there he will stay until he has stopped crying and is ready to comply. Parents sometimes get anxious when I explain this system. They ask me, "What if he just sits in there playing? What if he's screaming and yelling that he hates me? What if he stays in there for an hour? What if he doesn't feel punished? Does it still work?" It works. Not only is the Time-Away the best way to restore order to your home and get a wild toddler boy out of the driver's seat, but it will set up the parenting dynamic between you and your son that will last through his teenage years. (Yes, Mom, you will be sending him to his room when he's sixteen. Get used to the idea now.)

What if He Won't Stay Put?

Some parents have boys who will not stay in their rooms during a Time-Away. They just come roaring back out. I tell them it's okay to hold the bedroom door closed. Their son's tantrum will likely escalate. He will cry and may bang on the door, but he will eventually calm himself if you ignore all this. (Naturally, you would only do this if you know he is the type of boy who has never harmed himself in the past, such as banging his head against walls or biting himself.)

Do not talk to him or respond to anything he says or does until he is quiet. Don't ask him anything or say anything to him until he calms down. Over time and through practice, he should show a decrease in tantrums. He will find a new ability to go to his room on his own. Be patient and remain calm. This takes time, but it's worth the effort.

Wild Things

If you want to understand what your son experiences while he's alone in his room, you should read the wonderful story *Where the Wild Things Are* by Maurice Sendak. Sometimes I think this book was written more for parents to give them insight into the best way to handle wild boys. In the story, a young boy named Max wreaks havoc in his home. When his mother tells him to stop, he roars at her like a "wild thing," and she sends him to bed without supper. In his rage, he imagines his room has become a jungle. He imagines a boat that carries him to where the other Wild Things are. Max is so wild that the other Wild Things name him their king. But after a while, he smells the food his mother is making for dinner. He gets back on his boat and leaves the Wild Things even though they beg him to stay. When he gets home, his room is no longer a jungle, and he is himself again.

Although the mother never appears in this story, she is the crucial element because she sends Max on his voyage. Max's mother does several important things in just the right way.

1. *She doesn't yell at him or shame him.* Losing it emotionally is the wrong message to a young boy who is already overwhelmed by impulses he hasn't learned to control and emotions that he doesn't know how to describe. Yelling at him, holding him, and lecturing him are all additional sources of stimulation that will make him more frustrated and confused.

2. *She sends him to his room.* In the story, the room is not crowded with games and toys and distractions. It is a quiet place where he can be alone with all of his rage and energy. Here he can imagine all sorts of frightening things: that he is alone in a wild world, that his parents are gone or dead. A child becomes so mad at Mom and Dad that he imagines a world without them, then experiences that world, then wants back in, having to accept his parents' rules before he leaves his room. When he smells the

food and realizes that he wants to be with his family, he's ready to rejoin them.

3. *She doesn't check up on him.* This is a favorite technique of parents who are afraid of using discipline. They send the boy to his room, then knock on the door after a few minutes to say, "Are you okay, honey?" If you want to be sure there are no hard feelings, you are trying to control the emotional endgame of the conflict. You can't control this. He controls it. He must come back to you when he's finished being mad at your rules and ready to behave differently. He needs to struggle with the question of whether he can let go of his anger. He will not grow or learn to control his anger if he doesn't struggle with it alone.

4. *She doesn't take it personally.* When Max comes back to his room, his dinner is waiting for him. The family is ready to welcome him back from the land of the Wild Things. They start fresh.

As a parent, you have to earn your power. When you get overwhelmed, it's easy to feel sorry for yourself. You begin to tell yourself, "He's doing this to me on purpose. He's trying to make me angry." Yes, your son is trying to make you angry. He wants to see what happens next. You can take the upper hand here by refusing to take his tantrums, his bad behavior, personally. Instead, treat his behavior like the experiment it is. He steps over the line, and you give him a result, whatever it's going to be, a Time-Away or taking toys away. Do it without yelling. And resist the urge to check on him or make it all better.

It's Not Just a Punishment

You can use this technique of sending your son to his room whenever he has a meltdown or is so overexcited that he can't control himself. It will give him practice leaving situations when he's overstimulated, and it will offer him the chance to go to a quiet place to pull himself together. This is a skill, like any other, and it will take time for your son to learn it. The most important lesson a boy can learn about power is the power to control himself and to take care of himself when he's feeling overwhelmed.

As one mom said to me, "It was incredible. One day, he was getting frustrated and upset, and he just walked up to his room and closed the door. He was upset in there for a while. I could hear him. Then after about ten minutes he came back down, and he was calm again. He actually taught himself how to calm down. It was amazing." This is amazing, and it's one of the goals of the Time-Away. It is an important way for you to show your son that he can control his emotions. He can let them out in a safe place, then calm himself down, which will be incredibly empowering for him throughout his life. Imagine your son being fifteen, eighteen, or twenty-seven and knowing he needs to break from a situation that angers or worries him so he can regroup, calm himself, and think straight.

Diana's Story

Diana is a great example of a parent who got it right. We worked together in behavioral therapy for a few years after her son, Timmy, was diagnosed with ADHD at age five. At first, he was struggling in kindergarten and tearing up the house. Even though he took medication from time to time, Diana and her husband saw the best results through understanding Timmy, going with his temperament, and using basic behavioral techniques to guide him to become the great young man he is today (going off to college soon). Although he has used medication off and on over the years, he has dramatically reduced his need for it.

What Diana discovered in our work together was that her son was normal, that he had his own plan, his own way to get through the world. Diana understood that. She realized he was a separate soul. He had a journey that only he could make. He had to be responsible, ultimately, for who he was. Diana used many positive thoughts such as these to understand the complexities of how boys develop, their shifting needs, and their "take no prisoners" style. She stopped wrestling emotionally with Timmy. I coached her on letting him cry and have tantrums in his room as his mechanism to escape from Time-Away, and she was successfully able to ignore him and let him stay there as long as it took for him to calm down. Once he was calm, she would engage him in simple language, modeling control and calmness herself: "Timmy, are you ready? You can come out and start again now that you are calm."

Sometimes she said that from the kitchen, rather than walking up the hall to his room, because once he saw her, the tears started again, followed by more tantrums. Seeing a new opportunity to heighten his plight, he would play the whole drama out longer, grabbing more attention from the family. Diana learned to stay away and calmly say, "I'll check on you in a bit. You're not ready." Over time it worked. Timmy stopped using tears and angry words to solve the predicament he put himself in. He wanted out. He knew that his younger brother, James, had all the attention he could soak up while Timmy was jailed. He wanted to rejoin his wonderful family.

When he got out of Time-Away, Diana heeded my advice. She got down to Timmy's eye level and asked him to look at her. She asked him to listen and answer two questions. (1) Why were you sent to your room? and (2) Are you ready to come out and control yourself? Simple and short. Through drying tears and sniffles, Timmy answered her questions. Diana then would reinforce the fact that he went to his room when he got in trouble or was upset. She would say, "I'm proud of you. You did a great Time-Away. Let's start new!"

Timmy would get out and have a new chance to engage socially with the family. There were many of these events, several on some days. With my coaching, Diana stayed as calm and firm as possible. Her husband supported her. As discussed in previous chapters, sometimes the worst episodes were followed by developmental gains a few days or weeks later. The storm would pass, and Timmy might be using language better, able to brush his teeth better, listen better, write and identify his words better. So Diana knew not to panic whenever Timmy fell apart. Instead, she saw it as evidence of a new and better young guy emerging.

The Long View

If you don't give your son tangible consequences now, if you don't send him to his room and let him rage alone, then he won't learn to control his anger, and he won't learn that you are in charge. In a few years, when he's a teenager, you'll need to have established this system. You will need years of practice at providing rules and discipline because someday you will send him to his room and he'll say, "Screw you." I tell parents that someday their son is going to be bigger than they are. You have to establish the power now, while he's a little boy. Establish the routine of being able to send him to his room. When he's older, you want to be able to take the car keys away from him and make it stick.

I recall a very petite mom telling me about how she grounded her enormous son, Gabe, after she discovered that he stole a few beers from the refrigerator and drove with them to New Hampshire to party with his friends in someone's ski condo. On his return Gabe huffed and puffed, threw his car keys onto the floor, and said a few curses on his way to his room. Gabe must have traveled back to the place with the Wild Things, because when he emerged from his room a few hours later, he was a bit more civil, ate dinner silently, and went back to his room to brood. Meanwhile, his mom knew that no matter how angry he was at her, he was in the safest place in the world, in their house, and in his room. His anger was a small price to pay for his safety.

CHAPTER 7

He Has to Win, or Else

It is no surprise for me to learn that five-year-old Gareth loves NASCAR races. He watches them often with his father and has even been to the track a few times and met some drivers. On his own, Gareth stages races to see which of his Matchbox cars is the fastest. In fact, he has become obsessed with the idea of winning to the point where he is driving his mother and three-and-a-half-year-old sister crazy. All day long, he announces that he is the winner and that he is on the winning team. At mealtime, he asks for the red plate. When his mother gives it to him, he says to his sister, "Yay! I have the red plate. I win. The red plate is the winner." Of course, this makes his sister cry. When the family troops off to swimming lessons, Gareth runs ahead to get the red booster seat in the family car. Then he says, "I win! The red seat is the winner!" This makes his sister cry again.

Now Gareth's mother feels she needs to mediate who gets the red plate and the red seat. It becomes a point of discipline and fairness. Who had it last time? Who gets it this time? Gareth invents games that only he can win. "Whoever touches this bush is the winner," he says with his hand poised over the branches. What's worse, Gareth seems to have lost the ability to play games with his sister or even his playmates at preschool. He must win every hand, every game all the time, or he has a tantrum and throws the game onto the floor. His mother, who works part time as a paralegal and says she feels surrounded by impatient and highly competitive people at work, doesn't like seeing these same traits in her young son. She is furious when she tells me, "Gareth cheats! How is he ever going to have friends, how will the family ever play games at night, if he makes the experience such a nightmare?"

What Is Competition Good For?

Playing games can be the most powerful tool for driving social and cognitive growth for boys, and competition is the fuel. Boys love games. They need to see how they stack up against others. Most of all, they must win. Boys crave and learn from all types of games—board games, field games, made-up games. The game itself is actually inconsequential. It's a prop, a safe and controlled vehicle to pit two guys against each other. Games are a fundamental part of my practice, not only because boys love them, but because they are a wonderfully efficient means for building a boy's confidence, teaching him about consequences, and showing him how to deal with disappointments. At first, boys like Gareth are interested only in the ritual of gamesmanship, the notion that one person is a winner, and the rest are not. These boys want to set up a construct with a rigged outcome, so they can get a jolt of power (even if it's not real). Eventually, they will be interested in the actual game, the skills and strategies, along with the rules that maintain order and fairness. But not at age five or six. That takes time to develop. The drive to compete is natural in boys, and the need to compete and be the best is what pushes boys to learn and practice new skills, even those that are uncomfortable. Boys aren't hardwired to pay attention to a board game or wait their turn, but given the prospect of winning, they will gladly do these things.

While playing a game, a young boy is starting to look outside himself, and outside the close one-on-one relationship he has usually with his mother. Up to the age of three or so he is locked into a narrow version of himself viewed mostly through his mom's eyes. Slowly, as his brain develops, he branches out to notice other children and how they behave. He'll do this mostly by making direct comparisons. How fast does that boy run compared with me? How far did he throw the ball? So much of what a boy enjoys doing at these early ages of three, four, and five years old is going to be based on comparison, one that stresses who is better. They might compete about knowledge: "I know something you don't. I can spell my name. Can you?" Mostly, they compete over physical skills—who runs faster; who swings higher. To the winner go the bragging rights.

Maybe the legendary football coach Vince Lombardi was right—at least in regards to little boys. For them, winning isn't everything, it's the only thing. The trouble is that most parents and teachers are conditioned to see competition and winning and lording over others as wrong. Moms especially get caught up in micromanaging fairness and niceness among kids, especially boys. Many moms want everyone to win an equal number of times. They want everyone to be nice about winning and losing. This renders winning and losing meaningless for boys. In fact, these attempts to police or erase competitive urges may do more harm than good. To Gareth's mom, I would stress that this competitive talk all day long is not abnormal. It's his way of feeling that he can master his environment. Further, it gives him a way to explore the dynamics of power, which is a near obsession for boys of all ages. His need to turn everything into a competition will shift soon, when he starts playing more formal games and has something more concrete to compete over. I would tell her to put limits on this kind of talk only when it's out of control, when it leads to hitting or major meltdowns. When Gareth uses this talk to tease his sister about this plate or that seat, I would advise her to stay out of it. Tell the kids to work it out and send them to their rooms (or to different parts of the house) until they can work out their troubles on their own.

Age-Appropriate Games

Before boys are ready to play cooperatively with other kids, they play rudimentary games with themselves. In my office, they take the Barrel of Monkeys and spend time showing me how many they can link together. They want to link more monkeys each time, and they want my repeated acknowledgment that they have done more each time.

They make mock car races, in which they run two cars around an imaginary track. Here a boy gets to control the outcome and make a winner and a loser out of the cars. Fostering this type of play at home is important. It builds self-esteem before your son heads out to play with others, where there is real competition.

Very young boys, those age two and a half to three years old, can't play games in the way we think of games, with rules and turn taking. At those early ages, boys care most about mastery and power. Young boys shouldn't be pressed to wait for a turn or to lose gracefully. Let them experience early successes in everything they do.

Three- and four-year-olds can play simple games, such as Candy Land, but parents need to understand that these boys are going to try to cheat. They will take extra turns, skip over the board pieces, and just work things out so that they win every time. That's not a terrible thing. Let them cheat. It's a good thing, in fact, for boys (or girls) this age to gain self-esteem from winning. They still have plenty of time to learn about strict rules and turn taking later. At these ages, the point is that they are gaining a sense of mastery, having fun, and spending time with others.

Later, at age four to six, boys begin to understand what a true game is. A game imposes conditions on a boy's endless desire to be the strongest and the best. To take part in the ritual of the game, he has to know how to follow rules and participate in give-and-take. It's not until boys have reached this level of maturity that they can start to understand that the rules have to be constant over time in order for the game to work. Every time you play Go Fish, for instance, you start with a certain number of cards. Every time someone asks you if you have a certain card, you're supposed to answer truthfully. That doesn't mean he'll always follow the rules, even if he understands them by this age. He's a scientist, remember, and he'll test those rules over and over again.

Keep It Fun

One mom I know was struggling with her young son who wanted to play the game Sorry, but he couldn't get through the first few turns. He threw pieces and demanded to have extra turns. The mom felt as though she spent thirty minutes telling him what the rules were and explaining them over and over again: "Honey, it's not your turn yet." "No, this card means that you go back four steps." She would explain, and he would freak out, and neither of them would have any fun. Sorry is a game that requires players to draw cards, read written instructions on the cards, and follow those instructions. It also allows players to send each other back to square one. Even though her son could read, even though he had already turned six, this boy was not ready for all of this. There was too much stimulation, too much frustration. There were too many things to remember.

I often stress to parents that at first they should not spend much time drilling rules on how games should be played. It's always good to stick to the simplest games with the simplest rules or to alter rules to a level your son can comprehend. This mother's solution was to let her son be all the players of the game. What he really wanted to do is move the colored pieces around the board in his own little competition. Here he could control the outcome. And he provided himself with a lengthy commentary on the process as well. What a great solution. In this scenario he got to be the master of the rules.

It's actually a relief for young boys to be in charge at this stage, when they're just getting their feet wet with all the mental gymnastics and cognitive juggling that board games demand. Consider the typical board game from a child's perspective. Unlike the play he's enjoyed up to this time, which is spontaneous, often physical, dynamic, and exploratory, this play happens on a flat board. Rather than moving around freely, he has to sit still and pay close attention to small objects, such as plastic pieces, marbles, cards, and pictures. Rather than acting spontaneously from his imagination, he has to take part in a ritual, which means waiting for someone else's turn, paying attention to what happens to other players.

The ability to do all these things represents a huge social and developmental leap for a boy. The most challenging part is stifling his own natural tendency to grab, move around, or make the game do what he wants. Some games also require the cognitive skills of recognizing objects or colors, knowing how many spaces to move or pieces to collect. Others require reading letters or words. The best advice for parents is to layer in the rules slowly over time. Don't worry about following the game precisely. That will come with time. Remember, games are supposed to be fun, and you want your son to enjoy his first experiences with them so that he'll want to keep playing to the point where he's finally comfortabe with following the rules.

How Boys Learn About Winning and Losing

Many parents feel that their sons lack the maturity to play games well. They worry that their boys will grow up to be cheaters, or that they will lack character permanently because they don't win gracefully— never mind losing gracefully—and because they have tantrums and meltdowns during games, or because they seem to compete endlessly over silly things. (I have yet to meet a boy who doesn't do all of these things at some point.)

The truth is that games are highly sophisticated mini social situations. Many boys will use them to learn all sorts of skills they'll later need at school and in friendship. In my office, when I use games for teaching and modeling these skills, I'm careful to bring concepts of winning and losing into play in stages.

I worked for several years with a boy named Aaron. He was four years old when we first met. Aaron was at the time a very shy child who'd had a number of problems with his eyesight since birth. He had undergone two corrective surgeries to help his vision and would need several more. Aaron wore thick corrective glasses that were enormous on his gentle, small face. An elastic cord kept them tied to his head. He was having trouble adjusting to all the medical procedures he had to undergo, which is why his mother brought him to me.

It didn't take long for me to learn that Aaron was mad for Candy Land, a game in which players draw cards and race their pieces around the board of colored squares. The first player to get all the way around the board to the gingerbread house wins. Aaron was a fierce player, and in our early meetings, he won every single game. Now, Candy Land involves drawing cards from a stack. It's entirely based on luck. How is it possible that Aaron won every game? Because I cheated in his favor. Every few turns I peeked at the stack of cards and selected the ones that would hold me back or cause me to skip a turn. Aaron's visual impairments made this easy for me to do without his noticing. The point is that I wanted him to win many times before I challenged his ability to lose.

Letting a boy win when he first ventures into the world of board games is a good idea even at home. When parents tell me that their four- and five-year-old sons are not graceful losers, I often recommend that they give the boys a few more months of winning at home, or let them win more than they lose. Let them win, let them gloat. Be sure they win the last round of any game you play. Childhood is hard enough. Remember that when kids lose to an adult, it's devastating. When a boy plays against his older siblings or his peers, the game won't be rigged, and he has no choice but to endure the outcome. Let him learn to lose gracefully in those arenas. When he plays against his parents, let him be the master for a little while longer. As he grows up, he'll want to make the game more challenging, which means risking losing once in a while.

Also, let's remember that Aaron is learning so much from this one game. During our time together, he learned to sit down and focus on the board, despite his visual impairments. He learned to take turns. He learned to read a card and figure out where his piece will move next. He loved to track how he was doing in the game relative to me. I know this because he reminded me frequently that he was winning, that he had only "this far" to go before he won. And he definitely knew that the game always has a winner and a loser. I tell parents not to gloss over these important skills on our way to teaching perfect graciousness. That's not the goal. Soon, Aaron and I branched out to a few other board games, involving dice and spinners, but I still allowed him to win most of the time.

When a boy does win, he learns what it's like to be the winner. Boys must appreciate this side of the coin before they can try out the other side. Gracious, Aaron was not. He threw both fists into the air and shouted, "I win! I win!" Then he did a victory dance around the room. Every time. What did I do? I modeled for him what it's like to be a good loser. I complimented him on his skills, and I admitted that it's hard not to win, but that I enjoyed the game. I asked him if he wanted to play again, but he only wanted to gloat. After this had gone on for some weeks, I took the opportunity to tell him how his victory dances made me feel. This is different from lecturing him on why he shouldn't gloat. Instead, I said, "As happy as I am for you, when you jump around like that, I feel a little bit bad about myself. I'm wondering if I want to play again."

I know that at preschool and with his friends, Aaron had trouble playing games because it was hard for him to see. When he did play games at school, he invariably lost, because he couldn't keep up with the other kids. In my office, I was showing him two things. First, I was giving him chances at mastery, at being the best, which are an enormous boon to any boy this age. Second, he was learning that the feelings he has when he loses are feelings that others have when he wins. This was helping him to build empathy for others.

The First Loss

Eventually, Aaron needed to learn an inevitable fact about competition. He couldn't win every game, not even in my office. At a session a few weeks after his sixth birthday, I stopped cheating to let Aaron win. He won a round or two on his own, but then the inevitable happened. We played a close game, but I rolled the dice, and the number came up that sent my piece past his and to the end of the game board. Aaron stared at the board for a moment as though he couldn't believe it. He got up from the floor and went to the sofa, where he sat down hard. The tears began to stream underneath his large glasses. "That's not fair!" he shouted at me between his sobs. "I don't want you to win."

At this point, the instinct of most moms is to rush in to console and remove the pain with a hug or lots of talk. The lecture would fall along predictable lines: "You can't win every time. You have to be good about this. No one will play with you if you act like this. You'll win next time if you try harder."

Aaron was trying to grasp a new world order in which he could lose a game to someone he had previously always beaten. A boy who had suffered a loss like this could only relate to what was happening right then. I viewed this display of anger and sadness as an important developmental step for Aaron. He had to stretch his brain to accommodate this new information. He could lose. He was in a quandary. He didn't want the world to work this way; instead, he wanted it to go back to the way it was before, where he was always the best. He wanted me to say, "It was all a mistake. You're still the best. I shouldn't have won. You can win all the time." But I didn't. I said, "It's hard for me to lose, too."

The shift inside him would take some time. But he had to deal with the discomfort of losing, of this new way the world works, in order to grow. After a few minutes Aaron stopped crying. I asked him if he wanted to play another game. He refused to play unless he could win. I told him that he might win, or he might lose. That's the nature of the game. I told him that I felt sad when I lost, too, but that I enjoyed being with him and having a friend to play with. I reminded him that there were some things that I was better at than he was, and there were some things that he was better at than I was.

During this one-sided dialogue, I was careful not to tell him how he should feel. I only told him how I felt about losing and about what just happened in the moment. Aaron had to shift his entire worldview after losing the game, which is a very challenging task. He needed help processing what had just happened, not a lecture on how to lose or fit in or how to behave as others expect.

Parents who want to help their sons deal with the disappointments that come along in life should consider this as a model. When their sons don't get chosen for a team, don't win a contest, or perform poorly in an athletic event, many parents feel an enormous urge to try to talk the pain away, or even to tell their boys how to behave in a way that makes the parents feel better. They say, "Buck up"; or "It's okay"; or "Nobody wants to see you cry"; or "Stop whining"; or "It'll be better next time."

Another option is to let your son struggle with a disappointment and say simply, "That's happened to me, and it made me sad, too," or even just "I'm sad, too." Stay in the moment. Stay focused on what's just happened, because your son's not going to be able to focus on life lessons. Just be with him and don't work hard to fix it. A simple, encouraging statement is all that's needed while he's processing his disappointment.

Losing Gracefully—or Not at All

In the aftermath of disappointment, boys will come up with strategies for coping, some positive and some not. In the months that followed Aaron's first loss, he would agree to play games with me, but he would resort to cheating in order to win. As soon as he thought he might lose, he would stop playing or "accidentally" tip over the game board before asking to start over.

Then he began to make up rules. If he chose a card he didn't like, or rolled a number he didn't like, he would make up a rule about it. "Okay, when you pick a green card, that means you get to pick another one," he would say. Then he would take another card without looking at me. Once, he pushed my game piece back several steps when he thought I wasn't looking. All boys try out these behaviors. They want to win all the time, and they'll resort to cheating because the lure of winning, of being the best, is so strong.

I tell parents to model good behavior rather than lecturing their sons on the evils of cheating. Boys feel they must win, but they can't win if the other player quits. Every time Aaron cheated, I would say, "Hey, no fair! Let's both play fair." I told him that I wouldn't play unless we could both win sometimes. Having said that, I also admit that I did continue to let Aaron win more often than he lost. I always made sure that he won the last game or round that we played during a session. I think this is a good strategy to bring into the home as well. Young boys really do need to win more than an average number of times. Remember that games are inherently stacked in favor of the older, more experienced player. You can't teach him the social skills that surround board games if he's feeling discouraged and so frustrated that he won't play at all.

Over time, boys learn that while they don't like to lose (who does?), they like playing; they like the chance to win that is presented with every game. They learn to accept the fact that when you play a game with a friend, the two of you are taking a risk together. One of you will win, and one will lose, but by taking that risk, both of you experience and share the excitement of the game, the excitement of facing failure. By taking this risk over and over again, a boy learns that taking risks is exciting, and he will be more able to take all of the risks necessary in life, such as trying new activities and making new friends.

Aaron did make this shift, and he was able to use these experiences of winning and losing to deal with successes and disappointments in other areas of his life. It helped him face his frustrations and tolerate the mistakes he made in school. It also gave him more patience when trying to make new friends. It shifted his expectations to be more realistic, that not everything can go his way all the time.

The Battle Against Disappointment

Parents often ask me how long it will be before their sons will understand that cheating and having meltdowns during games is wrong. The subtext of this is, when will he knock it off? When will he be one of those straight-arrow kids who play by the rules and win or lose with perfect grace? To this I often want to ask, "Have you ever seen professional athletes at work?" Tantrums are a frequent occurrence in the big leagues, and there's a reason all those umpires and referees are running around.

In a boy's life, competition will be a constant factor. The stakes of this competition will get higher as he gets older. He will always have the urge to press his advantage against the rules of the game, against you, against his teachers, against his friends, against whatever system surrounds him. Your job is to push back. Let him know what the consequences are for cheating and misbehaving. Playing by the rules is something even adults struggle with.

I once worked with a boy named David, who liked to kick the checkerboard across the room and storm off when things didn't go his way. Instead of showing anger, I chose to report on the situation as calmly as possible. I often tried to use humor to ease the tension. "Wow, I guess the checkerboard decided to spill on the floor. It only wants you to win." At other times he would cheat, sneaking his hand across the table to snatch a piece, and I also made a joke of it at first. "Wait a minute, David, wait a minute. Did I just see those checkers magically disappear? You have special powers! One of my kings is in your hand now. No wonder you win all the time!" My goal was to make him aware that he had chosen to change the rules, and that I had noticed. Many parents feel very strongly about cheating as an issue of character, which it is. But not at this age. Before he can understand that cheating is wrong, a boy first needs to understand that cheating is transparent. The other player notices it and will call him on it.

In games against older boys, I will be more forceful and direct, telling them I will not play if they cheat or change the rules. But I avoid lectures. Instead, I pose questions: "Is it fair that I never have a chance to win? How would you feel if I cheated to win?" I use a kind, supportive voice without a trace of disappointment or anger, so it's easier for the message to get through. At this point, boys will typically try to negotiate to get an unfair advantage. I remember David picking up some of my game pieces and saying, "Well, let me have these back, and then we can play." Once he decided that he would only play if his pieces could move illegally. To that I said, "No, I don't think I want to play right now. Maybe another time." I knew that his desire to play would eventually trump his desire to cheat.

When he decides to play again but fairly this time, a boy will have learned something without getting a lecture. He will have picked up on my social cues, my body language, and voice intonation, in the same way he might if he were playing with another boy his age.

Cheating Is Developmental

Some parents complain that cheating becomes a kind of game. Boys try to cheat, and when Mom or Dad or a sibling says, "No fair," the boy just laughs. This is when parents really feel that their sons are on some kind of negative path. But I have to disagree.

I can think of many, many times when a young boy knew he was cheating but didn't think it was obvious to me during our office games. Then at some point, when his social skills developed and when he could better read my cues, he realized he'd been caught. I don't call boys on their cheating every time. After all, we often have other, more pressing concerns to discuss in sessions, and I sometimes use the game as a distraction, something to keep a boy's mind working, while he opens up about other issues. But I do call them on it sometimes. The interesting thing is that these boys think they're getting away with it the rest of the time, meaning they think I don't notice.

Later, at some point, it dawns on these boys that I always know where my pieces are supposed to be. They develop enough to read my body language, my little smirk when they palm one of my pieces, my raised eyebrow. The funny thing is, the cheating doesn't stop. Even after they figure it out, they often make a game out of how they can get away with more cheating. This is a great lesson for parents (and especially moms) about how boys play. Pushing the envelope is part of the way guys play with, and against, one another.

This happens mostly on the chessboard, where I'm a sitting duck. I learned to play the game late in life, after I had started my practice. Chess is a tricky game. Many adults can barely play it, and I know some five-year-olds who could give me a run for my money. When young boys play, they like to move their pieces around and try out different moves before they decide on what to do. Although taking your hand away from a piece and then changing your mind and moving it back is a major chess rule violation for serious players, boys need to move the pieces in order to better visualize the board. Some boys will then go a step further and move my pieces around, talking out what happened over the last few moves. All the while, they are changing where my pieces or their pieces land—always in their favor, strangely enough. It happens very fast, but they always look up at me to see if I caught the obvious cheating. I might say, "Funny thing, my mind is really going these days. I could have sworn my queen was over there instead. Oh well." I use sarcasm to make my point. The boy may laugh and agree that I'm getting old. I then might move my piece back to its rightful spot and smile, without saying I know what he was just up to.

As a parent, you can decide how to handle this moment. You can stop the game, or you can make your son's attempts to cheat part of the game. It's up to you. Many dads I know take the latter approach because they know that give-and-take and teasing and trying to get one over on your friend is part of boy play—even among men. The moms I know tend to take a harder line, and that's fine, too. Sometimes it's not easy for moms to feel comfortable with that aggressive type of play. If you can't do that comfortably, you don't need to. Tell your son what to expect from your games with him. He'll need to learn both sets of skills to play games with his peers.

Some parents tell me they just can't let their little boys cheat. "How will they get along in the world if he expects to win all the time?" they say. I remind them that there's a long time between now and then. And I tell them that when their son wins, that's not the only thing he's learning about games.

What's important to remember is that as his cognitive growth continues, as he continues to get more savvy about the world and about how people navigate through it, a boy's attitude toward these games will change in surprising ways. I recall Dexter, a boy I worked with several years ago. He first came to my office when he was in second grade to work on some problems he was having in school as a result of his ADHD diagnosis. During each session he wanted to play chess, and he sometimes cheated if he felt he was in danger of losing. He moved pieces out of turn, or he moved them illegally. A few times I questioned these illegal moves, but in most cases, I pretended not to notice. Sometimes, I pointed out moves that he'd missed and that would have allowed him to beat me. I then let him do his turn over again to take advantage of this new strategy. Over the chessboard we talked through all of the issues he had to deal with—social pressures, keeping up in school, dealing with his parents and their frustrations with him. Playing chess was a way to keep him engaged with me and keep up his confidence so that he would feel safe enough to be honest with me about his frustrations and fears. He was better able to listen to the advice I had to offer about his social and academic struggles at school because of his ADHD. He continued to meet with me at various times over the next several years. In these later sessions, we talked about emerging puberty, middle school, high school, girlfriends, and eventually the stress of applying to college. Many of these talks took place over the chessboard. Dexter no longer needed to cheat to win, and, in fact, he won every game honestly.

I saw him the other day, before he left for his freshman year of college. Before leaving the office he stopped at the door, turned, and pointed at the chessboard, my king tipped over in defeat. "You let me win all the time when I was younger, didn't you?" he said. I laughed, nodded, and admitted that I had in the beginning. But he was also a very good player for a little guy, and now he was an amazing player. "Can you keep a secret?" I asked him. "The truth is, there were a few times you did beat me on your own back then." Dexter hovered at the door, not ready to leave. I added, "I learned a lot from you—how to play, certain moves—just by watching how you did it." This was not a lie to beef up a young man's ego; it was true. Before leaving, he said, "I guess I taught you how to play chess, and you taught me about how to deal with stuff."

What About Athletic Games?

Many boys also struggle with the rigid rules imposed during athletic games. One young boy I know, Caleb, was in a major conflict with his father over backyard games. His father had bought a baseball mitt for him and was trying to teach him the rules of baseball. But at age six, Caleb wasn't ready for the rules. He wanted to hit the ball, and when he couldn't do that, he didn't want to play at all. At family gatherings when the older kids would play Wiffle ball or soccer together and have a great time, Caleb would lurk around watching but refuse to join in. Sometimes he would encroach on the game, stealing the ball or hovering near home plate to disrupt things, but he would refuse to play.

Caleb's father was really nagging him about this. "When are you going to try to play?" he would say. "Why don't you come outside now, and we'll play?" His mother felt that this nagging had ruined Caleb's interest in sports forever. My advice was to just drop the subject. Tell Caleb that he had to decide whether he was in the game or out during family picnics. He didn't have to play, but he needed to leave people alone who were playing. But more important, I told his parents to give him the chance to play a game he did like. At that time, he loved to play hide-and-seek, and he also loved to have races in the backyard with his dad (as long as he always won). I advised his parents to give him the chance to play these games and drop the baseball/Wiffle ball thing altogether.

They did, although they weren't happy about it. Both parents came from families in which backyard football and baseball games were an important part of family socialization. They didn't want their son to be a spoilsport.

Then a funny thing happened. Caleb went off to a summer day camp, where he was playing with kids all day long. They played dodge ball and tag, which Caleb had never tried before. And he found that he was pretty good. He was a fast runner and could think on his feet. Camp counselors also introduced Wiffle ball, and they made a big deal about playing a real baseball game at the end of the first week. The first day of camp, Caleb came home and began to nag his dad about playing baseball. He wanted to hurry up and learn so that he could play with his peers.

The push of his peer group made him change. Peer pressure is not always a bad thing. In Caleb's case, he wanted to be one of the guys and had to adjust to them if he wanted to be accepted and fit in. Peers don't coddle or help a boy along, as do many parents. Peers demand that you play or be left out. This is an important point for moms and dads. If you find yourself fixing things too much for your son in his peer group, back off to see if he can work it out for himself. As he moves off to join a group of friends, he will be challenged. He will struggle. Back him up with encouragement, but let him find his own solution to the problem of fitting in.

Older Boys Who Struggle with Competition

One boy I worked with, named Clive, was having meltdowns on the soccer field when he was eight years old. He had an overall pattern of reacting with super-sized emotions to all the events in his life. Anger came on like a flood, and small disappointments often triggered un-controllable crying. Clive had been diagnosed with ADHD and was taking some medication to help boost his ability to pay attention and remain calm at school. As with many boys on stimulant medications for ADHD, there's a limit to what could be expected. Often, in fact, the medications are a double-edged sword. When they wore off, Clive would become irritable, and his anger would become even more pronounced.

Fortunately, he was doing better with his behavior at school, and the emotional extremes were easing a bit as he matured. For many boys who struggle with big emotional responses, these will subside as they get older. The cortex, the part of the brain that allows us to control our emotions, continues to develop throughout childhood and adolescence. Even when the brain is fully grown, learning, or reworking the neurons, so to speak, never stops. In many areas of development, including this one, some boys will naturally lag, but more than likely they will make up the difference over time.

The one place where Clive was still struggling was on the soccer field. He was one of the best players on the team, yet he managed to embarrass his fellow players, his coaches, and his parents during every game and nearly every practice by throwing epic tantrums whenever the other team scored or when he made a mistake. He was rude to referees and abusive to other players. He threw things on the bench. And he was as hard on himself as anyone else, calling himself awful names if he missed a play or breaking down in tears when he botched a pass or sent the ball out of bounds. In some cases, I'd look to the parents to see if this behavior was being encouraged by them, but they were not pushing Clive into soccer or any other sport, nor were they driving his need for perfection on the field. They were mystified (and horrified) by his behavior and not excusing it at all.

The ADHD medication was of no use to Clive once he set foot on the soccer field. This was a real-life setting just too packed with stimulation and strong emotion. The coach had given Clive notice that he would be kicked off the team and out of the town's league if he didn't improve. As good a player as he was, Clive wasn't worth the hassle he brought to the field each game.

Clive told me that he did want to improve, that he wanted to continue to play on the team more than anything else. We developed a simple behavioral plan. First, I had to convince him and his parents that he was choosing his behavior and that experiencing real conse- quences would fix the problem. And together, he and I did just that— fixed the problem—in just two games. We clarified what he was actu- ally doing, breaking his actions down into levels, calling them "low," "medium," and "high." I told Clive and his father that Clive was al- lowed to give a low or medium response to events at the game but not a high response. We set up clear definitions for these. For example, yell- ing at a teammate or at an opposing player is a high response. Kicking at the grass or punching his fist into his hand is a medium response. Pouting is a low response. I told Clive's dad to remind him at the start of the next game that he was going to get yanked immediately from the game, removed from the field, and driven directly home for any high response. No warnings. No second chances. It's crucial that par- ents offer real and immediate consequences, and that they follow up on them without fail and without lots of lecturing. In Clive's case, he was not getting real consequences for his behavior because of his talent as a player. The coach kept giving him chances, the other players kept making allowances, and so did his parents. Remove this special treat- ment, and the behavior will change.

Clive did fine for the first half of that next game, but then he had a meltdown. True to his word, his dad removed him from the game and from the field. Clive begged for another chance and made all sorts of promises, but his father stood firm and silently drove him home. Clive found out later from his friends that his team had lost the game, in part because he wasn't there to play. Although he cried and pouted and seemed devastated about letting his team down, Clive went to the following game ready to play, and he had no incidents. Clive's father continued to give him the same pep talk before every game that season, but he never needed to pull Clive from a game again.

Several years later, I saw an item in a local newspaper about a beloved team player on a high school varsity baseball squad and rec- ognized the name immediately. Clive had grown up to excel in many sports, including baseball. But then he suffered a shoulder injury that ended his high school athletic career. Although that must have been enormously disappointing, Clive channeled his passion for sports into a new role with the team. He dressed for every game and cheered his teammates from the bench. He learned to assist the coach and became an enormous resource for his team.

The truth is, boys never give up their deep desire to be the best. Many boys always want to beat the other guys and show that they are better. Middle school, high school, and college-age guys dream about becoming professional athletes, rock stars, and multimillionaires, seeing themselves in the limelight and showing the world they are the best, fastest, smartest, coolest, biggest, and strongest. The basic desire to be better than everyone else never goes away; it only gets tempered by social skills and, later in life, channeled into coaching, teaching, and raising kids, passing on their skills to the next generation.

CHAPTER 8

He Wants to Be the Bad Guy

Thomas, age five and a half, is absolutely obsessed with the *Star Wars* movies, which he has seen several times with his older brother. His mother says that he has memorized the plot lines of all six movies and asks endless questions about them. He talks about one character who burns up in lava and about another who gets his hand cut off. The movies have become his one topic of conversation, his single source of inspiration for fantasy play. Thomas likes to act out scenes from the movies. He wields a stick like a light saber and pretends to engage in fight scenes from the movies, complete with eerily accurate sound effects. He does a chilling impression of Darth Vader. He even makes up scenes that might have happened in the movies.

His mother, Summer, refers to herself as a child of "hard-core hippies" who taught her to be suspicious of popular culture. Summer's parents, as she puts it, "hated meat and money." She's trying to be different. "I'm trying to be cool about the movie stuff, you know, the shooting and fighting, but I can't," she tells me. She has tried to limit Thomas's discussions of the film, telling him he can only talk about them for a few minutes at a time, but these limits make him very anxious. His questions are important to him, even though they make his mother uncomfortable. "Why do the bad guys want to hurt the good guys?" asks Thomas. "Why are there bad guys? Are there more bad guys than good guys? How can we stop the bad guys?" Underneath her pretense of tolerance, Summer really hates the *Star Wars* movies. She thinks they are too violent, too grown up for boys like Thomas. She says the movies and his obsession have damaged Thomas, made him both more aggressive and more fearful.

I hear this from a lot of mothers of boys this age, and I disagree with the sweeping conclusion that a love of bad guys or even moderately violent conflict can make boys worried, scared, or even aggressive. I think the reverse is true. It is a boy's inherent anxiety about the dangers of the real world that fuels his obsession with movies like these and the scary themes in them. There's nothing in a movie like this that isn't represented in many fairy tales loved by children and parents. It's shocking to realize that "Hansel and Gretel," for example, is about child abandonment, murder, and even cannibalism. "The Three Little Pigs" is about a wolf who comes to your door and tears your house down so he can eat you. These stories allow children to think about the unthinkable and desensitize themselves to it. War play and superhero play is no different for boys.

What's Good About Being Bad?

Lots of parents observe their young boys acting out fairly dark or aggressive fantasies, and they worry that this type of play is dangerous or proof that they've done something wrong as parents. Many moms say to me, "If he was into Superman or Spiderman or something like that, okay, but why does he have to idolize Darth Vader and Captain Hook?" It's true, boys love bad guys. As adults we often say of certain characters in dramas and novels that "he's the guy you love to hate." But boys aren't like this. They don't love to hate bad guys; they just love them. They act out bad boy behavior in their fantasy scenarios, and that means talking about (and making sound effects for) destroying things, stealing things, taking over the world, and killing off other characters. For girls, fantasy play also contains drama and conflict, but the themes tend to be wildly different. One mom I know overheard her two children playing and was nearly crying with laughter when she told me how they played together. Her son, age six, was busy acting out a scenario about killer dolphins eating the people who were falling off a bridge over the ocean. In this play, asteroids were falling down, while lava was boiling up out of the ocean. It was really elaborate, and while every element had its own sound, there wasn't a lot of talking, except, of course, for the screams of help from the people falling off the bridge. Meanwhile, her daughter, age four, was trying to take part in the scenario, so she was acting out both parts of a mother-daughter team of rescue cats. The cats, in contrast to the killer dolphins, had a lot to say to the people on the bridge and to each other. The cats were reassuring the people on the bridge that they would soon be rescued, while also chatting with each other about what kind of shoes to buy for the rescue. They also asked the dolphins what kind of snacks they might enjoy instead of eating the people on the bridge. Not all girls favor talking over action, and there are plenty of boys who love chatty narratives to go along with the action. Still, many boys favor dark and destructive themes in their play. They like to make drama and conflict and discord, even violence, in their play. In fact, the staging of the conflict, pitting characters against each other, is often the point of play.

These two children are acting out very different styles of play. One style favors talking to resolve the danger; the other favors sound effects to rev up the action and put the characters into more danger. Yet the goals of play are the same. Both kids are using it to deal with their anxiety. For one child (in this case, a girl), the fantasy play was an attempt to make things better, to save the people on the bridge, to feed the dolphins something more socially acceptable, and to have some fun shopping. Moms tell me that they get that right away. But the other style of play, which is generating all of these big events—lava that can burn you and things falling from space that can knock you down and violent animals—is just as valid. Here the boy is creating an absurdly violent and hostile world as a way of working out his real anxiety that sometimes bad things happen. They could happen to him or to someone he loves.

The next obvious questions from parents are these: Where does this anxiety come from? Why is he so anxious and upset about the world?

Why does he create turmoil and danger in his play? The answer is because he's growing up. He's now old enough to understand that he doesn't control everything (and that you as his parents can't control everything, either) and that a big, scary world exists outside the front door. The fact that he's interested in these themes doesn't mean he's surrounded by violence or that you've been a bad parent. It means his brain can now comprehend bigger themes, such as good guys who want to help people and bad guys who want to hurt people.

As adults we have anxiety, too. How do we deal with it? We read the newspaper to become more informed about the world so our fears don't become exaggerated. We also read books and go to the movies or the theater, which is our version of fantasy play. We have a lot of tools for dealing with our fears. Boys have fewer tools, but they use these tools in highly creative ways.

Role Playing

In its most primitive form, bad boy play is a fascination with power and the characters that have power. This means superheroes and the villains they fight. Boys as young as three will assign each other roles in play, and those roles tend to come in two flavors, bad guy and good guy. Boys don't play cops; they play cops and robbers, as in, I'm one, and you're the other. In this way, boys are creating teams and choosing sides, then playing out the obvious conflict. I want to steal, and you want to put me in jail. In such play, a boy is learning about categories, opposites, strong forces, and the conflict that comes with all of that. He is creating a battle with his friends with lots of drama, along with an outcome that he controls. When boys play, the good guy doesn't always have to win, just like in real life. These scenarios are played out with endless repetitions and the possibility of a different outcome each time depending on what a boy is thinking about, worrying about, or trying to get his head around in the complex new world around him.

A boy's love for villains doesn't mean that he'll never want to be a superhero. Those guys are a lot of fun, too. Your son will go back and forth in these years, wanting to be a bad guy and wanting to be a superhero, too. He'll try on each role in turn, exploring different sides of himself, a protecting, selfless hero side as well as a more destructive, angry, self-oriented villain side. Both are normal and part of everyone. It's healthy for him to explore and get to understand these darker parts of himself safely in play.

Further, his mind is ready to think about the big, scary things in life that are out there. Using these themes and characters in play allows him to juggle these notions in a safe and lighthearted way. Boys have very strong emotions at this age. As I've discussed before, because they tend not to talk out their feelings, these emotions can be overwhelming on occasion. By practicing bad guy behaviors in his fantasy play, a boy is rehearsing how the scary things in the world work and is channeling some of that safely. He is also enjoying some of the power of the darker side that's in all of us whether we want to admit it or not. That's why he wants to be the villain in the stories he makes up.

It may seem sometimes that he's lost in this endless fantasy play. Don't worry; by the time he's seven or eight, his love for movie villains and superheroes will fade a bit, and he'll shift into more reality-based superheroes, such as sports heroes and professional wrestlers, and games of strategy, including chess, cards, checkers, and sports.

It's important for moms like Summer to know that there's no age where boys are too young to be playing with characters who are bad guys. As soon as a boy understands the concepts of good guy and bad guy, he's going to be drawn to both at once, and he needs to explore both sides. Frankly, sometimes the bad guys just look cooler. They have green skin and black capes and wild hair. When these characters get a rise out of Mom, well, that just seals the deal. And the scarier the bad guy is, the better. It's like a Halloween mask: it feels powerful to be the one scaring others.

Violent Toys

Many parents dislike buying toys that suggest aggression and violence, and worry how to gracefully refuse such toys when they come in the form of birthday or holiday gifts from relatives. A lot of parents don't allow their children to play with toy guns because they don't own guns or want their sons playing with them. Of course, that's your choice.

You can choose whatever toys you want your son to have and can restrict him in any way that you believe is appropriate. I will warn you that keeping toy guns out of the house will not stop him from pretending to shoot people. Boys will make a gun out of a stick, a book, a piece of toast, or a teddy bear. You cannot keep boys from pretending to shoot each other. One mom of a three-year-old told me recently that her son likes to point his finger at her and make staccato sounds, sort of like laser gun fire. She told me that her son has never seen or owned a toy gun, and he has certainly never seen a real gun. The first time he did this, she asked him, "What are you doing?" and the boy said, "I'm shooting you." She looked at his empty hand and said, "With what?" and he answered, "With my shooter." This little boy didn't even know the word for gun, so he made one up.

Rather than worrying about whether he does or doesn't engage in play with imaginary guns, parents should pay attention to what kind of play their son invents for weapons. I coach parents to set limits on this type of play if it scares other people or crosses the line of good social behavior for kids. That means your son should only engage in this type of play with others who agree to play along. It's not okay to jump out of the bushes with a supersoaker and yell "Bang! You're dead" to the lady down the street. Even if he doesn't pull the trigger, it's not okay, because she's not in the game with him. Tell your son he can only do that with a friend who has agreed to play.

Little boys offend adults all the time by pointing fingers at them and pretending to shoot. There's nothing funny or cute about that, because many people have suffered the loss of someone who was shot. It's a parent's job to make it clear how this type of fantasy play works and where, and with whom, it can be done. When encased in good limits like these, this type of play can serve its useful purpose to help young boys process their own anxieties about bad things in the world, and respect objects of power.

How Much Is Too Much?

Boys have a great thirst for understanding bad and scary things far beyond what parents assume. One mom I know was shocked when her boy came home from kindergarten and asked how many people died on the *Titanic*. He also wanted to know how big icebergs are and if he could see one. She sent a note to the teacher, who explained that another child had come to school with a book about the *Titanic* and that she had read the book in class. It wasn't a book for adults; it was one aimed at young readers, yet it did mention that the boat sank and that people died. For weeks afterward, the boys in class were fighting over books about the *Titanic* in the school library. Boys have a great curiosity about natural disasters. And this one involved a huge ship with swimming pools on board and people wearing funny dresses and hats.

That doesn't mean that all disasters or scary true stories are appropriate for young boys. Kids need to encounter these things at a measured pace. Young boys, especially those under the age of five, can't understand the reasons for many types of violence or the context for violence. A PG or PG-13 movie or television show late at night that shows shooting and fistfights and other cruelties would be overwhelming for them.

Most young boys don't have a lot of experiences to help them understand violence or disasters. More important, these boys don't have a real understanding of probability. If your son sees news stories about flooding or fires, he's going to ask you when that will happen to him. When he's older, and in grade school, he'll be able to remind himself that bad things happen infrequently, even though we worry about them. At younger ages, he won't have any idea how often a bad thing he fears can happen.

Three-, four-, and five-year-olds are still at the age of what we call "magical thinking." This normally lasts until the start of grade school. Until that point, boys and girls have a hard time making distinctions between what's real and what's imaginary. They believe things happen because they think about them or wish for them. Monsters and dream images can be real to them.

A good rule for parents to remember is to respect and encourage your son's questions and natural curiosity to lead him to the things he wants to know. If he asks about a real-world disaster or about a violent period in history, it's his signal to you that he's ready to hear something about it. Give him a few facts, and let those simmer. Add a qualifier such as "This happened a long, long time ago" or "That won't happen to you." He will likely work this information into his play, and when he's ready for more, he will ask.

How to Join In

With my encouragement, Summer finally gave in to the *Star Wars* play her son, Thomas, was interested in. She bought him inflatable light sabers, one for Thomas and one for his little sister. Trouble is, his sister got bored with them after just a couple of pretend duels. This led Thomas to beg his mother to join in. She did just that, and they had a pretty good time in the living room, whacking each other with these soft inflatables. Summer was worried that he would begin to use sticks or pencils or spatulas to try to fight for real, but she set out the rules for Thomas. Soon, he was following her around the house all day, begging for more turns, more fights. She found this a bit trying, but she also really liked seeing him laughing and getting excited. After a few minutes of a "fight," Thomas would throw his arms up and keel over on the carpet. "What are you doing?" his mother asked. "I'm dead," said Thomas with his eyes still closed. "You killed me."

I'm amazed to report that she was okay with this. "I'm going to wake you up using my special powers," she said. And she tickled him. Of course, Thomas began to laugh, and then he sat up. Immediately, he wanted another fight. "This time *you* die," he said. "I'm going to use my tickle power on you." Eventually, Thomas had ideas for other special powers to wake his mother up. He wanted to use what he called "cold hand power," meaning he would lift up his mom's shirt and put his cold hands on her tummy or back. Then he wanted to use "fart power."

"I drew the line at that one," said Summer. It didn't take long for one of the light sabers to spring a leak, and then they were no good. Thomas still wanted to play, and he was willing to use pretend light sabers to do it. For him, the pantomime of fighting, of swinging his arms at someone as though he had a weapon and going through the ritual of winning or dying and then waking up, was more important than the weapon itself. He and his mom then did sword fights with invisible swords. Summer's only problem was that Thomas wanted to fight all the time. Once, as she was folding laundry, he wouldn't let up. He was hounding her about the fighting. Exasperatedly, she said, "When I'm done folding this laundry, I'll fight you." Thomas decided to help her so they could play sooner. He pawed through the pile of laundry to find his shirts, folded them (very badly, but still he tried), then took them to his room and put them in the drawer. "I couldn't believe it," said Summer.

Rules for Joining In

I encourage parents to join in with a boy's bad guy play. There are several ways to keep things positive and fun.

1. *Keep it safe.* You'll want to be sure that any fighting going on uses soft toys rather than sticklike objects that can actually poke an eye or cause physical damage to yourself, your son, or your home.

2. *Set rules.* This play should be confined to an area of the house where you're not going to run into sharp objects or break things. A playroom or area where there's very little furniture works best. Be sure he plays by the rules you set. Stop the play immediately if he uses real violence or is in danger of hurting himself or someone else.

3. *Set a time limit.* It's easy for boys to get wrapped up in this type of play and never want to stop. It will be easier for you to break away and get back to parenting, or doing something else, if you say up front how much time or how many rounds of play you're going to have together. Use a clock or timer. It's not easy for him to beg for extra time from a clock.

4. *Don't judge it.* It may be tempting to want to make this type of play into a moral lesson, to say to your son, "Well, after a fight we should make up and be friends again," or "We should take turns winning," or "Fighting isn't the best way to solve a

problem." Don't be a buzz kill. Remember that the ritual of fighting, the role playing of conflict, is what's important for him. It's pure fantasy and imagination at work. Let him go in whatever direction he wants, as long as it's safe.

How to Set Limits

Sometimes boys get so excited about this kind of play that they get violent, not out of a desire to hurt their parents or their playmates, but because they forget themselves.

One mom reported to me that her son's fantasy play sometimes included real violence. "Sometimes he hits me, not hard, but he does hit when he's trying to do pretend battle with me," she said. Her son liked to assign his mom characters in play. Many kids do this. In this case, the boy liked to say, "Let's have a dinosaur fight. I'm the big dinosaur." Then he would jump on his mom. "It doesn't feel right," she told me. "It's a bit scary to me."

This is a great example of when aggression steps out of the realm of pretend, imaginary play. This is the point at which you stop being a playmate and reassert your role as a parent. If he's acting aggressively with you, then he will do this with his friends, and that will get him into trouble at school or day care. Many young boys I know do get overstimulated by their aggressive thoughts when they are caught up in active play. What starts out as healthy play can spin off course (pretend sword fights turn into real jabs with sticks or toys). At that point you need to step in before the play degrades further. You need to reassert the boundaries and tell him that he can't play dinosaurs or swords or sharks, whatever the game is, if he's hitting.

Boys respond well to simple rules: "No touching unless you ask first." "No hitting." "No wrestling unless your friend says okay." I caution parents that they need to have rules for any type of play fighting. Otherwise, two willing boys will cheerfully hurt each other. They need to learn that pretend fighting has limits. "No hurting each other." "No touching faces and eyes." "No scratching." "Stop as soon as someone says stop."

End the play immediately and take a break from it when your son violates one of these rules. I tell parents that he needs a significant break from play if he violates a safety rule. Stopping for only a few minutes isn't effective. Put the play scenario away, including all props, for a few hours or until the next day. If he enjoys these games, he'll obey the rules. Also, this isn't permission for you or any adult to hover and jump in every time there's a mild complaint, an enthusiastic scream, or crocodile tears. If your son is playing with another kid, try to step back and let them work it out first, safely, if possible.

Even with these rules in place, some dustups are bound to happen. Boys are rambunctious, and they can get carried away. Recently, a boy I've been working with had a little trouble during a playdate, but one that had his mother Siobhan really worried about. Brendan, who is five, was playing with his friend James from school. They get really excited over their fantasy play about dinosaurs and firefighters. His mother says the living room sounds like a horror movie all the time, with screams and sirens and explosions. She doesn't mind because, as she says, "they're letting off steam."

But now James's mother has cut off their playdates. At first, Brendan didn't want to tell me why. His mother started the story. She said that the previous week, James had come over for a playdate, and the boys had started to play with a toy toolbox that Brendan's father had bought for him. "Brendan uses it when his dad is doing projects around the house. They work next to each other, and it's kind of cute," she said. She explained that the tools are made of plastic, but the saw is sharp enough to cut cardboard.

"I should have kept it stored away," Siobhan said. "I didn't know he'd gotten it out. I was in the kitchen."

As soon as James saw the tools, he wanted to use them as weapons in a battle. Brendan became Batman, and James became a bad guy. In a flash Brendan ran the saw over the top of James's head and cut his scalp. Blood was everywhere, and that scared both boys. Brendan stayed cowered in the corner while Siobhan called James's mother and held a cloth over the cut. It wasn't deep. The doctor used a butterfly bandage on it, but James's mom was not in a forgiving mood. "I can understand her concern," said Siobhan. "I shouldn't have let it happen. But she made it sound like Brendan needs help, like he's a bad kid, which he isn't."

I agree. Statistically speaking, boys go to emergency rooms far more often than girls do. They have more accidents because of their need for motion, high stimulation, and assertive, action-filled play. The boys in this case got excited and pulled all available toys into their well-rehearsed good guy/bad guy scenario. It was the toy itself that was mismatched to the situation. A toy that has such sharp edges should be tucked away and brought out only when a parent is ready to supervise its use.

Still, James's mother was probably pretty spooked by the incident. If the relationship between the two boys is close, Siobhan should give her a week or so to calm down. Then she can call and ask how James is doing. She can then test the waters for another playdate. She should promise closer supervision on future playdates. In this way, Brendan doesn't have to lose a friend because of a mistake they both made. If the boys do have another playtime together, Siobhan should sit both boys down and talk to them about safety. They can both learn from this experience.

When He Crosses the Line

A mom I know sent her six-year-old, Tyler, to a classmate's birthday party. Tyler had lots of fun, especially when the host mom handed out squirt guns to all the boys who launched a pretend war in the local park. The boys were squirting each other in the face, but when one of them got up close and did this to Tyler, his response was to pop the other boy in the chest and knock him down. Even the other kids were shocked. "I wasn't sure what to do," this mom said to me later. "It wasn't my party, but I felt I needed to say something." She called Tyler over and gave him a stern lecture, telling him not to hurt the other boys and to make it clear that if he couldn't handle being squirted at, he needed to stop playing. She also made him apologize to the boy he had pushed down. I assured Tyler's mom that this wasn't over-the-top aggression, and that it might be a lot to ask a group of excited six-year-old boys to handle a water gun fight while holding back from pushing or hitting. But she did the right thing by drawing a clear line in the sand for Tyler, telling him that hitting or pushing is different; it's real physical contact that is unacceptable under those conditions.

I also told her that boys do police each other's behavior and have a way of working through their issues without our interference. A kid who breaks the rules of fun play by getting violent is going to be called out on the misdeed by the other boys at some point. That's when he'll really learn not to act that way—because he wants back into the group. In the meantime, if his mom wants to teach him something or warn him of what's to come, she's going to need to take a hard line and do it as soon as he hits another kid like that. The answer is to give him a taste of what it's going to be like when the other boys tell him they don't want to play with him. That's right. Take him out of the game now and give him time on the sidelines to cool off. And give him a headline for what he can do next time: "Use your words first." "Say to the other boy, don't do that."

If you want to teach your son not to cross the line in active, good guy/bad guy play, you have to follow a simple plan.

1. *Give him the consequence first, before you give him the rule.* Pull him out of the game or stop the play immediately. There are no second chances. Typically, stopping the play involves removing a central play item, such as a ball, plastic sword, figurine, or water gun. Once you've acted, then you can speak.

2. *Tell him what he did wrong.* Restate the rule he violated. Your voice needs to be firm and calm in order to communicate authority. Make and sustain eye contact. Even good posture communicates authority, and so does a relaxed facial expression. There's no need for scowling or acting out anger or shame or disappointment. Imagine how a state trooper acts when pulling someone over for speeding on the highway. That's a good model. Troopers don't give a lecture; they just say it straight, firmly and calmly. Say to your son, "You lost the right to play just now because you were being dangerous. Play stops now. Take a break." Don't discuss right versus wrong or the merits of being

fair. He knows these ideas well by now, having heard the words hundreds of times. If you want, you can say, "We don't hit" or tell him briefly what rule he violated, but don't rely on the words. Stopping the play and taking the toy are the actions he'll remember.

3. *Wait for him to cool down.* Taking toys away or removing him from a game may cause a tantrum. Ignore the outburst until your son is ready to respond to you. If he is whining or begging or throwing a tantrum over the consequences, ignore him. If you give in now and say, "Okay, I'm giving you one more chance," you're reinforcing the original bad behavior as well as the whining and wheedling. You are creating a social monster. If the whining goes on and on, consider extending his loss of the toy or game. Otherwise, you are accidentally training him to whine or complain each time he has a similar consequence.

4. *Before you return his toy or game, make him tell you why it was taken away.* This makes him repeat out loud and recall the event, and the rules, which is a form of accountability. Don't accept a shoulder shrug. Don't fill in the silence with your worn-out rendition of the rules that he already knows. Make him do the work. If he refuses, say, "Okay, you need more time to remember. Come back when you remember why I stopped the play," and march him away. His memory will magically return. There are a few stubborn boys who will want to test how far you will go with this. Stand firm. He does know why the toy was taken away. It's likely that he remembers the event vividly.

5. *Ask him to tell you what will happen if he violates the rules again.* He should be able to predict the consequences of his actions, if he's going to follow the rules next time. When he does that, he is linking future bad behaviors (hitting) to future unwanted events (loss of fun), and his brain is making a stronger connection between the two. That way, when he's on the verge of committing another bad behavior, maybe an hour or a day later, his mind can do the right thing, suppressing his impulses and allowing him to behave better.

Why Consequences Work

This might strike parents as an overly simplistic approach. They might wonder how their son will learn right from wrong just by having toys taken away. They really want their son's character to grow. They want him to express empathy, to be the best boy around. But remember that boys are experiential learners. Losing the chance to play the game that he loves will force him to adjust and to suppress his aggressive urges in play. In time, he'll understand that if he wants to keep friends around, he'll have to treat them fairly and take into account their feelings and needs as well as his own. But he'll learn mostly through direct experience and consequences, moving slowly up the developmental ladder, and not through repeated reminders, prompts, or lectures on right versus wrong.

Whatever you do, don't discourage or label the play itself. Never say, "Why are you playing that spy game again?" or "Why don't you play something better than shooting each other?" That bad boy play belongs to him. It's his imagination at work, and he has some good developmentally appropriate reasons to be using this material to process his heavy-duty thoughts and fears.

How long should his weapons or toys be kept from him if he's misusing them? This depends on his age and the situation. Younger boys get the message after a few minutes or an hour. Older boys may need to have something removed for a whole day. If you've taken him out of an active game, such as the game at the birthday party, a few minutes may be enough time for him to cool off and think about what caused him to get yanked.

But don't expect him to feel remorse about what he's done. You'll see instead that he's upset about the consequences of losing a chance at enjoying some fun. Those consequences are what give him his motivation for changing his behavior.

He's Not Ready

Not all bad boy games or toys are appropriate for every boy. Just because your son's friends are engaging in role playing or squirt-gun fights or sword fights without getting into trouble doesn't mean that your son can handle this. Boys can want to play games and engage in fantasy play regardless of whether they're ready to control themselves emotionally. Especially when they are new to a type of play, they may not be able to dial back their emotions on cue.

If your son continues to break the rules during play or uses his bad guy persona to clock his siblings and jump on you or his friends, or if he seems obsessive about the play and wound up afterward, unable to transition to some other activity, you need to step in. Some things will be too stimulating for him when he first encounters them. You can then tell him, "You're just not ready to play with this toy," or "You're not ready to play pirate." Tell him it's okay that he's not ready. There's no need to be angry with him because he's not that grown up yet. He will be soon enough. Tell him he needs a bit more time before he can try playing with the toy again. Give him a timeline of a few days or, if needed, a few weeks, and tell him that he can try again later. A few days, weeks, or a month or two can make all the difference developmentally.

When He Obsesses

Many parents report to me that their sons are "obsessed" about a certain bad guy fantasy scenario or story line. I hear "He's obsessed with *Star Wars*" and "He's obsessed with Batman." A lot of times, parents use the term *obsessed* when what they mean is that the play is going on more than they would like. Boys can be insistent about wanting to know certain things. They want to pore over every nuance of a movie or cartoon or story idea until they feel they've mastered it and why everything happens. Most adults don't have the patience to answer fifty questions in a row about why a character in a movie behaves the way he does. There's no reason why you should. But boys are literal-minded. The reason a boy asks this many questions in a row is that he's trying to understand something about how the world works, even a fictional world. He's learning, and he's working hard at his learning. It's as if he's forcing his brain to accommodate new ideas. Later on, believe me, he'll annoy you with questions about where sweat comes from, why it's cold in space, what clouds are made of. He'll turn to other subjects. His obsession, if you call it that, is a sign of his ability to notice that there is a reason or an explanation for many things. And he wants that knowledge on the spot.

Still, it's okay to put limits on his play, if a boy becomes more anxious and wound up after his fantasy play about a certain superhero or bad guy, and on his questions if they seem excessive or if the answers make him anxious. Some parents tell their boys that they can have a designated time of day, say, right after school or right before dinner, in which to do their play about a certain subject. If there are too many *Star Wars* questions in a row, it's fine to tell your son that he can have five or ten questions and no more, or fifteen minutes of questions and no more. It's your house, and you set the rules. Or he can play a certain scenario in a certain room. He can play with his *Star Wars* figurines in his room, but not in any other part of the house. Again, you're setting limits that teach him to control himself around this type of play. Setting these kinds of limits won't squelch his imagination or bruise his self-esteem.

The Link Between Bad Guys and Fear

I worked with one boy, named Albert, who was seven and terribly afraid of the dark, afraid even to go to sleep at night alone in his own bed. By day he was a tough, confident boy, highly active. He could run all day long and was the leader of his gang of friends. He told them what to do, and they played whatever games he wanted. They acted out scenes from *Harry Potter* and played dinosaurs in which the little dinosaurs get eaten by the big ones. But at night he turned from warrior to worrier. He told his mother that monsters were out there, and he was afraid of them. His mother, Joanne, wondered how Albert could so quickly shift into fear at night. She thought she should take away the *Harry Potter* movies and the knights and dragon toys he loved. I told her that the fear and the toys didn't have much to do with each other. Most kids are afraid of the dark (most adults, too). Because people are primarily visual creatures, it's natural for us to get a bit more worried and hypervigilant at night. As adults, we've learned to screen out little noises when we go to sleep, but kids don't do that. Darkness, coupled with separation, brings about a natural fear.

Night fears come and go at this age. Usually boys encapsulate this general fear into something they can understand, such as monsters. Albert's monsters are his way of putting his fears and vulnerabilities into a humanlike form. He knows there are bad people in the world who act like monsters. Through stories and from things he has overheard, he has learned about real robbers who break into houses, people who steal kids from their parents, people who can hurt you or someone you love. These topics are unavoidable and have to be dealt with.

Instead of trying to sanitize what Albert plays with, it's better that he learn to soothe himself at bedtime and worry less. I worked with him and his mother on this. We created a positive bedtime routine in which he would choose an upbeat story to read. He got rewards for getting into bed, listening well to his bedtime story, and not complaining when it was time to say good night and turn off the light. For each one of these he got stickers on a colored piece of paper. If he does everything he's asked to in one night, he gets a treat, such as extra time watching a favorite television show or the chance to play his favorite game, checkers, with his dad.

We also worked out rituals for when he became afraid, such as reaching out for his favorite stuffed animal, and surrounding his bed and room with strong, protective stuffed dinosaurs that could "watch out for him" at night. This hooked his imagination into the ritual and allowed it to work in his favor.

Interestingly, during the day, Albert loves being afraid. He loves stories with scary parts and wants to have them read to him over and over. The scariest scene of "Hansel and Gretel," where the witch gets thrown into the oven, is his favorite. These stories offer him a thrill, no matter how many times he's heard them before. Here Albert is teasing himself with fear, playfully and safely, and slowly getting accustomed—or desensitized—to scary things as they go through his mind during each retelling. In a way, he's building immunity against his fears of real bad things in the real world.

Bad Boy Play Long Term

Eventually, boys begin to globalize the ideas they've discovered in play and learned about in children's books and movies. They begin to ask about bad guys in the real world. They begin to ask questions like "Who is the boss of all the bad guys? Can bad guys come to our house? Will they steal from us? Are there real wars?" They begin to pick up on similar themes in cartoons, comic books, video and computer games, and dramas on television and ask if they are real or not. This is how their brains sift through complex concepts of good and bad, love and hate. They can ask these bigger questions because they've rehearsed them safely first in play.

In years to come they will need to explore the unfortunate but basic truth that people do sometimes hurt each other and that scary things do really happen in the world. Many moms have the urge to protect their son from this reality. Don't. Through play and gradual exposure to these ideas, he will become better armed to handle the sad events and real dangers in later life. Allow him to be the bad guy and play freely, but safely, and with this he will learn to control his fears of the world.

CHAPTER 9

He's Suddenly Fragile

Lars is what his mother calls "a basket case." A few months earlier, just after he turned five, he seemed to collapse emotionally. Now every time she tries to punish him for something, even something really wrong, such as throwing a toy at his little sister's head and laughing when he gets a direct hit, he cries piteously. The crocodile tears flow harder than his sister's real tears. He cowers when being sent to his room and twists his face into exaggerated expressions. Not only that, he shouts, "You hate me," whenever he gets caught doing anything wrong. When asked about his school friends, he says, "No one likes me." When he's bored at home, he cries, complaining, "No one is playing with me. You don't like me." He insists that his mother likes his sister best.

His mother, Amber, was a grade school teacher before she decided to stay home to take care of her kids. She is used to wild boy activity from her years in the classroom, so Lars's early toddler behavior was no surprise to her. For example, Lars has always been easily frustrated when things go badly for him. He has had mini-meltdowns when his toys wouldn't do the things he wanted them to do. In these moments, he shrieks and tries to break the toys. Or he throws his plate when he can't get the food to stay on his fork. Now he also cries when he makes a mistake or whenever someone corrects his behavior. His parents wonder when the emotional roller coaster will end and how they can help him calm down. He seems too thin-skinned, too quick to become hurt and angry to get along in the world.

I hear this from a lot of parents. Young boys who have been swaggering their way through toddlerhood suddenly seem fragile for a period of weeks or months at a time. They can seem embattled at school, spooked by social situations, and unable to accept any form of criticism without a flood of tears or a tantrum. Other boys fly into a rage over every frustration, breaking toys and shouting, "I hate you." Oddly enough, most of these episodes are normal, nothing more than an indication that major leaps in development are about to take place.

Growing Up Isn't Easy

Boys do break down a bit after toddlerhood. In the years taking them through early grade school, they will be more emotional, less able to cope for weeks at a time. There are several reasons for this, each one having to do, in part, with the huge developmental struggle going on inside these boys.

One thing parents need to remember about boys is that their development is erratic. It's not the smooth, even process we would like to imagine. Boys this age are still developing the tools for learning new things. Unlike adults, who accumulate new information by layering it on top of old information and making links between facts and concepts they already know, a boy's brain is constantly reorganizing itself to accommodate new information and skills. He is still figuring out how to learn, how to use logic rather than just observations and direct experience. That tense and dynamic process of learning how to learn will unfold over several years. Young boys want to soak up so much, and they do, but they are also clumsy in their learning, just as they are clumsy in their first social and athletic experiences. As he makes leaps in learning, a boy will then have setbacks in which he seems to forget everything he's learned about a particular skill, whether it's tying a shoelace or spelling his name or catching a baseball. Don't worry; your son will pull it together again, but in the meantime, know that these setbacks are as frustrating and exhausting for him as they are for you.

Most boys really are on the two-steps-forward, one-step-back plan when it comes to learning new skills. Yet they are making progress, even when they seem to be at their worst.

For example, I worked with a wonderful little boy who had cerebral palsy, who wasn't able to swallow or chew food until after his fourth birthday. Up to that point, he had been fed through a tube in his stomach, so he had no idea how food tasted or felt in his mouth. Learning to eat was an enormous physical challenge to overcome. Every meal was a battle, first to touch food, then to taste it without gagging, and then to swallow.

Although his mother showed incredible patience with him and with the lengthy and frustrating ritual of feeding him, she was occasionally despondent, believing that he wasn't making any progress at all. She would tell me that he would have one or two good experiences, really trying and succeeding to take bites. Then at the next meal, he would get frustrated right away and melt down and quit. A few times, more ended up on the floor than in his mouth. Together we kept a chart, noting how many bites he was able to take and swallow at each meal. Although any given day might have seemed hopeless to his mother, we looked at the charts after a month and saw that he was making progress. Over time, he was averaging more bites, more food eaten.

This is a great model for how all boys learn. Whether it's zipping a coat or learning to read, they are likely to show great gains on some days. These gains will likely be followed by real frustration, real tantrums, and some setbacks. Only when you step back and check your son's progress over weeks and months will you recognize that, hey, he's really moving forward. You'll hear from relatives who don't see him as often that he's made changes. You don't see them because you are there every day, stuck in the trenches. So be patient.

The task, for you as a parent, is to stay calm; don't overreact. Remember that boys are like little scientists. They rely on experience to teach them, and they want to do it every wrong way first, which means they are likely to make many mistakes while learning. And they tend to show their frustrations in over-the-top ways with physical anger and meltdowns. It's a parent's job to focus on the big picture rather than the small tantrums. Your son is moving forward all the time.

He Wants to Be the Best

Hand in hand with this constant challenge to learn new things is a boy's intense need for mastery. A boy is in competition all the time, with his siblings, his peers, and even himself. He doesn't just want to learn a skill; he wants to wrestle it to the ground and own it. He wants to be the best at something right away, and when he can't because the skill is just too hard at first, he is going to be enraged or in tears. His drive to succeed is high, while his tolerance for failure is low. So he is likely to break down emotionally all through his early years of development.

This can happen easily in the classroom as well as at home. One mom I know told me that she went to her son's school to volunteer in the classroom. The class was doing an exercise where they were writing numbers on a piece of paper. Her son, Matthew, wrote a backward 2 and then realized his mistake. No one said anything about the mistake or even noticed it until he broke down crying. His teacher said, "It's okay, honey; just try again." Then Matthew became embarrassed about the fact that he was crying and just cried harder. This mom was embarrassed for her son and tried repeatedly to encourage him. She patted him on the back and whispered to him, but he shrugged her off and then cried harder. It went on for thirty minutes, and Matthew didn't actually stop crying until after his mother left the room. Later, she asked me what was wrong with him. She really wanted to know if he wasn't a good fit with the classroom. She feared that if he couldn't rebound from a simple mistake, he would be unable to keep up with his peers—even though he was only in kindergarten.

I told her that it was not that serious. What happens with many boys is that they want to be great at every skill all the time. I reminded her that her son was one of the youngest kids in the class. He had just turned five when all the other kindergartners were several months older. Some of the boys in that classroom were nine months older than

Mathew. But he didn't know that. Instead he was thinking: *I'm power-ful, and I want to be the best; why can't I do this?* He felt embarrassed that he couldn't perform perfectly.

Parents should understand that they can accidentally bring out the most regressive behavior in their own children, especially in a school setting. I don't mean that as an insult, but it's true. Your child will behave much better in the classroom when you're not there. He's more likely to misbehave and break down when Mom and Dad are watching. He is comfortable showing you all his vulnerability and is used to crying around you as a signal to you that he wants help. He saves his tears for you. When he is in the classroom, he makes his choices and deals with the consequences on his own. With Matthew, once his mom left the room, he was able to pull himself together and move on to the next task.

A mother's empathy can actually be a distraction for her son at this stage. Remember that Matthew, or any boy struggling with making mistakes or learning a skill, is not crying over deep pain. I tell moms that a boy's sadness is not like ours. Moms I know are raising kids while dealing with crises at work, aging parents, financial problems, a sudden illness in a sibling or good friend. These are big, big issues. The sadness and confusion that an adult will feel while dealing with these issues are not the same thing that your son feels while trying to build a robot out of plastic bricks. Yet it is so easy for a parent to automatically overempathize with the tears and screaming over a half-built toy. Many moms tell me they try to soothe these crying jags with hugs and lots of talk and encouragement. Or worse, they take away the offending object, the shoe that needs tying, the drawing that's not quite right, the tower that keeps falling down, and fix it for their son. They try to take away the frustration.

In my opinion, this is totally counterproductive, for several reasons.

First, this need to overempathize with your son robs him of the chance to feel reasonable emotional stressors and deal with them and learn better ways to cope with them. If you take away the thing that frustrates him as soon as he begins to squawk, then he doesn't get any practice experiencing frustration, and certainly no chance to try new and better ways to deal with the thousands of struggles and disappointments waiting for him down the road.

Second, you're communicating to your son that you really don't think he can accomplish anything on his own. "Here, let me do it" tells him he's not capable. A boy's source of confidence comes from your expectation that he can do something difficult and confusing. Better to leave him alone with his frustration or wait for him to ask for help. This will take longer, and he'll make a lot of noise, but he will gain confidence and self-esteem when you step aside and leave him alone to figure something out on his own. If you are intervening or coaching him too much, then any successes belong to you, not him. Let him own it all, successes and failures.

Finally, by hovering over him and his frustrations, you are accidentally promoting the very fragility you're complaining about. Remember that frustration at this age, while frequent, is transient. It needs minimal attention. If you hover and make a big deal over his tears, you reward him for being more dependent on your help. If you do that, expect more and longer bouts of frustration.

He Won't Leave My Side

Many parents notice a sudden bout of what experts call "separation anxiety" in school-age boys. This seems so startling to them. They often ask if this signals a problem.

Later in that same school year, Matthew's mom went to visit the classroom on Portfolio Day, in which the kindergarten class shows off artwork. After the art display, the kids went off to their gym class, and some of the parents elected to stay and watch. Matthew's mom couldn't stay; she had an appointment at Matthew's older sister's school. Matthew saw that some moms were staying, and he started to cry when his mom waved good-bye to him. He hugged her around the waist and said, "Don't go," which is unlike him. He normally leaves her side easily. Because we'd talked about this sort of thing in the office, she was able to say to him in a calm, direct voice, "I have to go. But I know you are going to have a great day. I'm proud of you. Go have fun."

She kissed him and walked away. He gave her the big tears and looked crushed, but she stayed firm. As she was walking out, she passed another mom whose little boy was wailing, "Mommy, don't go." The mother was on her knees hugging him, saying, "I'm so sorry. I have to leave," although she was making no move to leave. Next to them, the boy's teacher was trying to tug the mother away, saying, "It's okay, you can go. I've got him." But the mother in that situation couldn't let go. She kept saying, "It's okay, honey. Don't cry," but why would he stop when he had such a ready audience? This drama was likely to go on for some time. Mathew's mom said to me, "I'm glad that wasn't me." I'm glad, too. That kind of good-bye, if you think about it, is a vote of no confidence. You're telling your son that you have no confidence in his ability to feel sad and then go pull himself together and rejoin his classmates.

It may seem unfeeling to ignore his tears sometimes, but I urge parents to think about what other kinds of emotional frustrations their son inevitably will face in the next five to ten years: making friends, struggling with academics, trying out new sports, joining clubs, getting through middle school and high school, taking a driving test and SATs, signing up for summer jobs, and applying for college. He needs to be able to feel the pain of the many challenges and setbacks that are a part of every childhood. By allowing him to face smaller challenges now, you are giving him the chance to build the resiliency that he will need later.

The Empathy Check

Moms and dads need to remind themselves that a child's crying at day care drop-off, or while trying and failing to kick a soccer ball, is not like the pain you or I feel; his pain has a different purpose. It's an expression of not getting his way, of needing to shift gears and adapt to the world. He doesn't like that. His discomfort is developmental. It is not deeply emotional. It doesn't last like adult emotion. I tell parents to do an empathy check.

The empathy you feel for your son has helped you get this far as a parent. You needed it when he was a baby; you needed it to get up in the middle of the night to feed him, to maintain the exhausting vigilance required to keep him safe while he learned to eat and walk and explore the world as a young toddler. Now as he gets older, it's natural that parents find it difficult to relax and let him feel some frustration.

Parents often find it easier to handle a boy who is aggressive, enraged, or hyperactive, than one who is shy and timid. Sometimes, parents and teachers become flummoxed completely when these types of boys fall apart. They just don't seem tough enough to handle things on their own. It is tempting to rush in with comfort, with hugs, with an insistence that he's going to be okay, that the situation upsetting him "isn't so bad." But as with a tantrum, your boy's confusion, his sadness, his embarrassment, can't be talked away or hugged away. He might have to cry a bit, feel embarrassed, then see the emotion fade away, as it will, in order to feel that he can get control of himself again. It's tempting to believe that he can't learn until he calms down, but that's not true. In this case, it's his frustration and tears that are spurring his growth. The best you can do is say, "I know it's hard. I'll talk to you when you calm down." This is a battle he has to fight on his own.

Where Have I Seen This Before?

Moms ask me when their sons will stop freaking out over every frustration. The short answer is probably never. For all our strutting and muscle flexing, we guys tip over easily when it comes to emotions. Moms ask me, "Why does he break down so easily?" I tell them it happens to most men, myself included, but it's at a less visible level in adults. Moms are often surprised to learn that even as a psychologist, I often can't see my emotions coming. A lot of men feel that their feelings hit them from behind. Our minds can be like fuses, and they just short out for a moment. It's as though our mouths are temporarily disconnected from our brains, taking away our ability to put feelings into words. It would be great if men could better sense the emotions building inside them or could better signal their feelings and vent them with words, but often they don't. Part of this is how we're raised, and part of this is how we're wired. What's true for many men is even more true for little boys.

Moms who struggle with boys who short out frequently in late tod-dlerhood and early grade school sometimes notice that their husbands do the same thing. One mom I know, Cindy, told me about a situation she had recently with her son, Aaron, who is four. Aaron was playing, not quite happily, in the living room one morning. He was trying to balance a robot on top of a beach ball with predictable results. Cindy was at her wits' end. "He tries to do these things that are impossible," she told me. "No toy is going to balance on a beach ball. Then he just freaks out and screams every time it falls off." Cindy was rushing back and forth between the kitchen, which she was trying to clean up, and the living room, where she was trying to help Aaron calm down. Meanwhile, her husband, Chris, was rushing around, trying to get packed for a business trip. Cindy dumped some wilted vegetables into the sink and turned on the garbage disposal, and nothing happened. She casually said to her husband, "Where are the instructions for this thing?" Instead of finding the instructions, Chris dropped his luggage and attacked the problem. Every time Cindy said, "Honey, you'll be late. I'll take care of this," he answered, "I don't have time for this." She said, "Honey, go. It's okay." He said, "I have to fix this." He was at this point red-faced and enraged.

Cindy told me that at this exact moment Aaron had a huge melt-down in the living room. He punched the beach ball and broke apart the robot, then began screaming. Cindy felt completely torn. She wanted to stay in the kitchen and hover over her husband to encourage him to make the right choice to catch his train. And she wanted to rush into the living room and soothe Aaron with hugs and reassurances.

Instead, she had an epiphany. She left the kitchen without saying another word to her husband. "I thought, he's a grown-up. Let him do what he's going to do," she said. She went to the living room, re-trieved the half-deflated beach ball and the broken robot, and said to Aaron, "These are mine now." She put them on a high shelf, which sent Aaron into a stronger screaming outrage. She stepped over him and left the room. She gave him no lectures, no reassurances, no good reasons why he should calm down. Instead, she gave him no choice but to calm down.

"I'm not feeding the tantrum monster anymore," she said to me. "In either of them." She went to the bedroom with a magazine and left them, father and son, alone with their problems. Within two minutes, the house was quiet again. Chris had figured out how to fix the disposal and was feeling good about himself, and Aaron had forgotten about the beach ball and had picked another toy to play with.

Sounds good to me. Sometimes, withholding the urge to mother, to reassure, to fix, to talk through things is the best type of empathy you can offer your boy or partner.

In fact, by taking the toy away, this mom has created a tiny connection in her son's mind between having a tantrum and losing the toy. It's a small connection, and this lesson will likely be repeated a few hundred times over many different toys, computer games, scooters, bikes, and, finally, the car. But the connection will grow each time, and over time he will learn that continuing to freak out leads to something bad, while disengaging and asserting self-control leads to something more positive.

I Hate You

One of the things that invariably tags along when boys show their fragility is their clumsy use of language as a weapon. Many moms have called me in a panic the first time their son has turned from a sweet, rambunctious little boy to an angry monster, screaming, "I hate you! I hate you forever!" before storming off to his room.

In some boys, it starts early. Fiona is a polite, soft-spoken woman who is struggling with her three-year-old son, Todd. Lately, Todd has been yelling hateful things at her when she disciplines him for misbehaving. He tells her he hates her and that she's stupid. "It's so devastating to hear that," she said to me. "I know they're just words, but he sounds like he means it."

Yet Todd doesn't mean it in the way that his mother feels it. He has no idea what these words mean to her adult ears. Fiona is such a great mom that, if she took a deep breath and thought about it, she'd realize that he couldn't possibly feel true, deep hatred for someone who cares so much for him. Rather, Todd is like many young boys who express themselves with extreme emotions. He has latched onto a few shocking phrases that he knows get the attention of adults. In a few years your son will be trying out potty talk and even swear words on you, so it's time to develop your poker face now.

Understand that when he says these things to you, he's really saying, "I'm not getting my way right now." He's telling you that he's frustrated and angry. Admittedly, he can't go around telling people he hates them every time he doesn't get his way. That's not going to work in school and with his friends. Your job is to coach him toward better ways to communicate his frustration. I told Fiona to say, "I don't listen to yelling." She could even make the message shorter, "No yelling." She has to coach herself not to look hurt or shocked when he says these things, because that gives him more power in the situation. I told her to remove herself from the situation by turning away and, if necessary, to leave the room. Give him a simple reason. I tell moms who are dealing with this type of talk at any age to completely ignore their son until he's calm. If the anger doesn't subside on its own in a few minutes, send him to his room until he calms down.

Over-the-top emotions and overly dramatic phrases take many parents by surprise. I often get calls from parents who tell me, "He said he hates everything at school," or "He says all the kids hate him." These statements are usually accompanied by tears and screaming fits, only adding to a mom's worry that her son isn't able to succeed in class or is a social pariah. Neither is the case. It's nothing more than a temporary feeling, and likely an overreaction. It doesn't reflect anything very deep or long term. It won't last. For now, his emotional systems are highly reactive, and he wears his heart very much on his sleeve. Notice how he'll be laughing in a few minutes, or enjoying school and friends the next day. Be careful not to latch onto exaggerated statements and strong emotions, or you may reinforce these with the attention you give. Ignore them as best you can. They will pass.

I tell parents that if a single problem arises suddenly, for example, refusing to eat dinner or crying excessively before bed, complaints that the kids at school hate him, or sudden regressive behaviors such as clinginess, chances are it's probably not anything to worry about. As startling as these behaviors might be, they are part of the normal ups and downs of emotional development. Keep an eye on the problem without focusing too much attention on it, knowing that problems such as these should resolve themselves within a week or two. If they don't, then you might talk to your pediatrician.

However, if multiple problems erupt at once, and they seem fairly intense, then something more serious may be at work. For example, if a boy suddenly won't separate from his mother even at home and is also regressing with his potty training, he may have a more serious developmental issue. In this case, you wouldn't want to wait two weeks before acting to make an appointment with a pediatrician. Remember, too, that if a boy suffers a sudden loss of social skills or language at any age, he needs to be seen by a pediatrician or specialist.

Later, in Chapter 12, I discuss more sophisticated ways to determine if your son is showing real symptoms that may warrant evaluation or treatment. For example:

- Is the behavior serious enough to interfere with his functioning? Does it keep him from sleeping, eating, attending school, or staying safe?
- Does it persist over a few weeks or more? Does it show itself more than a few isolated times per day?
- Does it happen across different settings—at home and at school and at Grandma's and at playgroup—or is it happening in just one setting?
- Has the behavior been reported by multiple people, or is it observed by just one person?

If you are answering yes to these questions, your son may indeed have a symptom that needs to be addressed by a pediatrician. In most cases, however, you will not be answering yes to any of these questions. Most early childhood delays and problems are not serious and are transient.

The Mini-Manipulator

There are many reasons a boy might suddenly be crying more often or breaking down emotionally into tears and rage at home or at school. I've described the overwhelming nature of cognitive development and the need for competition and perfectionism that many boys feel. But there is another reason boys cry more at this young age, and it's also an important part of their development, even if it's a frustrating one for parents. Your son is trying out his ability to manipulate you.

Parents who have daughters as well as sons note that their girls knew how to use crocodile tears and a well-timed pout quite effectively before they turned three. These behaviors aren't as smoothly executed by your five- or six-year-old boy, but they are just as important developmentally.

In many cases, a dramatic "You hate me" or a sudden stream of tears may have little to do with deep internal angst. Even a boy who doesn't seem very socially sophisticated soon learns that crying, claiming to be hated and misunderstood, gets everyone's attention and gets him what he wants. He has seen these techniques at school, at day care, and at home, and he's trying them out. It's not evil intentions or sociopathic behavior. It's simply intelligence. We all behave in ways that we think motivate others to do what we want. Your son's version of it is just clumsier and a little more over the top.

Learning Self-Talk

One of the big steps in growing up is learning to talk yourself through a frustrating situation. Think of a stressor that any adult might encounter—getting cut off in traffic, say, or watching someone cut ahead of you to steal a parking space. You're frustrated, and the first thing you do is talk to yourself about it. *That guy's a jerk. Does he think he owns the road?* Then you talk to yourself about what to do next, maybe fantasize about getting out of the car and yelling. But you don't. You tell yourself to calm down, that it's not worth getting upset over, or you're late enough already, or it's potentially dangerous. It's better just to find another place to park and get on with the day. That's how adults negotiate the anger that arises from disappointments and setbacks all day long. They do it in their heads, using self-talk.

Because boys start out with lags in their language development, they come late to this skill. Many struggle with it up to and into their teenage years. When you think about it, this severely limits their choices when under stress. They have only gut reactions to guide them. In general, girls have an easier time with frustration because they tend to learn self-talk at an earlier age. You can hear them doing it. Many toddler girls have an ongoing external monologue, sometimes a singing monologue about whatever is going on in their heads. Some girls, though, are just as willing as boys to use behavior over words. In my experience this seems more true with little girls who have older brothers. As one preschool teacher said to me, "I can always tell when girls have an older brother. They tend to whack first and ask questions later."

An Anger Plan

If you've been working with your son on helping him manage his anger, then you've already sent him into Time-Away when he lashes out and breaks things. If he has some practice getting sent away from a situation in which he feels out of control, he likely will have developed some rudimentary skills for calming down. I tell parents that boys need a physical release first. They should have a pillow or a bean bag chair or something soft that they can punch or hit while they are mad to get the emotions out. (I remind parents to invest in pillows made of foam rather than feathers for the simple reason that feather pillows are actually too soft. They don't give enough resistance to punching. Also, if a feather pillow breaks, your son's room will look like a chicken coop.) Set up an "angry area" of his room into which you can march him and direct him to let out his anger physically. When I work with very young boys trying to deal with their emotions, I model this for them. I say, "You're mad. I'm mad, too." And I hit the pillow. They get excited by this. Here hitting is good; it helps your son exorcise the rage. Sadness is no different. When a boy is crying, he is getting it out of his system. You can label his feelings, but wait until he's calmed down a bit; otherwise, he's too upset to hear what you're saying and won't associate the label with the feelings he's just had. For example: "You are so mad because you couldn't have another cookie," or "You're upset because we can't go to the park." It's okay to reassure him a little, but resist the urge to rush in and tell him not to be sad or not to cry. Boys need to wallow a bit in any emotion to get the feel of it, to get the sense that it will fade on its own. Don't spend much time consoling. Once you get in the habit of directing his anger into safely hitting pillows, giving him a simple label for his feelings, and then letting him alone, you'll see how his strong emotions will quickly run their course.

Give Him Headlines

Boys will not listen to long monologues about how they should behave. When your son is raging or crying, he can't understand what you're saying. What can work instead is to try short bursts, or "headlines," that reinforce what feelings he's showing. You can say, "You are mad. Your toy doesn't work." "George hit you. That hurts." "Mommy took your toy away. You're sad." I know this is going to feel silly at first. Talking this way can make you feel like a character in a *Dick and Jane* book. But when you say these things, you are showing your son the link between the feelings inside him and the words he can use to describe them. The trick is to wait until he's relatively calm and to make your statement confidently and almost matter-of-factly.

After rehearsing these links between feelings and words many times over, he will begin to label his emotions. At the very least, he'll be able to nod or shake his head when you ask him about his feelings. Over time, you can try asking him to tell you what he is feeling, again making him do some of the work. Once he labels his own emotions, you can begin to make your explanations longer. You can talk about how actions make other people feel: "You hit Henry. That's why he's now mad at you, too, and doesn't want to play anymore." Eventually, you can ask your son why he thinks someone else is hurt or why someone else is angry, slowly encouraging his brain to empathize and connect the dots between his actions and other people's responses.

Over time, you will even be able to suggest another response from him that's more positive. A suggestion is often more powerful than a command. It allows your son to feel he has a choice. For example, you could say: "Honey, you're frustrated right now. Why don't you take a break?" or "When I'm sad, I like to be alone for a few minutes." He will likely ignore your suggestions at first, but slowly, he'll get better at letting his voice guide him through strong emotions, rather than relying solely on gut reactions. Remember that in ten to twelve years he will be behind the wheel of a car. When a cop stops him, he will need to hold it together. Or he might be cut from a sports team he loves or fired from a first job, and he will need to talk himself through strong emotions and regroup. He needs to be able to feel the pain of a setback and then pull himself together. By allowing him opportunities to experience fragility now, he is building resiliency that will serve him well as he grows up.

CHAPTER 10

He Hates School

J ack was so excited to go to kindergarten the first day. He was tugging at his mother's sleeve to get her out the door. He bounded into the classroom. His mother, Kim, says he was truly bored at home and couldn't wait to be a big boy who learns to read and make friends. He even longed to ride the bus like the older kids. But within a few weeks, he was complaining about school, saying he didn't like it. He told his mom that the teacher doesn't like him. Soon he was crying and screaming at the classroom door, absolutely refusing to go inside. Kim was beside herself, wondering why he hated to go to school, wondering if something had happened to upset him and whether this early reluctance meant that he was doomed to failure in school.

I met with Jack and Kim in my office. Jack told me that his teacher was mean and that school was too hard. These aren't unusual complaints even at this age level. Teachers who typically have to manage twenty or more children for a full school day have to develop a much stricter discipline style than boys are used to at home. Teachers tend to use and expect a lot of eye contact in the classroom, which many boys aren't comfortable with at such young ages. In addition, classroom work, even at the kindergarten level, demands a lot of sitting still and listening to directions and waiting your turn to speak. Not every boy is cut out for these behaviors at such an early age.

In our meeting, I found out that Jack saw his teacher as an unfamiliar species of adult. Many boys this age feel this way. Teachers have authority, but even if they are nurturing and caring, they don't mother. They aren't loving like the adults at home. Jack told me, "My teacher is like my mom, but she's not as nice." I asked why, and he added, "She tells me what to do and gets mad a lot." I explained to Kim that it takes some time for little guys to understand that other big people in the world will have control over them and expect things from them, tell them what to do, and can even discipline them. Lots of boys come home saying that a teacher is mean or that "she hates me." These boys just aren't used to someone calling them on their misdeeds for six hours at a time, someone who isn't Mom.

I also told Kim that meltdowns are frequent in the first few weeks of school among all types of boys. Their immature emotional regulation systems can get tripped off like oversensitive alarms by minor frustrations in a strange environment. Their clumsy social skills make sharing and waiting turns difficult. Their less developed language abilities make listening and following classroom rules a challenge. Piled onto all this is that many boys pick up on every mom's natural anxiety about having to leave her son behind in some new place, in the care of a stranger. This can make a boy even more resistant to sign on for his new school experience.

Why School Isn't a Good Fit

When I hear that a boy is struggling in his first year or two of elementary school, I immediately think of the specific areas in which the style of learning and socializing at school may be at odds with his own learning style and temperament:

The Gender Gap

Perhaps because of the challenging temperaments and behaviors of boys, one study has shown that preschool teachers view them more negatively than they do girls. When surveyed, teachers described boys as active, loud, aggressive, less teachable, and less easy to work with as students.

I'm not suggesting that this perception of boys is completely wrong, or even that it's wrong-headed. Moms often feel this way about their sons, too. They ask me these questions: "Why is he always yelling?" "Why does he break everything?" "Why is he making such a mess all the time?" "Why won't he just look at me and answer me when I ask him a question?"

Research shows that, on average, male teachers are less likely to see boys as troublesome and do not label as many of their behaviors as problems, but the vast majority—more than 95 percent—of kindergarten teachers are women. Many of them expect boys to sit still and pay attention while they teach a lesson, listen to their directions, and make good enough eye contact to pick up every subtle point. Not so. Boys are more likely to have trouble focusing and staying on task; they have higher energy and tend to need to fidget to work off steam, which teachers and classmates can find distracting. And as we've seen, many boys avoid eye contact; some even find it unnerving. Some teachers assume that students at this age will talk out their problems or ask for help. When girls are struggling in the classroom, more often than not they will initiate a dialogue about their problem, asking for advice from peers and from the teacher. Boys tend not to do this. They will wallow in their troubles and try to sort things out on their own, or get frustrated and lash out. When boys see their teachers' reactions to such behavior, they can easily get the idea early on that they aren't good at school. But these are developmental and stylistic differences between boys and girls, not an indication of delay, deficit, or scholastic ability or intelligence. Boys have a preference for hands-on activities, tactile learning, and physical movement rather than talking and listening.

Unfortunately for boys, most school days don't feature a lot of running and movement and lessons that involve taking things apart or making things. When boys are assigned a task or project, they very often need concrete directions to keep them focused. Some teachers assume several steps, saying, "Let's get ready to draw." Many boys need to hear every step: "Now we take out our pencils." "Now we take out a sheet of paper." Boys may need to hear the simplest instruction several times. When we shift the style of teaching to favor a boy's style of learning, boys do better. The differences are astounding.

Male teachers promote this style of learning and are more playful and emphasize the physical development of boys. Traditional classrooms tend to emphasize calm play and socializing. While social skills are important, young boys are highly curious and have a primary need to touch, explore, and be self-directed and assertive while learning. Not much research addresses this disparity of learning styles directly in young boys, but studies of middle school students show that having a male teacher increases a boy's interest in learning and may improve his achievement scores. Interestingly, girls tend to experience much the same positive effect with female teachers. However, since most elementary school teachers are women, most girls aren't deprived of teachers who are role models for learning.

Would putting male teachers into elementary school classrooms solve all our problems in education? In my opinion, no. I do wish that more men could be encouraged to teach these early grades. But we also need to give teachers the resources and support to do their jobs effectively. More often than not, having a smaller class size or having a co-teacher present would allow teachers to give girls and boys more direct encouragement and individualized approaches to learning.

There's a wonderful children's book called *No, David,* in which David is told "no" for all the things he does wrong all day. Well, when the Davids of the world go to school, they hear "no" all day there, too. What we sometimes fail to remember is that hearing "no" is as frustrating as having to say it. Yes, boys are exhausting in the classroom, but they are often exhausted themselves (and stressed) by trying to control impulses when their brains aren't yet equipped to do this so easily.

The Language Barrier

Many boys struggle with the sheer number of words they will hear over the course of a school day. An elementary school classroom is four-fifths language-based, and research suggests that many very young boys are not developmentally ready to process that much language during the course of a school day. Not only do they have to listen to the teacher's instructions about where to sit and what to do, but they also must engage in lessons that largely rely on language. Rarely are early elementary school lessons experiential in nature. Even experiential lessons (such as noticing how a seedling is growing or observing the weather) involve using language. Lessons learned must be verbalized or written, and in later grades, read about. Many boys will tire and zone out after a few hours of language overload, or they act out, becoming a distraction in the classroom, which attracts punishment.

Differing Conflict Styles

One reason boys get singled out as troublemakers early in school is that girls and boys use aggression differently and tend to be disciplined differently. This is true both at home and at school. As one mother put it to me: "When my daughter wants to annoy her brother, she does it quietly. She takes some of his toys away, sticks her feet in his face, and calls him stupid. And he never warns her or says 'no' to her. When he gets tired of it, he whacks her. Then she screams and cries. For months, I would hear the screams and come running into the living room. I'd turn right to him and demand to know what he'd done. It took me a long time to figure out that she had trained me to punish him even though she had started the fight. Now I don't get involved at all unless there's blood. I tell them to work it out themselves."

Studies of aggression in preschoolers found that boys primarily tend to use physical and direct verbal aggression, while girls prefer to use what's called relational aggression. That means that girls will use relationships to manipulate and exclude in order to hurt others. These behaviors are harder to spot in a busy classroom, but they can be very powerful and just as hurtful as a punch. The point is that a boy's style of aggression is a magnet for attention from a teacher, while a girl's style tends to go unnoticed. When boys and girls are in conflict with each other, the pattern is already set. A girl might say to a boy, "We don't want to play with you—you're not our friend," and then the boy comes out swinging or yelling. Usually, it is the boy who gets in trouble after such a conflict.

Differing Relational Styles

Boys tend to use gamesmanship and competition to relate to their friends and to blow off steam. Many times in classrooms I've seen a boy take a pencil or a piece of paper from a classmate as a type of benign teasing. Both boys seem in on the game; they're usually both giggling over the swipe. Or boys will try to edge each other out of a chair. Moving a boy out of his space or out of his chair is a game for them. (Although I've noticed anything can be a game. The rules may be opaque to grown-ups, but they are perfectly clear to the boys.) No one wants to lose, no one wants to be pushed or elbowed, and yet it's a game, not a fight. Both boys are smiling. But most teachers will view such behavior as a fight or, at the very least, a disruption—a situation in need of discipline.

It's worth keeping in mind that this is also how young men relate to one another. Watch high school and college age boys, and you'll see the same. They use teasing, small jabs, wrestling holds, and physical jousts as a sign of affection. It's just one of the ways boys socialize, and while certainly needing some limits in the classroom, it shouldn't be pathologized or completely discouraged. Very young boys will need to learn there's a time and a place for it. But if they had more frequent breaks to move around in their long school day, they would be more relaxed, better focused, and less likely to engage in as much of this guy-to-guy jousting.

Boosting His Behavior at School

Not every problem can be blamed on gender differences or bias. Sometimes the problems that occur in school are larger than a difference between boys and girls, or how boys are viewed by their mostly female teachers. Some boys seem completely overwhelmed by their exposure to the classroom. One boy I worked with, named Brian, had shut down entirely in school. He refused to speak to his teachers or peers. He needed help in overcoming his fears and his discomfort in the classroom.

I called Brian's teacher, and we came up with a simple plan. First, we stopped him from using his bolder classmates as behavioral crutches. In particular, there were two girls who had become like personal translators for Brian, getting things for him and answering for him when the teacher asked him questions. They were told to let Brian be a big boy who uses his words when he wants something. Second, I gave Brian's teacher a colorful chart to put on her desk or hang in the classroom along with a bunch of star stickers. Brian would get to put a sticker on his chart if he said "Hello" to his teacher in the morning. He would get to do the same thing if he said "Good-bye" at the end of the day. His mother reminded him of the stickers at school drop-off each morning. The teacher didn't put any pressure on him to comply. She said a happy "Good morning" to him, as she did to all of the other students. If he responded, he got to have the sticker. If he refused, she simply said, "That's okay. You can try again tomorrow." When Brian had earned both stickers in one day, he got a special activity or privilege at home, such as an extra game of cards before dinner or an extra story at bedtime.

For the first few days, Brian didn't go along with this program. Why would he? I'm sure he liked the status quo and wasn't interested in taking the risk of talking in class, even if there was a reward at the end of it. Many boys try to test teachers and parents before complying with a new standard of behavior. I told his mother to wait it out. On the fourth day, Brian whispered "Good morning" to his teacher. She got another barely audible "Good-bye" at the end of the day. He got the promised rewards and loved them. He seemed very proud of himself when he put the stickers on his chart. Because he couldn't use the little girls to speak for him, he began to whisper a few things during the school day as well.

After about a week, we upped the ante on Brian. I talked again to his mother and teacher to make sure we were in agreement. Then we told Brian: no more whispering. To get the stickers, he would have to use his big boy voice. The very next day, Brian shut down again and refused to say anything all day long. This confirmed to me that we had a smart little guy on our hands. I had no doubt that there was some actual shyness or social anxiety at work with him. The act of not speaking was his way of feeling powerful and having some control over others. That's why nagging him to talk or making a big deal out of the situation is not going to solve it. The key is to make the new behavior more rewarding for him than the current situation. I coached everyone to wait it out again. Within a couple of days, the lure of the rewards won out, and he began to talk in class using a louder voice. He complied on most days, and after a couple of weeks we increased the challenge again. We told him that he would have to approach a classmate once a day and ask him or her to play with him. We told him, "You get double stickers for that."

The program worked well for a few weeks until Brian got bored with the stickers. First we switched from stars to dinosaur stickers that he picked himself. Then we abandoned the stickers altogether. He was past them. At this point, his teacher could pull back a bit. Instead of measuring his compliance with stickers, she could verbally reward Brian for speaking out in class and for talking to his classmates. Things went on like this for about a month. Then after the school's two-week winter break, he went back to the classroom and was quiet and shy again, and didn't speak to anyone. He seemed to have forgotten all his progress. I talked again to his mother and teacher, telling them that this sort of setback is common when kids are learning new behaviors. I recommended a small sticker chart again and stressed that we would not be using it for another month. Instead, we tried it for one week. By the second day Brian was talking again and had reclaimed all his earlier skills. The point is that he hadn't forgotten how to talk. The learning had happened. He just needed a little jump start.

Although Brian never got to the point where he was as chatty as his classmates, and although he didn't tend to initiate friendships in his activities outside of school, he had made strides. At that point, I told his teacher and his mom that we were doing the best we could to encourage him. We had coached him toward the basic skills he needs. At that point, we just had to wait for his development to catch up, which it would do on its own. In time he would likely reach some sort of tipping point, and much of his reluctance to speak would vanish.

About two months later, Brian's mom called me to say that Brian was talking freely in small groups at school. His teacher said it was a dramatic change. While he will probably never be the class clown or the most talkative person in his grade school class, he had begun to engage in classroom discussions and had made steps toward making friends. If this change hadn't occurred, or if he had been unable to hang onto the progress he'd made with our behavior program, I might have considered giving Brian individual play therapy to help him address any fears or worries he might have. I might even have considered a short-term medication trial to help break his cycle of anxiety at school so that our behavioral program could have a chance to take hold.

The Short Course in Behavioral Adjustment

If your son has a couple of behaviors at home or at school that you want to change, here are the basic points to follow in creating your own method for helping him change.

1. *Stay calm.* Don't infuse the situation with your own anxiety. Approach the situation with an attitude that this is workable and that your son's behavior is a developmental issue rather than some scary disorder.

2. *Start small.* Reward your son for very small first steps. Don't pile on new behaviors until the first simple behaviors are happening at least 80 to 100 percent of the time. Keep track of these behaviors for a week or two, and once they seem stable, you can increase the challenge. Many behavior programs fail because we expect too much too soon. Build slowly on early successes.

3. *Don't punish noncompliance.* There is a real temptation to nag or cajole young boys when they first turn their backs on our reward system. After all, we've spent so much time drawing charts, buying stickers. Some parents want to give lots of prompting or to give second or third chances for a boy to comply. We adults seem to want to get to the reward even more than he does at first. Instead, it's best to be completely nonchalant. Say, "That's okay. You can earn your sticker another time. It's your choice."

4. *Stay consistent.* Be sure you stick to your end of the bargain.

Give rewards as promised. Many behavior programs fail because we don't do our part.

5. *Choose the right rewards.* Select rewards he won't otherwise get. If a reward is TV or computer playtime, that only works if it's a commodity he's not getting much of. Offering an extra ten minutes of TV time when he's already watching a couple of hours a day isn't going to be very exciting to him. Boys do best with new privileges, such as getting to feed the family pet (if he doesn't normally get to do that) or getting to choose what's for dinner.

6. *Keep it challenging.* In time, adjust the program so that he doesn't get bored. Increase the challenge once he has mastered one skill. He's growing and developing all the time, so rewarding him for the same behaviors over and over makes no sense. Instead, find new big boy behaviors for him to master.

Making Home More Like School

Not every boy is shy like Brian. Other boys can be too aggressive, or active, or inattentive and can't be taught effectively in an early elementary school classroom, where sitting quietly and waiting your turn is the standard approach. I refer to these guys as "little warriors." The classroom can accommodate them only so much. But that's where I start asking questions about what can change in the classroom to make it a better fit for boys like these. Teachers can use sticker charts, brief time-outs, better structure, and clear rules; they can give boys chores to channel their energy and rewards for making strides toward better, less disruptive behavior. We can capitalize on a boy's strengths and interests, which tend to be learning by doing, touching, or getting outdoors.

I always ask teachers to outline clear, concrete consequences and expectations for these types of boys. They need to know exactly how the plan to shape up and improve works. They also need us to increase our expectations of their behavior slowly, predictably, rather than expecting too much too soon. Parents can help by making their home life more like school, structured and predictable, teaching their little warriors to use words over screams, grabby hands, and kicking feet. Changes such

as these, when done at school and at home, push forward the development of assertive boys and allow them to stay in their classrooms. It's
not easy, but it works when everyone is on the same page.

Tell your son that the big rules are pretty much the same no matter
where we are, at home or at school. Ask him to recite the rules he's
learned at school. These might include no hitting or using mean words;
using an indoor voice and not screaming; using words to ask for things
instead of grabbing; observing personal space; being a good listener.
You will likely be amazed by all the social rules he knows and can
repeat, even if he isn't using them at home. One reason early elementary school teachers are so successful at getting boys to learn these rules
is the sheer amount of energy they spend on repeating them. A large
part of the kindergarten experience for most kids is learning rules.
They are told to be good listeners; they draw pictures of themselves
trying to listen; they are quizzed about listening skills. The same goes
for other rules and skills: lining up for recess, cleaning up after craft
time, sharing school supplies, and being safe while using scissors.

Parents can benefit enormously if they use some of these same skills.
Come up with a list of a few rules you would like to better enforce at
home. You can use a sticker chart at home with these rules, depending
on which behaviors you would like to reinforce. Your list might include
getting through dinner without a meltdown, putting dirty clothes in
the hamper rather than on the floor, sitting on the couch rather than
jumping on it, or simply saying "yes" and looking up at you when you
say his name.

Then you have to behave a bit more like your son's teacher. State
the rules clearly several times. Ask him to repeat them back to you.
Warn him before the situation occurs that he's got to comply: "Now,
we're sitting down to dinner; what's the rule about dinner? And what
do you get if you're good during dinner?" It might feel silly, but you're
helping him, coaching him to do what you expect. Also, use Time-
Aways when he's acting out and being aggressive or when you find
yourself in an endless verbal fight over the rules. This is what teachers
do at school. They remove a child from the situation until he or she
can calm down and rejoin the group.

Relating to the Teacher

Establishing and maintaining a good relationship with your son's teacher may be the most important factor in his long-term school success. I recently met with Melanie, a mom who invested much love and effort in raising her two young sons, Jeffrey, who was seven, and Kyle, who was five. Melanie wanted help for Jeffrey's extreme shyness, which was a particular problem for him in school. I was immediately struck by Jeffrey's relationship with his brother and asked Kyle to join us in the office so that I could observe them together.

By watching both boys together, I saw that Kyle acted as the big brother in the family, even though he was two years younger than Jeffrey. That's a developmental chasm that's pretty wide at this young age. Yet when Kyle talked to Jeffrey, he used a voice that mimicked that of an adult. In our first meeting Jeffrey showed interest in a chessboard, which is developmentally appropriate for an older boy. To this, Kyle said, "Jeffrey, no. Leave that alone. Come over here." And Jeffrey complied, joining Kyle at the pile of LEGOs. On the surface this seems benign and endearing, yet it wasn't a good thing for Jeffrey's role to be limited to that of assistant to his younger brother's play. And this was exactly how it unfolded in several sessions. Melanie told me that Kyle also liked to play the role of parent in the home, especially when her husband was away on business. Kyle helped put Jeffrey to bed at night and calmed his fears about the dark. Jeffrey was utterly compliant to his brother, even more than he would have been to a parent. I wasn't surprised to hear that Jeffrey was having trouble socializing at school. Jeffrey's teacher had told Melanie that he was morose and timid in the classroom. He wouldn't interact with the other kids at all, and he rarely spoke. Melanie was quick to say that things would work out fine. "Now that Kyle has started kindergarten, Jeffrey feels better at school," she told me. "I've asked the teachers to let them play together when their recess overlaps."

Jeffrey had two months to acclimate to first grade, and I wanted to start pushing him to be less shy. I told Melanie that it was time to help Jeffrey face his worries about socializing with the other kids. Sure, some kids are shyer than others. In this case, though, I saw that Jeffrey's reticence, while okay to an extent, had been accidentally reinforced at home by his mother. We needed to take a new approach. Rather than setting up the school to allow Kyle to be a parent there, too, we needed to think about how to bring Jeffrey out of his shell. First grade is an important year, a time when a boy can really grow. I outlined for Melanie some goals for Jeffrey in first grade, including developing some newer, big boy behaviors by midyear. I also wanted him to make a couple of friends at school, kids his own age with big boy interests. To do that, Melanie would have to have a good relationship with Jeffrey's teacher because we needed to have Jeffery practice new skills at school that could be rewarded by his teacher. If the behavior was to change, we had to practice it in the place it was most problematic.

At this point, Melanie balked. In the first two months of the year, she'd formed a negative opinion of Jeffrey's teacher. The teacher had sent home a few notes about Jeffrey's shyness, but when Melanie tried to talk to her after school one day to explain how to deal with Jeffrey, she said the teacher was impatient with her. "I had the feeling she thought I was ignoring the problem," said Melanie. Meanwhile, Jeffrey complained that his teacher was "mean," that she "picked on him" and made him join group activities and speak out in class. Further, Jeffrey had attached himself to a girl in his class who took care of him in the same way that Kyle did. She treated him like a baby doll, telling him what to do and answering for him in class and with other kids. Melanie thought this was cute, but the teacher intervened, keeping them separate in class. "This teacher doesn't understand him," Melanie said to me.

This is an impasse I see a lot. On one side, we had a teacher with her own approach, a teacher who had dealt with hundreds of children this age and who couldn't devote her entire day to the care of one child. On the other side, we had a mother who wanted to protect her young son from pain and discomfort, and who wanted the teacher to use a different and gentler approach. The first order of business was to repair this relationship between mother and teacher, to make sure that they were both working on the same problem rather than working against each other.

Practice Adult Empathy First

When a mom tells me that her son's teacher isn't a good fit for him, or that she's struggling to relate to his new teacher, I often ask her: "Would you want to be a teacher?" Let's first envision what the job entails. Remember that your son's teacher, whoever she is, may be a mom herself. In addition, she has to care for, educate, socialize, and monitor the safety of twenty or more kids, five days a week, for as long as six hours a day. The work can be stimulating, enormously rewarding, and sometimes fun, but I've visited many early elementary school classrooms and many preschool classrooms, and I'm always astonished at how draining and overstimulating the experience can be for me, when I'm not even in charge. In a kindergarten classroom alone, the teacher is instructing kids about how to line up, how to stay seated and quiet while she gives instructions, how to ask questions, how to wash hands after using the bathroom—all this alongside lessons on how to read, count, make patterns, cut with scissors, and follow directions in a craft project. It's daunting. A teacher needs an enormous amount of energy to do all of this every day.

A teacher also comes to the job with her own personality, her own set of skills—both strengths and weaknesses. She must deal with the administrative expectations of the school and often has to conduct her job in a system with limited resources and a restrictive budget.

When parents feel the urge to criticize the teacher, or they feel the need to rush in to protect their son, I tell them to start here, to keep all this in mind, all the effort, skills, passion, and work teachers bring to their jobs each day. This is the first step in ensuring a good working relationship between parents and teachers.

Making the Home–School Connection

First, Melanie needed to make an appointment to meet with Jeffrey's teacher. That didn't mean trying to have a harried conversation at the beginning of the school day while dropping Jeffrey off or in the parking lot after school when the teacher would be exhausted and trying to get home. It meant sending a note to school and asking to schedule a real face-to-face conversation. Melanie said, "I'll e-mail her. That's probably easiest for both of us." I strongly advised against this and told her, "You need to talk to his teacher, face to face, not e-mail." She could use e-mail to schedule a meeting with the teacher, but I cautioned her to avoid airing her concerns in the e-mail. Just use it to set a time to meet. We all have busy lives, so it's always tempting to fire off an e-mail to a teacher to raise questions about behavior or discipline or conditions in the classroom. Don't use e-mail as a forum for questioning the teacher until you have created a rapport with her. The funny thing about e-mail is that while it is a quick and direct way of getting information across, it is a poor tool for communicating emotions and the nuances of emotion, particularly sympathy and concern. I've seen many parents get off on the wrong foot with teachers and school administrators by sending a few terse or poorly worded e-mails. Make the effort to meet in person, and resort to e-mail once you have created a good relationship with the teacher.

Next, I coached Melanie on how to listen and pull out the essence of what Jeffrey's teacher is saying without making a lot of assumptions about what else she might mean to say. Lots of parents hear a teacher's comments about a child's behavior as a personal criticism. A teacher sends home a note that says, "Your son is hitting other kids," and what the parents hear is, "Don't you ever discipline him at home?" I have to tell parents again and again, listen to what's being said. There's no need to assume an accusation. All kids have some trouble with behavior at some point, with boys as a whole leading the pack. Teachers know this. When a teacher communicates to you about your son, about a problem he's having, try to be positive. You can say, "Great. I appreciate your letting me know this." You can even say, "What's your plan, and how can I help?" Even if you disagree, rather than challenging the teacher, you can say, "I haven't noticed that at home. Tell me more about what you are seeing."

In Jeffrey's case, Melanie had avoided responding to the teacher's concerns. This caused frustration on the teacher's part. She had also taken the teacher's comments personally, believing that the teacher was blaming her for his shy behavior. Finally, she started to blame the teacher for Jeffrey's problems in the classroom. I've worked with many parents who have alienated their son's teacher by coming into the situation with the assumption that the teacher is wrong or insensitive. By taking the opposite approach and bonding with the teacher, really listening to her and asking how to help her, parent and teacher can work together to help boys like Jeffrey. It's possible to be a caring parent without taking your son's side against the teacher.

I encouraged Melanie to acknowledge that Jeffrey was extremely shy, that he just came into the world that way, and that the behaviors she and Kyle used at home to accommodate Jeffrey weren't working at school. The longer Jeffrey was coddled, the more ingrained these behaviors would be. Now, when he was young and school was less academically challenging, was the time for Jeffrey to try out new social skills and to learn that he didn't need to be so afraid.

I told Melanie that the first thing she needed to do was to shore up her relationship with Jeffrey's teacher, to let the teacher know that they both had the same goal, which was to help Jeffrey fit in, make friends, and feel safe at school so that he can learn. His problems were not caused by a conflict between Jeffrey and his teacher, even if he said it was. Although there are certainly instances where teachers and students have conflicting personalities, it's not very common in these early grades. The conflict in this case was between Jeffrey and his fear.

The home–school relationship is two way. I also encourage teachers to reach out to parents early in a new school year. I liken this to welcoming someone new to the neighborhood. You reach out once and say hello and here's who I am and I'm looking forward to the school year. It can work wonders. Otherwise, you can get a couple of months into the year without saying anything more to each other than a stilted hello or good-bye during drop-off and pickup. Negative feelings can fester in those two months, and over nothing specific. One heartfelt welcoming with a warm handshake sets up good feelings that will begin the relationship on a high note. Until now, the "no news is good news" approach to home–school communication has been the norm, and, in my opinion, it's not working.

Talking to Your Son

Melanie and many other parents don't always know how to talk to their children about their struggles at school. I coach parents to stay positive. Never, ever say bad things about the teacher to your son. No good can come of this. Many parents think they are supporting their child by agreeing with him, to validate his feelings. Not true. When kids come home from school, they do what adults do: they blow off steam by complaining. These complaints are very often exaggerations and overshadow all the positive things that happen as well. By agreeing with him and offering overt sympathy, you are encouraging more of the same, more exaggerated accounts. You're telling him that whatever picture he's painted of his classroom is justified. You're encouraging him to vilify the person he has to learn from all day. Don't do it, no matter how frustrated you are with the school situation. You can offer support instead by saying, "Yep. I had some tough days in school, too. Tomorrow will be better. What could you do to help make it better? Let's think of a few ways." You can even support the teacher by saying, "Well, that's a tough job. Your teacher works really hard." You can tell him that teachers have to be tough sometimes to keep control of the classroom, just like you do at home.

Remember that what you tell your son about his teacher now is the message he's going to take forward through all his future classrooms. If your message to him now is, "No one should ever talk to you like that," then he's going to struggle with every authority figure every year. Instead, you should give him one statement about how it's going to be better tomorrow, or how learning is tough, but it's great that he's still hanging in there and trying. Then let the matter drop or change the subject.

If it's a long-term, more serious problem, you will find that it continues day after day. After a week or so, you have better reason to be concerned and to address the situation with your son's teacher. In most cases, though, you'll likely find that the "problem" magically vanishes within a day or two, signaling it was only a temporary expression of your son's frustration with fitting in and having to challenge himself developmentally.

Take the Direct Approach at Home

Some boys struggle because they lack some of the skills they need in the classroom in order to feel good about themselves and to do well in school. You can work with your son at home to practice a few basic skills that he can bring with him to school.

Melanie and I worked on some techniques at home to get Jeffrey to open up more there. When a boy can learn a new skill at home, he is more likely to eventually transfer those skills to new environments. That meant that Jeffrey was going to need to play independently of Kyle and to get Kyle out of his parenting role at home. We set up a system of rewards at home for Jeffrey when he did things we wanted him to do, such as putting himself to bed at night and asking for things rather than letting Kyle speak for him.

When Melanie went in to meet with Jeffrey's teacher, she kept an open mind and listened carefully. At our next meeting she said that she felt much better, that the teacher was essentially doing the same things for Jeffrey at school, asking him to speak for himself and using small check marks on a chart to reward his efforts. The program was very similar to the one we discussed for Brian, the socially shy boy we talked about previously. But in this situation, there was a longer road to getting the problem fixed. First, Melanie was resistant to working with the teacher, and second, the family had been encouraging Jeffrey to behave like the youngest boy. Change didn't happen overnight, but it did significantly improve after a couple of months. After a few ups and downs at the start, Jeffery gained more social confidence. Then he made a sudden leap, making friends and talking for himself in class. As with any new skill we're learning, we're awkward and clumsy in the beginning. Some days we get it better than others, and then once we've learned the basics, we seem to move ahead really well.

Labels Aren't Always the Answer

Another boy I've worked with, named Jordan, has struggled in school with a different issue. His first-grade teacher scheduled a meeting with Jordan's parents to talk about the fact that he's inflexible in the classroom. He can't make the switch between activities. He hunkers down during craft time, something he loves, and won't finish and turn in his art project when it's time to move on to story time, or literacy stations, both things he likes a lot less. In addition, he's often fidgety and makes a distraction when the class is working on a lesson he doesn't like. The teacher told Jordan's mom that he might have a form of ADHD because of these two problems: he's either overfocused on one thing, or he can't focus on the lesson at hand. In this situation, I like to remind parents that there are many possible reasons why their sons are struggling to do what's expected of them in school. ADHD tends to be far down on my personal list at this age, because so many kids—boys and girls—struggle to pay attention to things they find boring (adults, too, when you think about it).

If we look at the behavior alone, Jordan's inability to move from activity to activity on demand, we might see several possible reasons. Note that none of these is a disorder or requires major interventions to fix. They are developmental issues, and also reflect the natural differences between how kids (and adults) are built:

1. *Anxiety.* Some boys who are anxious or more naturally shy, for whatever reason, tend to look stubborn and inflexible. These types of boys are a bit more hypervigilant, can feel overwhelmed and overstimulated in the classroom, and so they may want to hang on to an activity they like and are good at rather than giving it up in favor of something that might be more difficult or less fun. They are not risk takers and generally need more time and encouragement to try new things.

2. *Attentional immaturity.* Many young boys don't have a lot of control over their powers of concentration, and once they bore into an activity they really love, they can be unable to switch gears easily. More often they flit from one thing that grabs their attention to the next. In most cases, they don't need medication at these young ages. It's not an inability to pay attention. Their brains will catch up and develop this ability over time.

3. *Fast processing ability.* Some boys are processing the world around them faster than their classmates at an early age. A boy

who isn't challenged by an activity might see it as just busy work and can seem inflexible to the teacher. He's going to legitimately get bored more easily and will need extra challenging tasks.

4. *Routine-oriented boy.* Those boys who really cling to a routine are going to be sensitive to changes in that routine. When a change occurs at home or at school, it becomes more difficult for them to move fluidly from subject to subject or activity to activity, which has been the normal sequence of things up to that point. Their somewhat staid style serves them well later in schoolwork that has multiple, detailed steps to follow, such as science and math.

Any one of these four factors could explain why Jordan behaves the way he does in a classroom at his age. None of them mean that he has ADHD or that he will struggle in school long term. As boys get older, their anxiety will likely fade as they get used to school. Any difficulties controlling their ability to pay attention will improve through practice at school and normal brain growth. Boys who readily process information will do much better in higher grades, where they will have more challenging tasks. A boy who prefers routine will have an easier time in grades where he knows what to expect all day.

Techniques for Home and Classroom

When a boy has behavioral problems in a classroom, there are several ways for parents and teachers to work together to help things improve.

One technique I favor is a simple chart with stickers. It's the most common behavior program that teachers can use, and it's easy. For example, there was a boy I worked with named Ezra who daydreamed and chatted his way through most of the day. The teacher was experienced and immediately figured out that Ezra was very bright and that he was getting bored with first-grade work. She told me she notices one or two of these kids in her class every year in September. It takes a few weeks before she can get the whole class up to speed and move them onto more challenging work. Meanwhile, review and practice of basic concepts can drive these very bright kids crazy.

We used a chart with stickers that Ezra could earn for not chatting or interrupting every ten minutes or so. He could also earn a sticker when he raised his hand to speak. He chose creepy Halloween stickers and worked hard to get as many as he could. The chart went home every day, and his mom would go out in the yard and play catch with him on those days when he did well.

Some parents feel that they don't want to suggest such a solution to a teacher because they think they are being pushy or demanding special treatment for their child. Remember that this technique is for troublesome behaviors that are eating up energy in the classroom. Putting a sticker on a chart is a small amount of effort expended by the teacher that can yield enormous positive results. But remember, this is an idea best introduced in a meeting with the teacher first. Explain the idea and say, "Let's try it for a couple of weeks. I'll supply what you need." When the behavior changes, then you can fade out the stickers so that they're not a permanent feature of your son's day.

Keep the Relationship Positive

If your son is having a tough time at school, your goals are to keep the relationship positive with his teacher and to keep him positive about the rest of the school year. Things will likely get better for him in a few months as he matures, as he gets used to the classroom setting, and as he works to improve his classroom skills. Even small, positive comments will build on themselves and yield results. Here are some other techniques that will help you keep a positive relationship with the teacher.

End every interaction on a positive note

Last impressions count heavily in people's opinions of one another. As your son's advocate, you want to be as effective as possible in all your interactions with his teacher. If the teacher brings up a problem or addresses an issue at the end of the school day, it's best to hear her out first. Next, say you'll try to work on it at home, which communicates compassion and respect for the teacher as a person. One mom I know was recently taken aside by her son's preschool teacher, who said, "Andrew has been telling a few of the other boys that he hates them, that they can't be his friend anymore." This mom knew that her son had been the victim of some bullying on the playground. She replied, "Oh, no. He shouldn't do that. But I think he's saying this because he's had it said to him, and it hurt. I think this might be a new weapon for him." The teacher nodded and said, "You're probably right. But I have rules about this in the classroom, so I really talked to him today about it." And the mom said, "You're right. I'll talk to him tonight, too. Thanks for telling me this; it's helpful. Don't let me keep you. Have a great weekend." If you end the conversation by acknowledging that the teacher has her own life and that you appreciate her efforts, you express that you see her as a person and not as an employee hired by the school to instruct your child. That goes a long way to gaining her help and support for your son over the school year. Surprisingly, such simple diplomatic efforts help tremendously in bringing teachers and other school staff into a positive mind-set around your son, despite the normal but often challenging school struggles many young boys face.

Be available and flexible

I recently spoke to a friend of mine who is the mother of a sweet but somewhat socially aggressive first grader. I think of him as a little CEO, who likes to manage rather than cooperate with his friends in play. He's extremely verbal and well liked. He's the guy who makes up a game and the rules, recruits friends to join in, then anoints himself as referee. This is a fine style of play if you can pull it off, and he's making it work for him. In fact, he tends to attract shyer kids who need a little help getting going in a group. His mother has a similar style in her workplace, and she is highly successful, too. Where her style doesn't work so well is in her relationship with her son's teacher. I listened to this mom's litany of complaints against the teacher, how she's not organized enough and how her notes and handouts sometimes contain spelling and grammatical mistakes. She feels that the teacher is too soft-spoken, not forceful enough. Lately, the teacher has sent home several notes to this mom saying that her son has brought some swear words to school, that he is talking back to the teacher and is refusing to do some of the classroom activities. The reason he gives is that they are not interesting enough to him.

I asked about the latest round of parent–teacher conferences, and she sighed. "I haven't had time to get to a meeting yet," she said to me. I was surprised to hear this. Then she explained that she had e-mailed the teacher a list of possible available times for a meeting. She had sent a separate list of available time slots for her husband, who travels a lot. "We'll have to meet with her separately. There's no other way," she told me. She went on to say that she had already made and broken two appointments with the teacher, and as she was getting ready to launch into the list of reasons why she's so busy, I stopped her. I asked her, "Is this the message you want to be sending to your son's teacher?"

All parents are busy. Working parents face so many complications at work and at home. These parents often tell me that the two halves of their lives are always intruding on each other. Free time at home is taken up with work issues, and time at work is always being interrupted by snags in child care, doctors' appointments, early release days, and other chores to keep the home front organized. I know that juggling the schedules of two working parents along with those of multiple children can be a daily headache. I know that many parents who work feel that they are failing a bit in both halves of their lives.

Yet, when you are unavailable, when you are too busy to meet with a teacher, you are sending the message that the teacher works for you and that your time is more valuable than hers. Being available and flexible sends the more positive message that the teacher's concerns are important to you, too. Again, simple signs of respect, appreciating the challenging work of your son's teacher, and being flexible to meet will make all the difference in fixing these developmental and behavioral snags that pop up for many boys.

Enlist the teacher's help first

When a teacher identifies a problem behavior or a troublesome situation in the classroom, it's often tempting for parents to jump right in with a proposed solution. In fact, some feel embarrassed by their sons' behaviors and want to announce right away what they're going to do to fix the situation without waiting to hear what the teacher proposes. I always urge them to listen first, even to ask a teacher, "What do you think we should do?" Allow the teacher to be in charge and be the expert. Ask for a possible solution. Afterward, chip in with your ideas. You do know your son better than the teacher does. Everyone understands that. But teachers have had experience with all kinds of kids, and many of them know how well boys rise to a challenge, or how quickly they can learn to behave differently when expectations are high, or when there's no alternative.

When I work with teachers I always get their ideas about a situation first. I know that I am getting a viewpoint of that child's behavior in their setting, where they see them every day for several hours. I then find that these same teachers are much more open to my ideas after they've been heard.

When a dialogue between a teacher and a parent is unproductive, most often it's because one or both people are feeling stressed and defensive. To support a real give-and-take between yourself and the teacher, one that builds toward a solution you can both live with, it helps to be aware of your tone of voice, have a friendly smile, make eye contact, and don't push the teacher to fix the problem. Once you hear what she has to say, offer up some helpful solutions that have worked at home, and be willing to make the needed changes at home that will support changes in the classroom. Both parents and teachers who have challenging boys can learn from one another, and the solution often requires a coordinated effort.

Problems Are Often Situational

Oliver, age seven, is very bright. He has flaming red hair and glasses and is the youngest of three children. He is chatty and precocious and used to being the center of attention at home. He is also used to getting his way. I can say with certainty that he is as headstrong as his father, who works as an architect in his own firm. Oliver believes that there is one right way to do everything, and he won't let anyone join him on a task to complete something, particularly drawings or art projects, at which he is adept. In fact, Oliver will talk back to his teacher if she tries to correct him on anything. He has fought verbally with his teacher, telling her she's wrong, that the things she's asking him to do are stupid. If he can't do everything his way, he yells or breaks down and cries.

Still, the boy I see in my office is loving and sensitive and doesn't understand why he's having so many problems at school. The teacher has had it with him; the other students don't like him and won't sit next to him. These things upset him terribly. And his problems at school are now causing stress at home for every family member, in part because every dinner table discussion focuses on what went wrong for Oliver that day.

I spoke to his teacher, who told me that she's tried everything. She has sent notes home to his parents; she has sent him to the hallway when he talks back; she has sent him to the principal's office. I spoke to Oliver's mother at length, and she blames herself for raising such a difficult boy. She admits that he has been stubborn like this since he was a baby. Yet she is also very angry at this teacher, who she thinks doesn't understand her son's unique gifts, his beautiful artwork, his high intelligence.

Unfortunately, this situation has gone on for so many months that the school administration is now involved. They are pushing to have Oliver evaluated, to see if he qualifies for special education classes based on his behavioral problems. From their perspective, he needs to be in a smaller classroom with other behaviorally challenging kids.

I knew right away that if Oliver could be enrolled instead in a tiny private school classroom with more one-on-one adult attention, he would do much better. He'd still need some help with his stubborn, know-it-all style, but there would be more of the individual attention that he craves. Also, if he were in a school where he could spend a lot of time working independently, he would do much better. Headstrong kids of high intelligence do better in arenas where they can have more control of what they do moment to moment. Of course, the family couldn't afford this as a solution (most families can't), so we had to work within the system.

The first task in a situation like this is to help everyone understand that no one is to blame. This young boy is going to be like this wherever he goes. We can work to modify his sometimes pushy style of talking to others, but in the end, he'll grow out of much of that as peer groups in later grades take him to task. Most important is to realize that what's going on for Oliver isn't the parents' fault, the teacher's fault, or the school's fault alone. Still, certain ways of running a classroom or a household can make the situation better—or worse.

For example, spending a lot of time in verbal arguments with Oliver over trivial issues is feeding the problem. It gives him an audience and only serves to increase his negative, combative behavior. I urged the teacher and the parents both to pick a few battles carefully. There are certain things in the classroom that he cannot do, just as there are certain things at home he can't do. He can't talk back to the teacher. He can't have a tantrum when he doesn't get his way. When he does these things, he needs to be removed from the classroom for a time-out. The teacher is absolutely right in doing this, and Oliver's parents needed to understand this. His teacher does need to have control of her classroom.

I encouraged his teacher and his parents to separate Oliver's issues into two groups, before they arise. What's crucial for you to control? This you fight over. What's less important? Here you let him have some control.

The trick here, especially with a bright guy like Oliver, is to tell him, "It's your choice, Oliver, to talk that way to me, and every time you choose to do that, you'll need to leave the class. So it's up to you— you decide if you want to go out of the class or not. I'm not going to fight with you." This removes the power struggle and gives control to Oliver over the outcome.

The truth is that problems in the classroom are most often related to the environment and likely a developmental phase that will shift later on. A good match in the classroom could come down to the mix of other students in the room. Remember that your son's trouble, whatever it is, is not a reflection on his character or your parenting, or even the teacher's personality. When we look at the environment for things that trigger behavior we want to change, we might learn, for example, that a boy does better in the morning than in the afternoon or vice versa. He might do better with quiet time activities first before entering into groups where activity overwhelms him. He might be reaching out to make a friend but gets upset when his social skills don't guide him well enough. Maybe all those things are going on at once and slam together to cause a crying episode. If your son misbehaves in school, and the teacher brings it to your attention, you should treat the incident seriously. One mom I know, a woman named Eve, has two children. Her older daughter is nine years old and very compliant and helpful. She's so good in school that teachers practically swoon over her in conferences with Eve. Her younger son, Jon, is quite the opposite. He's a great example of how a situation can draw out behavioral problems. He's a contrarian, a boy who doesn't like to sit in first grade and listen to long directions. He fidgets and often starts projects or rushes through assignments ahead of the class. This is typical for active, smart, and confident boys his age. Jon is struggling a bit with writing his letters, although his reading comprehension is ahead of his peers. Jon's teacher has a lot of experience with boys and seems to be working well to keep Jon occupied and interested in classroom activities. However, some of these activities don't challenge him enough.

One day Jon finished an assignment early, and the teacher caught him drawing a superhero on his desk. She took his pencil away and gave him a wet wipe and told him to clean it up, which he did. That would have been the end of it, I'm sure, except that Jon's teacher mentioned the incident to his mom at the end of the day.

When moms tell me of incidents like this, I'm always very interested in how they respond and what reasons they use to explain their sons' behaviors. First, Eve said to me, "The teacher would be crushed to hear this, but I think Jon is a little bored in class." I agreed, but I worried that Eve was making excuses for Jon's behavior. Before I could point this out, she said, "But no kid of mine is going to write on furniture!" Eve's response was to send Jon to school the next day with a sponge and some window cleaner. "I told him that he was going to stay after school and wash every one of those desks. And he did, too," she said. In fact, when Eve went to pick him up that day, the teacher was laughing. Not only had Jon washed all of the tops of the desks, he had washed the seats, the legs, and the undersides. He had a grand time doing it, too, according to his teacher. This isn't surprising, given that he is such an active, task-oriented boy. Most important, Eve had supported the teacher's authority and encouraged Jon to be more respectful of school property.

The Pressure to Fix It

Come mid to late September, my phone rings off the hook. It's been just long enough for the stress of school to kick in. Teachers start sending home notes and calling parents in for meetings—the honeymoon is over. Sometimes, teachers communicate poorly and make a mom feel she has to "fix" her son's problem. When it's not an isolated issue, moms can be driven to worry unnecessarily about each call or note, with worry and tension mounting for each new "incident," and they often report feeling like a failure as a parent. You have to drop that way of thinking altogether. You can't do your job as a parent if you worry like that or feel so terrible inside. It's absolutely absurd to expect yourself to magically control things that your son does when he's away from you at school. Your son is an independent agent—he has free will—and you can't control him by remote. Your job is only to keep working at ways to improve and support him, to allow him to make his mistakes and find ways to move him forward and develop. Try to keep in mind that teachers are supposed to send notes and call home to give feedback. It's not always an implicit message that you have to change him immediately. You are just being kept in the loop.

I know a parent who has this down pat. Her son is very difficult at times and challenges his teachers. Many notes and phone calls go back and forth between home and school. She will say, in a calm voice, "Thanks for keeping me informed. It really helps me to know what's going on at school so we can go over this at home. We will talk about it tonight. Let me know how things go on your end, too." Remember to put bad events and challenging moments into proper context. Your son is having hundreds of successful moments every week that don't, unfortunately, get reported to you.

The End of Summer

Recently, I got an e-mail from a mom who has a little guy named Paul, who was starting second grade in two weeks. He had just turned seven. I had started seeing him the previous year at the start of first grade. Paul had a horrible first six months of school. He would scream and cry each morning and refuse to go to school. He struggled in the classroom for the first couple of hours each day—he would shut down, refuse to participate in classroom activities, and demand to go home. Then, by the middle of each day, he would pull it together and do fine in the classroom. He enjoyed the time after lunch and fully participated in class, only to start the whole cycle over the very next morning. I interpreted his behavior as purely developmental. He had to ride out the storm. After winter break, he came back to school and had a stellar rest of the year. His teacher's comment was, "He's an entirely different little boy." His mom was thrilled and felt that the storm had ended.

Paul went to summer camp and had a wonderful time. He learned to swim; he played dodge ball; he went on hikes; he even learned to play chess. As an activity-driven kid, he loved all the playtime, the free movement, the athleticism, and the outdoor time of camp. He was beloved by his counselors, who saw him as energetic, fearless, and happy. He behaved perfectly, until the last three days of camp. That's when his mother got a call from the camp leader, saying, "We don't recognize your son anymore." Paul was hitting other kids, having tantrums, and refusing to join in camp activities. He came home crying, saying that he hated camp. Paul's mother called me. On her own, she had guessed what had gone wrong, but she was at a loss about what to do.

What was happening with Paul is what happens with a lot of kids at the end of summer, especially kids who have struggled at some point in the previous school year. The summer, and all of its wonderful playtime, ends, and it's time to face the risk of meeting another teacher, another group of kids with whom you might not get along. Paul was grieving for the end of a season and remembering how hard last fall was for him. His mother said, "But wait! The year ended great for him. It really did." Sure it did, but it's now fall again, and he's remembering last fall. Adults do this, too. We have a fancy term for it; we call these "anniversary feelings." It's the same thing for little guys facing school in the fall. You remember your emotional state from a previous year. It's locked into the season itself.

Boys like Paul who have struggled in school the past year are going to enter a new school year with a great deal of anxiety. It's as though they are waiting for something to go wrong. Parents sometimes do this, too. They can accidentally give a young boy the message that things are likely to go wrong at school. Here is another area where you can communicate failure to your son if you're not careful.

Paul's mom asked me, "What do I do?" Here's what you do if your son is anxious about going back to school.

1. *Don't panic.* It's easy to say to yourself, "Here we go again." But keep in mind that the new year brings a new teacher, new kids in his class, new opportunities to learn, and he will be facing them as a new boy. A lot can happen in a boy's development in three to six months. In Paul's case, he had a lot of social and emotional and physical successes during the summer. He can build on those this year.

2. *Words can help.* I'm not talking about lectures or pep talks. Just give him the chance to say that he's sad. Don't downplay his feelings or rush in to fix it or take away those genuine feelings and memories. You can remind him how much fun he had. You can tell him that you're sad the summer's over, too. You can remind him, also, that he ended last year on a great note. Remind him of his past successes.

3. *Give him an outlet.* As adults, we sometimes pace when we're anxious. We might go out and run a few miles; we call our friends and complain; some of us have a glass of wine or garden the heck

out of the backyard. Boys need an outlet, too, although none of the above will work for them. In Paul's case, I suggested drawing, which is his passion. I never suggested, though, that he draw a picture of a happy teacher or of himself in a pleasant classroom. Therapy doesn't have to be corny. I encouraged him to use his creative energy to draw whatever he wanted, which in most cases was knights defending castles against jet-powered dragons. The drawings are pretty impressive.

4. *Do a drive-by before the end of summer.* Go see the building where he'll be at school. Treat it as a field trip. Bring a lunch, let him romp on the playground at the school. This personalizes the school and makes it a part of his community, rather than just a place he goes to work.

5. *Join in and admit that it's hard for you to go back to work after the summer is over, too.* Tell him you'll miss the fun of summer, the beach, the vacations. But remind him that there are fun things coming up in the fall, such as Halloween or family birthdays. Young boys have trouble looking into the future; it's good to show them there are other things to look forward to.

The primary advice I give to parents is to listen to the teacher, get as much information as possible, and keep her on your side. Give her the power. Acknowledge that she is in charge of the classroom. Having said all that, I do know that not all teachers are effective in managing students and conflicts in class. I know of one mom who learned that her son's first-grade teacher was making the kids put their heads down on their desks as a punishment. She saw it herself, and it felt wrong to her. Her son was really struggling with this teacher and had a lot of privileges taken away. He was spending time every day with his head down on his desk and having no free playtime during the day.

This mom wanted to know how to deal with this. I told her that she's right. This is not a nurturing or helpful way to handle the many common problems that come up in classrooms. The teacher, in my opinion, is wrong, and there are better ways to help kids regroup and get back on task. These might include taking a few minutes of quiet time, running outside for a few minutes, and playing music. Still, she has to work with this teacher. Her main job is to realize and to make her son realize that some teachers are tough, but you stick with it, do your best, and next year you will have someone else. All his life, he's going to be working with teachers and managers he doesn't agree with and who may not be entirely fair. With positive encouragement from you, he can get through the year and be stronger for it.

CHAPTER 11

The Teacher Thinks He Needs Testing

I get a lot of questions from parents about testing. In most cases, these parents have been told that their sons should be tested for a possible learning disability or developmental delay. They want to know why their sons have been singled out for this. There are two reasons teachers recommend that boys get tested.

Boys who aren't doing what the rest of the class is doing are assumed to be lagging behind their peers. An example would be a boy who is not talking and socializing as much as the other kids or who doesn't acknowledge teachers as the other children do. Perhaps he doesn't seem to be recognizing letters and numbers as early as his peers or other information about himself, such as his birth date. Most often the classroom average is used to judge what is "normal" in development, which is not appropriate in many cases because it fails to take into account that development is uneven among children, especially boys. A classroom average is limited to those few kids who happen to be in the room at the time. If your child is a few months younger than his classmates, he'll seem to lag behind them more than he really does.

Boys who are behaving in ways that are strikingly different from other children in the class. An example would be a boy who stays in the corner during group activities and avoids circle time, or a boy who needs repetitive or ritualized actions to calm himself, such as rocking or hand flapping, particularly if he can't seem to stop when asked, or a boy who fidgets so excessively that he creates a distraction in class. Some of these actions might signal a developmental problem, yet they might not.

In general, I think it is important to listen to whatever information a teacher gives you about how your son is getting along in a school or preschool setting. Remember that a teacher is a more objective observer of your son. She's not as emotionally attached to him as you are, even if she is a very caring and nurturing educator. Teachers spend time with lots of children over the course of their careers, and they have experience in dealing with many different types of children and many different learning styles. The classroom is also a more controlled environment in which your son is facing tasks that challenge him, and those tasks are likely to flush out any developmental lags he's experiencing.

Having said that, in many situations, I don't think parents need to run out and get an evaluation or seek a child expert for a diagnosis without first taking a short wait-and-see approach. This allows a child time to adjust or develop, as long as he is making progress with some reasonable help and not falling backward.

When Is Testing Helpful?

In very young kids, those between two and three years old, serious social concerns or serious language problems might be an indication that testing is a good idea, specifically for autism and autism-related disorders (also known as autism spectrum disorders). With autism, early detection is better than a wait-and-see approach.

Let me define what I mean by serious social concerns and language delays. A delay is not just shyness. It's a profound difficulty interacting with most people.

Sometimes these kids get overstimulated in even small groups, and they shut down, or they engage in repetitive, odd behaviors and can't break from them even if they want to. These behaviors tend to be striking. The following are some of the red flags for autism spectrum disorders:

- No babbling at twelve months
- No gesturing by age twelve months, no pointing or waving by twelve months
- No single words by sixteen months
- No two-word phrases by twenty-four months
- Does not respond to his own name
- Doesn't smile
- At times seems to be hearing-impaired
- Has suffered any loss of any language or social skills at any age

These can alert parents to seek an evaluation, but I want to stress that just because a boy has one or more of these symptoms doesn't mean that he has autism. These are scary symptoms, and because they are so scary, we look for them more. We are overvigilant in looking for them. But because autism should be accurately diagnosed as early as possible in order to take advantage of early intervention, an evaluation is a good idea when any of these symptoms are present.

Another signal to look for early problems and test is when there's a family history of learning disabilities, such as dyslexia. In this case, a parent is justified in showing concern and testing a child earlier than would otherwise be warranted. If a boy's older siblings have suffered from dyslexia or other serious language delay, for example, and he's reversing numbers and letters in kindergarten, by all means do some testing. In cases such as these, testing can tease apart if it's a true learning disability or some emotional or social problem, or even just a developmental lag that's getting in the way of learning.

When Is Testing Not Useful?

For other problems that boys may struggle with, such as ADHD and Asperger's syndrome, a wait-and-see approach works much better. Testing for ADHD or Asperger's shouldn't occur until a boy is at least five or six years old, preferably older. Asperger's can't be accurately diagnosed until kids are older and are facing much more sophisticated social situations and more demanding educational environments where more group learning occurs. And ADHD is about executive functioning, planning, thinking ahead, and suppressing urges, most of which preschool kids can't do yet, nor should they have to.

Testing tends to be less useful in children younger than age six. The brain is developing so quickly in very young children, and their skills and abilities are changing so rapidly, that testing them is like trying to measure a moving target. It's normal for a boy's development to be all over the place at this age and to find many skills not really up and running. The exception to this is when a child under six exhibits extreme, persistent, or highly compulsive behaviors (such as self-biting, rocking, and head banging) or a profound developmental delay (if a boy is not able to use words by sixteen months or is unable to socialize with his peers). Any of these would warrant early testing.

When Testing Goes Awry

Jill made an appointment with me while she was on a several-month-long waiting list to get her son seen by a pediatric neurologist. "I couldn't wait any longer," she told me. "I have to talk to someone." Her question to me was whether her son had Asperger's syndrome, which is often referred to as a high-functioning form of autism. Her son, Aaron, had turned three just a few months before, and it's unusual to think a child this age has any disorder unless there is something clear and startling to be concerned about. For example, if a child is autistic, there would be something dramatic in his behavior. A child might have no language or use just a few words. Fortunately, that wasn't the situation with Aaron. Asperger's specifically is characterized by very poor social skills, something you wouldn't pick up until a boy is a little older and around more kids in more complicated social situations. Aaron was quiet at school and preferred to play alone, although he did play side by side with a few other boys and girls. This syndrome also features restricted, repetitive patterns of behavior, which his mother didn't report at all.

I noticed right away that Aaron was a quiet boy. He looked around my office and seemed to study it, the books on the shelves, the toys that were sitting on my desk. He took note of these things but didn't immediately run to them or grab them or ask me if it was okay to play. Instead, Jill fetched a couple of toy trucks for him, and he sat happily playing with them, moving them back and forth, crashing them into each other without looking up or making any noise when he played.

I told Jill that from what little I observed so far I couldn't see the necessity of testing Aaron for Asperger's. I was willing to talk with his teacher and get her view, but he just didn't meet the basic criteria. "How can you be so sure he doesn't have it?" she asked. I told her that we should never be asking the question that way, assuming a diagnosis "could" be there unless proven otherwise. Diagnosis works completely the other way around. The burden of proof is on showing symptoms that reach the severity level of whatever criteria are set out, not digging and digging or wondering until you might see something of concern. That's the "guilty until proven innocent" approach to diagnosing kids, and it's dangerous.

While Aaron played, Jill told more of her story, one that began a month earlier when she was summoned to Aaron's preschool for a meeting with his teacher. "She told me he wasn't socializing properly," Jill said, and I asked her what she thought that meant. She nodded right away.

"That's what I asked his teacher," she said. "I mean, he's three. And he is shy; he always has been. So am I. So is his dad. We're not social. We don't go to parties. We don't chat. What's the big deal?"

Still, this preschool teacher kept insisting that something was wrong with Aaron. She reported that Aaron never made eye contact with teachers. He never spoke to his classmates; he played next to them but not with them. He often ignored directions. She pushed Jill to contact the town's public school system, which has a program to diagnose and treat early developmental disorders, including speech delays and impediments. The school's program is great at getting kids with moderate to severe learning or physical disabilities ready to enter mainstream classrooms. But Jill didn't think her son fit into this category—after all, he doesn't have a hearing problem or a problem with eyesight. He knows his numbers and letters. In Jill's opinion, Aaron is just a quiet boy who likes to do his own thing.

When she contacted the school system, Jill was interviewed over the phone by a school psychologist, who asked her questions about Aaron's behavior. Does he like to line up his trucks? Does he like to look at fans? Does he avoid eye contact? When Jill answered yes, the counselor said, "I thought so." Jill asked what this might mean, and the counselor said, "Well, he rings all the bells for Asperger's." Jill was incredulous. "She's never even laid eyes on my son," she said to me. The counselor was pressuring Jill for immediate testing to see if Aaron had a problem that warranted enrollment in the town's special education preschool. "But they've already made up their minds," said Jill. In fact, the counselor was indeed telling Jill that she should enroll Aaron now in an expensive summer socialization program run by two of the town's preschool teachers. Jill was afraid that she was getting railroaded along with her son. She told me that she knew kids who had individual education programs, generally called IEPs, in preschool or kindergarten, and she feared this would be a stigma for her son. "Those records haunt those kids," she said. "Once you're labeled, the school treats you differently. Forever."

What's an IEP, Anyway?

IEP stands for individualized education program. It's used when a learning disability has been identified in a child. It's an important part of the Individuals with Disabilities Education Act (IDEA). It documents "present levels of a child's academic achievement and functional performance." It also contains a statement of a child's academic goals and his or her performance toward those goals.

Since 2004 the method by which schools identify a learning disability has significantly changed. And schools are slowly moving toward this new approach. Prior to this, a child who was suspected of having a learning problem or disability would be referred for comprehensive testing from someone in the school system. Many of these kids were on long waiting lists to be tested and meanwhile underperforming for months and months at school while waiting to get tested. When a learning disability was identified, these children were often pulled out of the classroom and given highly specialized services.

The new system, which many people prefer, is called response to intervention, or RTI. It's a system that seems to understand that a significant subset of children will fall behind in school and will need extra help, but they aren't necessarily suffering from a learning disability. It offers more help and intervention to many children before testing a few of them and labeling them with a learning disability.

For example, in an average first-grade classroom, perhaps 20 or 30 percent of the kids will struggle with moving from simple counting to solving math-based story problems. That group of kids will be targeted for more intensive teaching in the classroom in this area. The teachers are given research-based teaching methods to give these kids a boost. For several of them, this will remove the problem. The remaining kids who still struggle with math will be given additional help in the classroom using new, more targeted methods. This guides teachers in using multiple means to teach a diverse group of children. Again, for most of the children who struggle, this second level of intervention will remove the problem. Any children who still struggle after these interventions in the classroom will be candidates for testing. Only at that point can a learning disability be diagnosed so that an IEP can be drawn up.

Ignore Diagnostic Language

I can see why Jill was so angry and worried. In her case, the whole process to get a diagnosis was unnecessarily rushed. This would make anyone distrustful of signing on for special education services. In Aaron's case, the teacher hadn't adjusted the teaching methods to help him make better eye contact. No one was helping him specifically with the social aspects of learning in a classroom.

What she wanted from me was a second opinion about Aaron's behavior. She also wanted to know what her rights were with respect to testing and getting entangled in the school's special education system. Also, she feared that maybe they were right, that something was wrong with Aaron, and that if she didn't act right away, she was somehow hurting him long term.

My colleagues and I hear this story, or variations of it, quite a bit in our practice. Very often, well-meaning teachers and school counselors or school administrators make fast diagnoses, or rather, they float theories that sound like diagnoses, and these statements cause total panic on the home front. There is a tendency among many parents to feel that teachers and school counselors, people who work with children every day, should have all the answers about behavior because they are experts who work with kids, but they don't. They shouldn't be diagnosing children. They shouldn't be using language that's diagnostic. That doesn't mean they shouldn't be telling you what they've observed in the classroom. One mom I know was taken aside by a preschool teacher, who said to her, "Your son is very cautious in class. He tends to stand apart from the group during music time. He's slow to join in any activities. He seems to have social anxiety problems." Everything the teacher said up to that last bit about social anxiety is very helpful. But it was those last three words that sent this mom over the edge. She heard it as a diagnosis.

Most teachers don't think they are diagnosing when they say these things. They are trying to be helpful. They are struggling to understand quirky kids, just as I am, alongside pediatricians, psychiatrists, and other child experts.

In the pervasive environment of overcrowded classrooms and high academic expectations of today (including preschool, and sometimes especially in preschool), teachers don't feel they have the luxury of letting unusual behaviors play themselves out and let development take its natural course. They are pressured to keep curriculums moving and kids performing on set targets. They don't always have time to teach the impulsive kids to sit still, and the shy kids to reach out, and the grabby kids to learn better personal boundaries. The temptation is strong to find some reason for this behavior and to get some specialists involved to help with the kids who use up most of the classroom energy. In many cases, boys with a minor developmental lag can end up being tested and labeled with a diagnosis that just doesn't fit, and that causes needless panic and distress.

If They Say Your Son Needs Testing

I remind parents in these situations of a few important things to remember before they react in panic to something a teacher says, or the suggestion that their son needs testing for a developmental disorder:

Many boys experience developmental setbacks and erratic shifts that can look like disorders. They exhibit such behaviors as impulsivity, delays in socialization and language, resistance to making eye contact, problems making smooth transitions between activities, showing extreme shyness, problems with toileting, flying into sudden fits when frustrated, biting their fingers, or chewing their shirts until they are soaked. Almost all of these are temporary and not signs of disorder. They are in fact evidence that much is happening deep inside a boy's rapidly and ever-changing brain. One day they make gains, and the next they fall apart. This is how learning works, particularly in young boys.

With rare exceptions, almost every boy who shows such quirky behaviors grows up to be just fine, even better than fine. If we want to look at the actual diagnostic numbers being reported, we would see that the number of young kids diagnosed with serious, long-term problems such as autism spectrum disorder (autism, Asperger's, or pervasive developmental disorder) is about 1 in 150, mostly boys. While this number is upsetting, it's still a very small number relative to the many kids who will face screening procedures and possible diagnoses in early elementary school.

No matter how your son is behaving right now, he's going to be different in six months. That's how aggressive brain development is at young ages. A boy who is three years old is going to be a completely different child at three and a half, and again at age four. Even at the older ages of six, seven, and eight, a boy's brain is developing and changing, making new connections and learning new social and intellectual skills all the time. Rather than rushing into a program to "help" troublesome behaviors, many boys benefit from a wait-and-see approach. Given time, the brain is likely to sort things out itself, with the exception of those red flags as discussed for autism.

A behavioral problem nearly always benefits from a behavioral program. Rather than worrying about getting the right diagnosis, many boys benefit when the adults around them provide better structure and reasonable expectations while rewarding positive behaviors and discouraging negative ones. Also, moderate short-term tutoring helps with temporary learning problems, putting a child's development back on course or facilitating acquiring new skills.

Keep these four ideas in mind when someone tells you your son has a problem and needs immediate, aggressive intervention. This will help keep the panic at bay so that you can make informed decisions at every juncture.

Listen Even if You Don't Agree

When parents come to me with news that a school official or teacher thinks their son has a problem, I tell them to listen to what's being said. Although it's true that some teachers may have a one-size-fits-all approach to dealing with students, most teachers aren't like this and are great observers, picking up on important behaviors you may want to be aware of. They are trying to share information about what they see in their classroom, information that can be really important to hear. Every time your son's teacher communicates with you, she's giving you valuable information. Hear it first, then respond to what's being asked of you. In this case, she's offering information that may or may not be accurate long term, but describes what's been happening recently. A classroom teacher isn't qualified to tell you that your son definitely has ADHD or Asperger's syndrome or any other disorder. A teacher is, however, on the front lines of seeing your son every day and under controlled learning situations where a potential problem might show itself.

It may be that your son is going through a temporary developmental glitch, and that's what his teacher is actually seeing and reporting to you. Time and some form of accommodation in the classroom or at home will help him work through it. There is another issue to think about, however, if your son's teacher tells you there are repeated, longer-term adjustment problems in her classroom: for example, if your son is bored and causing problems, if he's zoning out often during the day, if he refuses to participate in activities or ignores the teachers, or if he gets overwhelmed in group activities. This may indicate that the school's style doesn't fit your son's learning style. In preschool, learning styles are very different among different children, as they are among adults. Keep in mind that just because one style works for one set of students doesn't mean that it works for all students.

Your son might benefit from a few simple accommodations in the classroom that can help him better meet the classroom's expectations. A teacher might be able to keep him on track by simply asking him to repeat instructions given to him. He might be seated near the teacher or away from distractions, such as doors and windows. He might benefit from warnings before transitions occur in the classroom. He might need more time to complete complex tasks. You might also find that he can be moved to another classroom down the hall, where the teacher has a different style, and a new mix of students might work better for him. Sometimes, the mission and teaching philosophy of the school are just too different from your son's learning style. His problems are not an indication that he has a serious disorder and can't learn. In those rarer situations, I coach parents to look around and see if it's possible to change schools within their districts or entertain the possibility of finding an affordable private school, keeping in mind that any new school needs to be a better match between teaching approach and their son's learning style. It's not worth changing schools or threatening to do so unless you know there is a better alternative available.

In the above example, I have to agree with Jill that the school psychologist was out of line to offer a diagnosis over the phone for a child she had never met. Plugging for an expensive class run as a sideline by school officials is a red flag for me, too. In that instance, I would tell a mother to resist the pressure. Don't rush to get the screening done, and begin the process of getting a second opinion outside of the school system. Her family's pediatrician was a great resource for trusted and independent child development specialists, in this case a pediatric neurologist, who could evaluate her son.

Jill went to her appointment with the pediatric neurologist, an older doctor with a lot of experience. He reviewed the packet of tests and did a basic neurologic exam, which took about ten to fifteen minutes. At the end, he said, "This boy is perfectly normal," and ruled out autism. He told Jill that he doesn't screen children for Asperger's unless they are much older, around six or seven, and having significant social difficulties.

Aaron recently turned six, and he still struggles in new situations when social demands on him increase. He's not very comfortable speaking in front of his class and is sometimes shy with his teacher. Still, he is more outgoing in small groups and is forming relationships with one or two boys he trusts.

Know Your Own Style

When moms and dads react to the stress of being told they should have their son evaluated, they often exhibit what I call their "anxiety style." Some become instantly tough. They shut down emotionally and just want facts. They want a plan in place, and they want it to happen right now. That can seem intimidating and angry from the other side of the desk. Other parents become emotional and upset quickly, or combative. Still others side exclusively with the teacher, taking whatever's being said as the absolute and only truth. When someone tells you that there's something wrong in your child's life or in his school environment, your stress level is going to skyrocket. Parents in this situation tell me that when the phone rings and they look down at the caller ID and see the school's number, they can feel the panic taking over. I advise them to take a deep breath and try to relax a bit instead. Sometimes grabbing a piece of paper and just writing down what's being said to you is a way to keep the stress at bay. It gives you something to focus on other than fear. If you're panicking, you won't process the information, or remember the details, and you might accidentally inflame the situation with a defensive or hostile reaction. Get all the teacher's thoughts down, thank her, and tell her you will be needing some time to digest this new information and to check in with your spouse and/or pediatrician.

The Parent-Teacher Conference

When your teacher or school administrator says to you that your son's struggles in the classroom warrant testing, the first thing you should do is schedule a conference with this teacher. It's possible, and in many cases very likely, that the two of you can work together to create simple accommodations in the classroom and at home to help your son improve his behavior and his academic performance.

Generally, these conferences are nothing to worry about. They are common and informal, and it can be very helpful to get uninterrupted one-on-one time with a teacher to discuss how to address the situation at school. Take the opportunity to prepare any questions you may have ahead of time, and try to get as much information as you can about how your son is doing in relation to other children. Don't worry if your son is behind other kids in some areas. Many boys need more time because their skills are uneven through the early grades. Also, it helps to remember that development isn't like a marathon race, where it's hard to make up for lost distance and where you are unlikely to come quickly from far behind to win. It's very common for young boys to be the last in their class in some skill one year and near the top just a year or two later. Skills and abilities shift dramatically all the time.

Encourage the teacher to outline your son's strengths as well as his struggles. When she is describing problems in the classroom, stay focused on solutions. Always ask your son's teacher, "What should we do at home, and what might you plan to do at school, so we can help him?"

Keep Track of What's Said

For most parents the first inkling they have that there may be a behavioral problem in the classroom occurs in the parent–teacher conference. Here the teacher may identify for you a problem that she feels is learning-based, such as a learning disability, or a behavior-based disorder that might lead to a psychiatric diagnosis. You should always ask for as much information as you can get.

Take notes, not as an interrogator, but as a journalist, say—as someone who wants to understand the situation. Otherwise, even a few hours after the meeting, you will have forgotten much of what was actually said, remembering instead only a few phrases and your emotional state. Keeping track of what was said gives you a chance to remember the positives and the negatives of the conversation. It also allows you to be armed with information that educates you. I take lots of notes in my work, because it helps me to keep track of the details of stories told to me. It helps me get perspective on what's being said. Most parents have no clue, nor should they, of what the difference is between ADD and ADHD, a nonverbal learning disorder versus Asperger's syndrome or autism, or one of several other possible labels being commonly used these days. You need to get details of what the teacher saw, specific behaviors in the classroom that made her think your son has ADHD, for example. Make the teacher give you specifics about the incidents she describes. She can tell you who was there, what time of day, what day of the week, what was happening in the class when the problem arose. Otherwise, you will leave a meeting or get off the phone with a label that is based only on someone's opinion. If your child is given a diagnosis, it will have been built on someone else's observations of your child, and unless those are based on specific, observable details, there aren't enough reliable data to be making a diagnosis in the first place.

Updates from Home

If you do choose to have your son evaluated by professionals for a behavioral or developmental problem or a learning disability, you'll want to keep the teacher informed of how this is progressing. In some areas of the country, it can take many months to get an appointment with a neurologist, neuropsychologist, or other developmental specialist. If you let the teacher know, send a note into school that says, "Just so you know, we're working on it, but his appointment isn't until next month." That can relieve a lot of pressure for your son in the classroom environment. His teacher will feel included in the process instead of feeling that her concerns are being ignored.

Teachers can also find it helpful to get behavioral updates from the home front. I got this idea from a woman who has taught special education to severely disabled kids in a Boston elementary school where home–school communication is crucial. She says that she encourages parents to update her when their kids reach a new milestone at home, when they show a new positive behavior or skill. If one of her students tries out a skill at home—eating with a fork, asking to use the bathroom, or saying hello to a new acquaintance, for example—she wants to hear about it, so that she can look for these behaviors at school. This is an ideal approach for parents to use. When Jill told me that she and her husband had been working with Aaron to get him to open up and that he had been asking more questions and making better eye contact at home, I encouraged her to pass this along to the teacher. Frame it as happy, exciting news, which it is. Milestones are wonderful. Be sure to ask the teacher to look for these new behaviors at school.

Communication Breakdown

One mom I know, Cynthia, has a son, Stephen, who is an active, highly verbal second grader. At age seven, he's got multiple behavioral issues in the classroom and at home. Some of his problems concern impulsivity. He's the boy who will climb the bookshelves at home, not realizing that he's likely to pull them down on himself. At school, he grabs everything, touches everything, tries to balance on everything. He's the boy who can't quite find his inside voice. He's the boy who shouts out answers in class instead of waiting his turn. In addition, he's not doing very well at following directions or going with the flow of the day. He has multiple tantrums per day, whether he's at home or at school, because he wants his own way, and when he doesn't get it, he digs in his heels. He's terrible at making transitions at school from one activity to another, and he fights both with his siblings and with his classmates.

Cynthia is a dedicated mom and has had many meetings with the teacher and school administrators to try to get a handle on his behavior. Early on in the year, Stephen's teacher thought he had ADHD and pressed for an evaluation. Now his teacher reports to Cynthia that he must have what some experts are calling explosive child syndrome.

I began working with Stephen at the beginning of the school year, to help him learn some new behaviors and to practice the skills he desperately needed to help turn things around in school. Although Stephen has made some strides in changing his behavior at home, his situation at school is getting worse. Cynthia has been great at keeping communication open with Stephen's teacher. She has stayed positive during all of her meetings with the teacher and with administrators. Yet one day she calls me in tears to say that the teacher is insisting that Stephen needs an evaluation for ADHD and medication that will calm him down. The teacher has told Cynthia that she is meeting with school counselors and the school principal to see what they can do to move Stephen to special education services. She asked Cynthia to come in for a parent-teacher conference, but when Cynthia arrived, she found that the meeting also included the school's two counselors, a regional school psychologist, and the administrator in charge of special education.

Intervention-Style Meetings

Sometimes parents arrive at the school for what they assume to be a routine parent–teacher conference, the equivalent of an educational checkup, but find instead a group of professionals ready to discuss their son's behavior. These meetings can include school psychologists, counselors, resource teachers, and administrative staff who handle special education. This signals that the school feels there is a serious problem. School administrators may be very concerned about your son's fit into their program. I tell parents that if such a meeting is sprung on them, they should feel free to reschedule until they have some idea of what's going to be discussed. The administrators may want to talk about achievement scores, recommendations for various assessments, options for formal special education evaluations or services, and accommodations to which your son is or is not entitled. If you aren't prepared for a meeting of this kind, you may be overwhelmed by the amount of information and the technical nature of the information given.

These meetings tend to be emotionally overwhelming as well. You will be hearing different people offer opinions on your son's behavior and educational readiness, his social relationships, and his development. Much of this can be frightening. Parents who are themselves teachers, who are familiar with how these meetings work, tell me that even they are uncomfortable and overwhelmed when they have to go to such a meeting and sit on the parents' side of the table. Parents who are accomplished lawyers or corporate officers, used to fast and demanding group meetings, have told me that they are easily emotionally overwhelmed when they go to meetings like this, meetings at which the topic is their own son. Try not to go to one of these meetings alone. You might want to have another parent or family member join you. Further, many group meetings may end with an administrator asking you to sign forms, which you should not do until you have an opportunity to take them home and review them, and perhaps get some third party to consult with you about them. Don't be afraid to ask for extra time, to take forms home with you, and to delay reacting to anything that is said at one of these meetings. The problem is not going to be fixed in that room. Get the support you need in the room by talking directly with those people you know and trust the most, perhaps your son's teacher or a counselor or a principal with whom you've had a good working relationship.

Here are some statements I've coached parents to use in this situation. We practice them in the office ahead of time, or I'll jot them down for them to use as an example. I encourage parents to use the first names of professionals, particularly if they are being addressed by their first names. If a professional is too uncomfortable with that informality, certainly you must respect that, but I log that into the back of my mind and consider it a possible warning sign that the school staff member is not very flexible or not highly interested in using a team approach to solving your son's problems. I've been wrong about that from time to time, but generally, it's a pretty good litmus test of openness and fairness. Here are some examples of what you could say in such a meeting:

"As his principal, Kathleen, what do you think we can do here to help Josh?"

"You can appreciate how hard this is for me. Melanie has been a great teacher, and we have had many meetings to help Josh in the classroom, and I thought we were making progress."

"Let's pause here. This is all a bit overwhelming, and I'll need to take this home and get back to you when I've had time to digest this. I know we all have Josh in mind here, and I appreciate that."

The overall goal is not to get angry, defensive, or too emotional (not an easy thing to accomplish), but to keep your eyes on the long-term well-being of your son, rather than on short-term interventions being thrown at you in that room. You ultimately have control. He's your son. The school officials are there to offer resources and suggestions. While most educators are sincere, devoted professionals wanting to help your son, the system they work in is set up to serve the school and its goals. Most public schools are trying to meet the needs of the student body as a whole while dealing with serious budgetary restrictions. Don't rush into any major change or testing for diagnosis, particularly with boys who are very young. Be sure to insist on positive and supportive changes, including behavioral coaching and reasonable academic accommodations first.

Practice Moderation

Having said all that, try not to fall into the trap of taking an extreme position or viewpoint at the outset. In Jill's case, she immediately assumed Aaron was being railroaded into a diagnosis, that the preschool teacher wanted to kick him out. That's not an assumption that's going to help you advocate for your son. Some other parents take the opposite view, that the system is set up to do the right thing for their son and that they should trust the process without questioning it.

The best approach is cheerful skepticism. When in doubt, ask lots of questions. Some parents think they're being pressured, but when they ask a simple question—"What if we don't get him tested? What if we wait a couple of months and see?"—they find that the teacher or administrator agrees. With so many parents focused on demanding special education services, schools aren't used to parents saying, "No, let's wait a bit." A child in kindergarten or first grade has many years ahead of him to fit into his school and reach his potential. Don't feel obligated or pressured to make everything perfect at such an early age. Early ages should be about making missteps and experimentation. You have time to watch and learn which programs and teaching styles fit your child best and which do not work for him.

Even if you are getting direct pressure from a school administrator to take immediate action, there is no harm in asking questions about all the possible options, not just the ones proposed by the school. In the meantime, get informed. Schools are required to inform you of your rights with regard to special education screenings, services, and other accommodations they can make in a classroom. Yes, these usually come in the form of brochures written in tiny type, but you need to read them.

But I Don't Want Him Tested

Is an evaluation going to lead inevitably to a diagnosis and special education services and—as Jill worries—an indelible label on a boy?

I used to caution parents to question any attempt by the school to formally assess a young boy when these typical developmental glitches occurred. Now that the special education laws have been updated to include RTIs, I now encourage parents to accept the recommendation to allow minor screenings by the school and be willing to try accommodations that might help their son fit into his current classroom a bit better. Any lengthy and special assessments recommended and done by the school should be administered by a licensed and experienced professional, such as a school psychologist, at no cost to the parent. Parents should always ask up front exactly what types of tests will be conducted, and why; they should be told what questions or problems the testing is intended to address. The answers should make sense, even if you're not familiar with all the fancy jargon or terms we psychologists use. Push the tester to explain things in simple language you can understand.

In some cases, the school is looking to do extensive, prolonged, and involved tests, and you have the right to ask them to do only those tests required to evaluate a specific issue they've identified. Some schools have a policy of testing for everything from emotional problems to learning disabilities, even if the problem is a single physical behavioral tic or a few fights on the playground. One reason to avoid a lengthy battery of psychological tests is that these results become part of the school's file on your son, a file that will follow him from grade to grade regardless of how dramatically his behavior and skills improve. Further, some testing elicits highly personal and emotional information that has no business being held in records to which many people will have access, and where it could be misinterpreted or even used inappropriately.

It's also important for you to know up front that tests have limitations. Most test results don't have a long shelf life. Most aren't accurate or useful a year after testing on very young children. Depending on the quality of the test and a child's age, these tests have varying levels of error (tests are far from 100 percent accurate), and because a boy's brain is developing and changing so quickly, you can't use tests to accurately predict his behavior or skills in later years. For example, I've seen test results on three- and four-year-old boys that seemed to show significant delays in processing visual information only to learn that these same boys had become facile at playing checkers or chess or other games that require decoding patterns, memorizing moves, and planning visually by the time they turned five or six.

Think of tests as one-time snapshots to answer a question at the moment, and not much else. You don't want too much data lying around in your son's school files where people can make incorrect assumptions about him based on old test scores. And you don't want extensive, unnecessary testing that fishes around for "potential" weaknesses or problems. That only invites misdiagnosis.

Be wary of things that lead to bad test data. A boy might have a bad day. He might be tired or feeling ill on the day he's tested, and that will certainly affect his performance. If this is a reevaluation of a child already on medication, such as a stimulant for ADHD, a boy might be temporarily pulled off medications with the assumption that this will yield a clearer reading of his true abilities, when in fact he will be thrown off by the changing levels of medication in his bloodstream. An inexperienced or unqualified tester can draw incorrect conclusions or misread findings.

Sometimes we all forget that testing isn't only a tool for diagnosing and medicating kids. Its real purpose is to measure a child's strengths and weaknesses and guide his further development. Overall, however, testing can yield helpful results when administered appropriately and when the person administering the tests understands the tests' limitations. When the testing is completed, you should always sit down with the person who administered the tests to get a written report that states the reasons for the testing, the specific tests used, the results, the conclusions based on the results, and a list of specific recommendations to enact in the classroom and at home to help your son. There should be references to his strengths as well as his weaknesses. If the only recommendation you see is to assign a diagnosis and use medication, this is not a valid, well-done assessment. Seek a second, independent opinion if possible.

Useful Accommodations

When a boy is struggling in a classroom, some schools will offer accommodations or minor adjustments to help him stay on track and keep up academically. These are well worth considering. Your goal is to allow his teacher flexibility to find the methods to best teach him and encourage his growth and development. More and more, schools are offering accommodations without having to go through the formal IEP process, or without getting a formal diagnosis, so ask for these adjustments first.

Given that so many young boys have uneven development and are behind in language and social skills, it's little wonder that the majority of accommodations and special education services provided to students are being offered to boys. Here are some types that can be very useful for many boys struggling in school.

1. *Simple accommodations.* These can include preferential seating, which would be near the teacher or away from distractions, such as windows and doors. Your son may need more frequent breaks in class to get up and walk off pent-up energy (almost all boys would benefit from this—as would most adults I know). There is a trend among some schools to move some science lessons outdoors, where there is hands-on learning and opportunities to get out of chairs. These programs have shown that trips outside not only help decrease behavioral problems and lower student stress, but improve learning as well. Some schools can also arrange visits to the school counselor in order to participate in social clubs or to chat about what's going on in class. In later years, some boys need exposure to more challenging material to stay focused in class. Almost anything can be written into an accommodation, if your son needs one. Don't be afraid to ask.

2. *More time to work.* Most young boys don't have to worry about standardized testing with strict time limits in early elementary school. Still, if your son does face some multistep school tasks, giving him more time and instruction will help him master the tasks his classmates are working on.

3. *Help in the classroom.* This is one of the most effective ways to improve classroom behaviors and quality of education. It essentially lowers the student-teacher ratio. This, along with smaller class size, is one of the most significant variables shown by research to produce a better outcome in education for kids. Since most problem behaviors are situational, having a second or third adult in the room helps shift the behaviors of all students. There will be less conflict, fewer scuffles, less noise, and less disorganization overall. These adults could include part-time teacher's aides, tutors, educational specialists, student teachers, or adult volunteers. Why are families willing to spend large sums of money to send their children to private schools? Parents are attracted to the idea of a small number of students assigned to each teacher and the cap placed on the total number of students who are in each classroom. A teacher's aide who comes into the

classroom to spend time one on one with your child is giving him essentially some private tutoring. You need to ask, though, which specific times and situations the teacher's aide will be working with your son, because sometimes an aide will be enlisted to help several students in one classroom.

4. *Resource room.* When more intensive teaching methods don't work, the school may offer services provided by a specialist in a room separate from the classroom. Children who are struggling to stay organized, to keep on pace with their reading skills, or who lag in socialization skills or have speech impediments, for example, can spend time working on these problems in the resource room. Until recently, these rooms have been reserved for children with significant learning disabilities, and formal IEPs, but more and more they are being used to help kids learn all kinds of skills they need in class. Still, the school may ask you to go through the process of getting an IEP before offering these special services. Be sure to ask how much time your son will be spending away from his peers. A boy's time outside the classroom should not make up the major part of his day and should be focused only on what he truly needs, academically or socially. Some resource room lessons are done in fun group activity formats, and many boys like having that as a small part of their day at school. Generally, boys age seven and younger don't feel as ostracized or "different" from their peers going to such resource rooms for small amounts of tutoring. However, later on, when kids become more aware of themselves socially, they are very self-conscious of being "different." For now, resource room lessons will likely be a helpful and positive experience provided they are geared toward your son's educational needs.

When to Refuse Accommodations

In some cases, you may want to refuse accommodations offered to your son if you think they are rushed, if they are too simple to address the problem, if they completely miss the boat, or if they seem over the top.

You should feel free to refuse an accommodation that's thrust on you with no warning, or if the school enrolls your son in special education services without consulting you.

I know of schools that have something called a "lunch bunch" and put a few socially shy or aggressive kids together during the twenty to thirty minutes of lunch. They sit with a counselor or teacher's aide a few times a week to help them with social skills. Not a bad idea, and a great start for some boys, but it's important to consider if this is a sufficient accommodation to address this issue. It's easy to look at a boy who is aggressive or overly shy and say that a lunch program is the answer, when in reality, an overcrowded or disorganized classroom, or some subtle learning delay, is more likely the problem. In this case, such an accommodation is likely to have a limited impact.

In other cases the proposed accommodation can be too aggressive to help a boy. I've worked with many boys who have trouble sitting still in class, which makes them a distraction to their classmates. Any accommodation that helps such a boy to improve his behavioral skills or his ability to focus would be appropriate. If, on the other hand, a teacher or administrator advocates pulling this boy out of the classroom for large chunks of the day to enroll in occupational therapy sessions to work on his "fine motor skills" or into a group for emotionally challenged boys or even into an academic program to boost reading skills, you should feel free to refuse these accommodations, or at least to question their validity. In this instance, I'd ask what occupational therapy has to do with sitting still and being a good listener. The answer is, probably nothing. Sometimes, even with good intentions, schools may shuffle students around and miss opportunities to meet their needs appropriately. Remember, schools are supposed to address your son's struggles in the classroom first, using a variety of teaching methods that have been proven to work in other classrooms.

Changing Schools

Michael is six and having problems fitting in at his kindergarten. He is rowdy, very physical, can't keep his hands and feet to himself, and having trouble following directions. An evaluation didn't find anything of concern, except "developmental immaturity." That's an evaluation that is pretty straightforward. It indicates that he needs more time to grow up. Michael's parents are thinking of holding him back a year or looking for a different school that would fit better. There is an all-boy private school, kindergarten through eighth grade, in a nearby town that his parents have been considering. I told Michael's mom that an all-boy school wouldn't necessarily fix this problem, nor would holding him back. Most likely, he's going to grow into a set of skills that work better at school. He will achieve an ability to control his impulses and learn to pay attention in school in a few more months with appropriate coaching and feedback from his parents and teacher.

Changing schools is a serious step. I tell parents that when deciding on changing schools, it's best to determine first what the new school is like in terms of class size and educational style. With regard to class size, smaller is always better for boys whose development is lagging a bit in one or more areas. The next thing to look at is the physical layout of the class and school. Is it large and open? Many boys do better in spaces that have rooms and dividers between learning areas. They face fewer distractions, as well as less noise, and can better focus on the task at hand. I would ask how many opportunities there are for physical activity during the day. Boys with attentional delays and trouble with impulse control do better when they have chances to burn off more energy and get frequent breaks to move about. Actually, all children do better with frequent activity, more chances to run and yell and be energetic, followed by quiet time in which to focus.

I would also ask how much time students get for breaks, lunch, and recess. I recently heard about one school policy that asked kindergarten students to put on their coats and wear them during lunch, to save time before going to recess. The five- and six-year-old kids who lagged at putting on their coats had less time to eat lunch. Some parents complained that their kids came home from school not having eaten any lunch one or two days a week, because they didn't have time. Any school that views lunch break as disposable time is valuing efficiency over student needs.

I know a boy named Ruben who struggled through kindergarten and first grade, mainly because he challenged authority, is very bright, and got frustrated easily because he'd plow through material or tasks quickly. This is a profile of a kid who would likely struggle through the first few years of school no matter where he was. We spent the first two years doing damage control, helping him stay positive and learn some important self-control and cooperation skills, and wait it out. By that I mean Ruben needed more time to grow and develop. Meanwhile I told his parents to be on the lookout for a school that would be a better fit. They got the help of an educational advocate who knew many schools in the area. They started to consider schools and programs first in their town, and even thought of moving as an option at one point. Fortunately, with help from grandparents and some scholarship money, Ruben was able to get into a private Montessori school that was a perfect fit because he was allotted much more in-depth material to cover and could control how he learned. The smaller class size and hands-on approach also made the learning environment better for him. Interestingly, this reduced his tendency to challenge his teachers.

We didn't rush him out to another school. We got the two early years behind him and then found a better fit. If Ruben's family hadn't been able to change schools, we would have doubled up our efforts to work within the current school system. It was easier on Ruben to have changed schools at this age, versus waiting it out and pulling him away later on (such as third or fourth grade), when boys are far more sensitive and angry about leaving the familiar school and friends they have. Some parents want to wait to make a change until middle school, because kids are changing schools anyway. But boys can find it more difficult to go into a school system and find a place after the social patterns are already established. It's not the end of the world to change schools at that age, but it's easier socially to change before middle school.

Getting More Support and Help

If your relationship with a school has become too contentious or emotional, if you feel that you cannot get through a meeting with a teacher or a school official without breaking down or becoming upset, you might consider hiring an educational advocate to work with the school on your behalf. Educational advocates are familiar with local school systems, school policies, and the rights and benefits of special education services. They know what benefits parents and students are entitled to, what the criteria are for special education services. Most important, these advocates are experienced, tough negotiators. Many were former teachers or administrators themselves. Some are parents whose children have gone through the special education system and who therefore have become experts in that system. The goal here is to decrease your stress, get more information, and work more productively with the school to improve your son's education.

As with any profession, there is a wide range of skill levels and personality types among advocates. In my experience, the best advocates are those who are thoughtful, reflective, open to many options, and diplomatic in their approach. These are people who ultimately keep your son's educational needs front and center. Some parents have told me their advocate makes them feel protected or vindicated. That is fine, but keep in mind the real goal is getting the best educational fit, one that allows your child to succeed academically, emotionally, and socially, and then move on. Battles can go on and on; meanwhile your son is not getting the real help or attention he might need in his current placement. When hiring an advocate, stress to that person that you want to use the least invasive and least disruptive course of action first. Be accommodating, willing to listen, and flexible, and move slowly before considering more drastic changes, such as demanding new school placement.

CHAPTER 12

He Has Already Been Labeled

Diagnoses are powerful, descriptive tools to guide us toward providing the best possible treatments. When used correctly, they are invaluable. Yet, so often, the word *diagnosis* is thrown around in a casual manner, or a diagnosis is affixed like a permanent tattoo, when in fact it can signify something far more vague and inconclusive. Some mothers come into my office and say that their son has been diagnosed with "sensory processing disorder" or "explosive disorder," or he has been diagnosed as a "spirited child." More and more I hear diagnoses of bipolar disorder and Asperger's syndrome applied to difficult young boys, even more commonly in recent years than the once very popular ADHD label. When I ask about who made the diagnosis and under what circumstances, more often than not I discover that it was a well-intentioned school administrator or a preschool teacher or a friend of the family. In some cases a parent will say that she's read a certain book and feels that it describes her son completely and now wants to have him evaluated to see if that is the right diagnosis. These are typically very caring parents critically concerned about their son and who are, in some cases, under a lot of pressure from the school system to assign him a diagnosis, sometimes to help a boy in genuine trouble, but other times to move a troublesome boy out of his classroom and into special education services. Making a diagnosis is a serious step and should be thought out carefully.

A problem with aggressively seeking a diagnosis is that it nearly always leads to treatment. That's the purpose of a diagnosis. In many cases, this will be a pill with real, potentially serious side effects. I caution parents not to think so narrowly. Pills are not the only treatment for behavioral problems, let alone developmental challenges. Nor are they always the best treatment. Many boys respond extremely well to shifting their environment, tutoring, coaching, behavioral therapy, and changes in diet and nutrition.

Even when medication is used, it is often the combination of the right medication with behavioral and educational interventions that leads to the best long-term outcome.

In this chapter, I want to lay out for parents what a diagnosis is, what it means, and what to expect when you go down the road toward assigning a medical label for your son's behavior. I will include in this a sampling of screening techniques and tests often given to boys of this age and what they mean and don't mean. In some cases, a test or screening technique is used as proof of something that it may not be designed to prove at all. In other cases, a well-designed test can give helpful objective information about how your son is doing, but it should be considered merely as a starting point. "Screening" instruments, such as checklists, are the most common type of assessment your son is likely to receive. They seem very scientific and official, but when used alone, they are not the most accurate path to diagnosis. They should only be a first step in deciding if the situation is serious enough to warrant going further to obtain an evaluation or a formal diagnosis.

For example, I worked with a wonderful six-year-old named Connor who has struggled with compulsive behaviors. He had to smell the floor when he got up in the morning. His parents were okay with this at first, hoping that this habit would go away if they ignored it. But then he started doing it more often during the day. He developed new rituals for hand washing and touching different surfaces or smelling them a certain number of times. He took a lot of teasing at school for this. Connor told his mother that he wanted to stop doing these things, but he couldn't. His mother told me that Connor's uncle had been diagnosed as an adult with obsessive-compulsive disorder (OCD), and she wanted to know if a diagnosis and perhaps some form of medication could help ease Connor's compulsions as well.

Many times parents refer to common childhood struggles as symptoms that represent a problem. But *symptom* is a clinical term that has a specific meaning. Given that we're talking about very young boys here, I think it's best that we use a strict definition. A symptom is a behavior that (1) is seriously disruptive to your son's life; (2) persists over time and across situations, not something that comes and goes; and (3) is problematic and resistant to simple interventions to change it. In this case, Connor really did have symptoms. His behaviors were symptomatic of a problem that would benefit from a diagnosis that could put us on track to give him appropriate treatment.

In Connor's case, he did very well with an established behavioral technique known as "exposure and response prevention." It sounds complicated, but it's really a simple two-step procedure. First, Connor was guided to think more about whatever was worrying him (the "exposure" part). His thoughts were mostly about catching bad germs and getting sick. Connor was encouraged to think of germs by using his imagination. He told me they looked like big, gross bugs. Next, I asked him to wait longer and longer before he rushed off to wash his hands or touched and sniffed things (the "response prevention" part). He practiced these two steps in my office. Then his parents practiced at home several times a day, extending the time he held onto his scary thoughts and delaying the time until he did his compulsive behavior (such as hand washing). He was rewarded for successfully delaying his ritual. He received points that could get him special time playing an electronic game he enjoyed. Very soon, about a week later, his parents noticed a dramatic change. His sniffing, touching, and hand-washing behaviors decreased significantly.

Medication was also an option to help control Connor's OCD symptoms, but his pediatrician and I agreed that he was too young to use psychiatric drugs unless it was absolutely necessary, particularly when there was a viable, nonmedical option available. I told Connor's parents that his symptoms would likely flare up over time when he was feeling stressed or going through developmental changes, but some rehearsal of these techniques should keep his OCD symptoms at bay. In some older boys with more pronounced OCD, and in whom behavioral techniques aren't effective by themselves, I refer them for a short-term trial of medication. This combination approach works very well when symptoms are particularly disruptive.

The Criteria of a Symptom

Diagnoses are built on the symptoms we report. I remind parents that the word *symptom* is a clinical term with a specific meaning. Here are four criteria I use when considering if a young child's behavior is a symptom.

1. *It must be serious.* Is this behavior getting in the way of your son's ability to function in a significant way? Usually, the answer is no. Is the child grossly unhappy? Again, usually the answer is no. Can it be explained by stress or changes in the family? If so, then it's not a symptom that stands alone and is rooted in a child's hardwiring. Chances are you are seeing normal, if quirky, boy behavior. It deserves intervention but not necessarily a formal diagnosis. Some parents say to me, "But he's disrupting the classroom. How can he be functioning if he's doing that?" The term *functioning* is arbitrary. In some classrooms, a teacher may be able to reduce this disruption through accommodations. In Connor's case, his growing routine of rituals had taken over his life. If he was prevented from carrying out these rituals, he was incapacitated with fear. He shook and cried and refused to do anything until he could perform his ritual. That's very serious.

2. *It must persist over time.* The behavior shouldn't show up Monday and be gone by Tuesday, only to show up again on Thursday. Single events, no matter how severe, are rarely meaningful. If a boy hits a kid at school, wets the bed, or tells you he hates himself, that's not a symptom if it happens only once or

twice. Don't focus too much on it, or it will gain a life of its own. Paying too much attention to it, especially negative attention such as yelling and nagging, will encourage this behavior because your son will still be getting something for it. In Connor's case, his parents tried to ignore the ritualistic behaviors, and they didn't go away. At this point, his behaviors were so entrenched that no amount of nagging or ignoring could interrupt them.

3. *It must occur across situations.* If we're talking about a trait or a problem that is primarily biologically based, warranting diagnosis and perhaps even medicine (such as chronic hyperactivity, an inability to use language, an inability to identify letters or numbers, or poor motor control), it will occur in many different places. For example, ADHD symptoms such as distractibility and hyperactivity in your son shouldn't completely disappear for hours on end while he watches a movie or colors in a coloring book. If he's hyperactive at home but not at school, that's not a symptom that needs medical intervention up front. It means the routines at home have to be a bit more like those at school, more structured, less chaotic, and the rules must be applied more consistently. In Connor's case, he was using compulsive rituals at home and at school, although at school his OCD-like behaviors were less notable because he worked so hard to suppress them. Yet, despite his efforts, they still spilled out at school.

4. *It should be reported by more than one trusted observer.* More than one person who encounters the child regularly should report this behavior. This includes teachers, babysitters, and relatives. Before you seek a diagnosis from someone, ask people who see your child regularly if they've noticed these behaviors. Why? Because it's too easy to affix diagnoses onto very young boys who are undergoing such rapid changes in their development. So, if you just have your fear or suspicion about your child, and you want a diagnosis to confirm or deny it, you're in a very vulnerable position. Some highly specialized diagnosticians have become myopic by focusing only on what they are looking for day in and day out. They will confirm a parent's suspected diagnosis because

that's what they are used to seeing. Many of my colleagues steer me away from very respected specialists, saying, "Don't go to him unless you want a diagnosis of bipolar or ADD. That's what he always gives." In Connor's case, several of his teachers and the adults who care for him have seen these compulsive rituals.

Let's contrast Connor with Trevor, who is a five-year-old also struggling with behavioral issues. Trevor doesn't seem to have any personal boundaries. He touches other kids on the face and hugs them and hangs on them even when they are clear about not wanting this. His mother can't get him through a playdate or a social event without constantly reminding him not to touch the other kids. "Hands to yourself," she says again and again. He complies, then waits until she's distracted, and away he goes again. In school, he has fewer problems with the teachers, who set boundaries and provide consequences. His mother, who describes his development in terms of several delays and minor tics, wants to know if a diagnosis would help because he could get special services at school.

While Trevor's behavior can be seriously disruptive at times, it doesn't persist all the time or across most situations. It can come and go, depending on his mood, what's happening in the classroom, who is watching over him, and a range of other factors. Some people really enjoy this aspect of his personality. He's loving and free to share affection. He's socially clumsy but engaging, and this is an endearing characteristic to many of the adults that know him. In fact, few of his classmates complain about his behavior. They may push him away from time to time, and then he gets the hint and wanders off. By using some behavioral techniques to establish personal boundaries and reward him when he complies, he has been able to adjust his behavior at school and in playdates.

Trevor did well with a simple "no touching" rule. Before entering a classroom or the park, he was reminded that touching others was completely off limits, no exceptions, unless he asked permission first. Making it a simple black-and-white rule gave Trevor a better chance of success. It also kept the adults more consistent with delivering their consequences. Trevor was rewarded for listening to the rule, usually, getting a sticker and lots of praise. If he broke the no touching rule, he was asked to sit out briefly from the group. At the start, Trevor was almost spending as much time outside the group as in, but over a few weeks he got greater control over his impulses to grab and hug others. Eventually his teachers could reward him for long periods of time—such as a whole morning, or during lunch, or during the whole afternoon—in which he didn't touch other kids inappropriately. This last type of reward is very important. We often forget to reward kids for the absence of a problem. During that time, they are working very hard to suppress impulses.

Tracking His Behavior—Is It a Real Problem?

A first step is to try to define the problem behavior clearly. Is it hitting? Is it running around excessively? Is it crying? Is it avoiding other kids? Stay away from vague descriptors, such as "He's been difficult and not listening," or "He's apprehensive about learning." Next, you should track these specific behaviors and keep a notebook to record individual incidents. You can ask a teacher to do this, too, when you're trying to decide if this is a serious problem.

Impulsive behaviors, hyperactivity, and a lack of focus are the hallmarks of ADHD, and this is the most common boy problem likely to get diagnosed. At times I have made my own quick and dirty checklists for these three areas. I ask a parent to fill them out every day, keeping track of which behaviors showed up and which didn't. Here's an example. I ask parents to jot down two or three behaviors with which their sons struggle. I ask them to do this in each of three hallmark areas: impulsive behaviors, hyperactivity, and lack of focus. The first asks parents to measure two or three impulsive behaviors, such as getting into situations without thinking, taking or grabbing things he knows he shouldn't, or hitting other kids instead of using his words. The second one measures hyperactive behaviors. How often did he run around uncontrollably, or fidget excessively? Third, they measure two or three areas concerning focus, such as staying on task, looking up when called, and following directions. These lists can be as informal as a grocery list. Let's say a mom or teacher records two or three behaviors in each area per day, recorded over several days. We pool the checklists at the end of a week or two and try to see a pattern across times, people, and situations, if there is one. Is a boy bothering one or two specific kids only? Is this happening in the morning when he first gets to school or later in the day when he's tired or cranky? Is it happening when the classroom is supposed to be still and quiet or during unstructured, active playtimes or during transitions between rooms or activities? There is almost always a pattern that shows the effect of external factors on his behavior, more than his behavior's effect on his external world. Situations at home often play a part. For example, he might be worse at the beginning of the school week because he's not getting enough sleep over the weekend due to overscheduling of activities, or he's worse right before Mom or Dad leaves for a business trip because his routines at home have been disrupted.

I often give this type of simple charting task to parents who are wondering about an ADHD diagnosis to help illustrate how much of their son's challenging behavior is driven from inside (from within his brain) and how much is caused by things outside his brain. Tracking information from home and school over time and pooling it is much more likely to yield an accurate picture than relying on a single incident to indicate your son's condition. Having a chart like this will also prepare you for discussions with any doctor or school professional who attempts to make a diagnosis. Unfortunately, most professionals don't look at long-term tracking when making a diagnosis. One outburst in the office, a few incidents at school, and a diagnosis can be easily affixed. The process is often rushed. This happens in medicine as well. Dr. Jerome Groopman, professor of medicine at Harvard Medical School, reports that even experienced physicians tend to diagnose prematurely and make their judgments in the first few seconds or minutes of a meeting. This, in part, leads to one out of five diagnoses being wrong. If it's happening every day with common medical diagnoses such as strep or rashes, imagine the potential for error when deciding if throwing crayons is part of a psychiatric disorder like ADHD. Even a good diagnostician should collect information over time to make sure what's observed isn't a fluke. Putting in the dipstick on any one bad day isn't going to give you a true reading. A bad day or isolated incident might be just that, and not evidence of any underlying biological disorder.

The rate of psychiatric misdiagnosis in very young boys is unknown, but I would estimate it to be high, at around one third or more, depending on what is being diagnosed. This isn't wild speculation. A 2007 study in the *Archives of General Psychiatry* found the misdiagnosis rate for adult clinical depression, which is among the most researched of disorders in psychiatry, is about one out of every four (25 percent). The error rate in diagnosing the emotional and behavioral problems of very young boys has to be higher. Whereas most depressed adults can self-report their feelings or behaviors, young kids do not report their own symptoms, and most don't think they are having a problem in the first place. Also, because boys develop and change quickly, from time to time, their moods and behaviors are going to seem erratic simply as a part of normal growth.

In real-life terms, think of it this way. If you are having your son evaluated for ADHD and are sitting in a waiting room along with two other moms with their sons, it's possible that one of your boys will receive a misdiagnosis and, further, be prescribed medicine inappropriately. Given such inaccuracy, we must treat diagnostic labels put on preschool boys with caution, and never as static, long-term conditions. Boys are just too young and in the process of too much growth to view problems or difficulties as set in stone.

Here's an extreme example of misdiagnosis to illustrate the point. Parents I know of were concerned about the fact that their son seemed especially clumsy. He ran into walls and knocked things down. He seemed uncomfortable in his own skin; he fidgeted against the tags in his clothes. He wouldn't wear any pants with buttons or zippers, or shirts with collars. Loud sounds bothered him and frightened him excessively. He was evaluated at an occupational therapy practice, where the therapist told his parents at the first session that he had all the classic traits of sensory integration disorder, which is presumed to be a neurologic developmental condition in which the brain is not processing information from the senses in the best and most coordinated way. The therapist told his mother, "This is a lifelong brain issue. Your son will never be a varsity athlete. Team sports are out. So get over it now." The mom was flustered by this statement. Because her son was only four, she had never assumed that he was supposed to excel at sports. In fact, she hadn't thought ahead much about what his interests might be in high school. She was more concerned about him getting along at preschool and being able to play on the playground without hurting himself.

Fortunately, her next stop was to her family pediatrician, who suggested an eye exam as a more logical first step before beginning any occupational therapy for sensory integration disorder. The eye exam revealed that this young boy needed glasses. The boy was walking into walls and doorways because he couldn't see them well enough to avoid them. The mother was shocked, both by the turnaround in her son's behavior after he came home with glasses and by the realization that she almost signed up for a rather strict course of occupational therapy for her son. After all, the therapist had seemed so sure. She told me later that her son is now on the Pop Warner Peewee football team in his town and that he plays as well as the other kids. He still hates the feel of tags in his shirts (but so do I).

This extreme example is not to dismiss the value of diagnosing sensory integration disorder, but rather to illustrate how easily an incorrect diagnosis can be made. Higher specialization narrows a professional's diagnostic lens. Rushed appointments result in practitioners jumping to conclusions before getting enough history and data that allow them to consider alternative explanations. And the topsy-turvy nature of a young boy's rapid development leads some behaviors to masquerade as symptoms.

What Are the Tests?

First of all, diagnosing these types of childhood disorders isn't like diagnosing an earache or a bruised bone; there is no standard approach or standard set of tools to see or measure them. Therefore, you want to look for practitioners who take their time, using more than one instrument. Practitioners should contact others who know the child, such as teachers, during an evaluation process. For ADHD, which is among the most common diagnostic categories for boys, you will likely see a checklist that you and teachers will be asked to fill out. Most often, this is the Conners' Rating Scales-Revised (CRS-R), by Keith Conners. Another test frequently used is the second edition of the Behavior Assessment System for Children (BASC-2), by Cecil Reynolds and Randy Kamphaus, which assesses ADHD and other social and emotional problems. The BASC-2 and a long version of the Conners are better with differential diagnosing, where we try to tease apart the possible reasons why a boy is having trouble focusing and behaving at school or is having problems making friends. These are two commonly used checklists. Practitioners will also review the criteria of ADHD with you one by one.

Another commonly used resource is the *Diagnostic and Statistical Manual of Mental Disorders, fourth edition (DSM-IV)*, from the American Psychiatric Association. The DSM-IV breaks out descriptions for inattention, hyperactivity, and impulsivity as part of a diagnosis of ADHD. What follows are the criteria as they appear on the website for the centers for Disease Control and Prevention.

INATTENTION

1. Often does not give close attention to details or makes careless mistakes in schoolwork, work, or other activities
2. Often has trouble keeping attention on tasks or play activities
3. Often does not seem to listen when spoken to directly
4. Often does not follow instructions and fails to finish schoolwork, chores, or duties in the workplace (not due to oppositional behavior or failure to understand instructions)
5. Often has trouble organizing activities
6 Often avoids, dislikes, or doesn't want to do things that take a lot of mental effort for a long period of time (such as schoolwork or homework)

7. Often loses things needed for tasks and activities (for example, toys, school assignments, pencils, books, or tools)
8. Is often easily distracted
9. Is often forgetful in daily activities

HYPERACTIVITY

1. Often fidgets with hands or feet or squirms in seat
2. Often gets up from seat when remaining in seat is expected
3. Often runs about or climbs when and where it is not appropriate (adolescents or adults may feel very restless)
4. Often has trouble playing or enjoying leisure activities quietly
5. Is often "on the go" or often acts as if "driven by a motor"
6. Often talks excessively

IMPULSIVITY

1. Often blurts out answers before questions have been finished
2. Often has trouble waiting one's turn
3. Often interrupts or intrudes on others (for example, butts into conversations or games)

I point out to parents a few things about this checklist of ADHD symptoms that makes it an easy diagnosis to hand out. While this list of symptoms does describe a child with ADHD, it also describes a lot of kids who don't have ADHD, particularly very young or immature kids who are still developing. First there is no adjusting the symptoms for a child's age. A four-year-old is expected to "interrupt others" more than a five-year-old, and certainly interrupt much more than a seven- or ten-year-old. Without adjusting for a child's age, younger kids who are active and challenging are more likely to get tagged with the disorder, especially when the evaluator is inexperienced. I would also question any diagnostic tool that relies so heavily on the words *often* and *some*, which are purely subjective and not quantifiable. This invites opinion and personal judgment into the rating process. It would be preferable if these symptoms could be quantifiable, for example, "fails to finish schoolwork 30 percent or more of the time," or "loses things needed for tasks and activities more than three times a day."

But my biggest criticism of this symptom checklist is the "symptoms" themselves. Each is a normal characteristic of all children, and most adults as well. These aren't symptoms in the way that unwanted behaviors and uncomfortable conditions are, such as sleeping too much or too little, loss of appetite, headaches, fears, disorientation, memory loss, prolonged sadness, or persistent problems learning how to read and write. I sometimes tell parents this checklist would better fit what I call PIN (pain-in-the-neck) disorder. There's nothing on this list as written that would fit my definition of a symptom belonging to a serious psychiatric disorder.

I caution parents not to let professionals use only the *DSM* checklist in diagnosing ADHD in their young child. The use of at least one rating scale like the Conners or the BASC–2 helps compare your child's behavior to other kids his age and across settings, such as home and school.

Other Tests You May Encounter

Many learning problems that have nothing to do with focusing or motor activity can look like ADHD, when in fact a boy may be acting out or avoiding a task because he's frustrated, unable to learn, or bored. In these cases, more sophisticated individual testing is warranted. Specifically, a cognitive and educational assessment can be very useful. The Wechsler Intelligence Scale for Children (WISC) is one of the most commonly used tests of intellectual skills for kids six to sixteen years old. It tries to assess a child's basic mental aptitudes, such as reasoning, visual-spatial skills, memory, and planning skills. There is another version called the Wechsler Preschool and Primary Scale of Intelligence (WPPSI) that can be administered to children as young as two and a half. Educational assessments are instruments that measure how much your son has learned and can do in areas such as numbers or basic math, letters or basic reading and writing, compared with others his same age. When given together, cognitive and educational tests are sometimes known as neuropsychological testing and are often supplemented with a few other shorter tests that look to measure specific neurologic skills, such as fine motor performance, integrating visual and spatial information, focus, processing speed, and storing and retrieving information. Mostly these involve a bunch of blocks, puzzles, and drawings that a good examiner uses in a standard way to see where your son's mental abilities and learning skills are, compared with other kids of the same age. These typically require one to two sessions' worth of testing in the examiner's office. The quality varies based on who is giving the tests. They should be administered only by well-trained, certified professionals.

The most common scenario for young boys, however, isn't this type of long, careful testing, but a quick review by a pediatrician or other health professional who goes down a checklist of symptoms with a parent. Diagnosing at pediatric visits is likely to be quicker because the current insurance system forces doctors to see patients under tight time restraints, where the opportunity to misdiagnose, particularly ADHD, is higher. Beware of this, and consider second opinions and possibly more formal testing if your son receives a diagnosis quickly and without using any type of standard rating scale (e.g., the Conner's Scale or the BASC–2 mentioned above), or if his problems persist even though the pediatric visit yielded no concerns.

In general, the more thorough one-on-one testing will yield the most accurate findings and will more likely reveal possible reasons your son is struggling in school. In some cases, a child who tests high on the Conner's checklist for ADHD may not really have ADHD. One possibility is that he has a high IQ; he's fidgety and unable to concentrate in school because he's bored. No quick checklist can tease that apart. Generally, if the school officials are pushing for special education without first trying reasonable accommodations in the classroom, or if they are urging a quick diagnosis and medication, you'll want to do more extensive testing. Ask if the school will do a full neuropsychological evaluation (cognitive and educational tests), and be sure to get a second opinion outside the school system if you have concerns about the skill level of the school's examiner. Getting another opinion that is not tied to the school's program is often a good idea. If separate testers yield the same results, you can have more confidence that a diagnosis or learning problem is real. Another reason to get a second opinion is that it can stretch out the time between testing and assigning a diagnosis. You'd be surprised how often behaviors sort themselves out on their own in this span of time due to normal developmental changes that take place.

What's the Rush?

Unfortunately, diagnoses are all too often assigned to kids on their first and only visit with a professional. I consider this a red flag. Yet many parents are themselves in a rush to get an answer and to act on the problem. They believe that the earliest possible intervention will yield the best results in terms of treatment. Parents often say to me, "We can't wait; things will only get worse, won't they?" I call this the "nip it in the bud" theory, and I think it is well meaning but mistaken.

For some of the more serious disorders, such as autism, it is indeed advantageous to get an accurate diagnosis as early as possible so that helpful interventions can begin. But for most children, it's not helpful to give them a diagnosis just to categorize their developmental struggles. Because the nature of a young child's development is erratic, particularly for boys, we need to be cautious not to rush to use labels that don't fit for the longer term. A hurried diagnosis can lead to a course of treatments that may be inappropriate, can interfere with development, and can unnecessarily stigmatize a young boy.

I completely understand why we like to diagnose challenges and problems. It helps us deal with something scary and gives us some plan to deal with it. A diagnosis puts a set of behaviors into a box, which is great if you've found the right box. But the younger the child, the more likely it is that the diagnostic box is wrong. It wasn't very long ago that we believed that boys diagnosed with ADHD had a disease of the brain, a lifelong, progressive disorder always requiring medication. Now we know that many of these boys are just lagging developmentally and will catch up, whether medication is used or not.

What a Diagnosis Fails to Say

I also like to remind parents who seek a diagnosis of what they will actually have when they get one.

So many times, I see mothers in my office who bring me thick folders of testing results, along with the diagnostic label for their sons. These mothers are every bit as anxious and troubled as they were when they started the process. Their sons have a diagnosis and often a prescription, yet they still face a troublesome situation at home and at school with their behavior. I say to them, "This diagnosis doesn't matter right now. A little boy is a work in progress. No matter what his behavior is now, it will be different in six months, a year, two years."

I remind them that diagnoses are static, flat descriptors, meaning they put a label on a set of behaviors but don't actually explain them. A diagnosis doesn't tell you what led up to and set off the behavior or what controls the behavior. A diagnosis will never tell you why your son behaves the way he does or why he is struggling. In fact, a diagnosis is like the photo on your driver's license, accurate only at that moment. It's just a flat, two-dimensional representation. You change, while it stays the same. Just as you wouldn't want to be judged forever on that photo, your son's behavioral challenges shouldn't be explained forever by a medical-sounding diagnosis based on a few checked items on a list or a few bad days at school. A boy's mind and body are dynamic, changing, and growing, and will be for years. His developmental hiccup this month could be gone in a week, part of the ups and downs your son needed to go through as part of growing up. That's why seasoned pediatricians, health professionals, and educators don't worry about any single event and don't push to diagnose. They take a wait-and-see approach, knowing that many problems sort themselves out.

Get a Second Opinion

Parents should always get a second opinion on a diagnosis when it is serious or when the proposed treatment is invasive, such as a prescription for psychopharmacological drugs, or when the child's social and educational settings will be drastically changed. Parents of younger children, those in preschool, who have received any type of diagnosis should always request a second opinion. In this age range, the most likely concerns are profound delays in language or socialization. Diagnoses that involve attentional problems, impulsivity, or hyperactivity are not recommended much before ages six and seven, when it's normal for children to have very underdeveloped executive functioning. At these very early age ranges, such labels are unreliable and often meaningless in the long run.

I'm astonished how often second opinions and evaluations result in different diagnoses and different treatment recommendations. It's not that most practitioners are inept. Rather, we're dealing with young human beings who are elusive, ever-shifting, and developing. It's illogical and frankly arrogant for someone to see a boy one time for ten or fifteen minutes, listen to a list of vague problems, affix a label to them, and send him out the door with medication or therapy. I tell parents not to let any doctor do this to their child, no matter how knowledgeable or certain he or she seems to be. A parent's first job is to advocate for his or her child's development, and that means securing a second opinion to increase the accuracy of finding out what might (or might not) be wrong.

Medication

Beware of clinicians in a hurry to attach a label to and prescribe medication for your child. Some clinicians rush because insurers promote this type of medical practice. These clinicians have an overload of cases and very little time or resources to accurately get to know your child or ask all the right questions. Another warning I give is don't let anyone use medications to help them diagnose your son's problems. I know of too many practitioners who like to take a stab at a diagnosis by seeing what happens when medications are given. When the symptoms change, these practitioners use this as a confirmation of the diagnosis. This is unacceptable medical practice. Don't allow someone to diagnose your son's behavioral issues via a response to medication. This happens most often with attention deficit disorder (ADD) and ADHD-like problems. The truth is that everyone focuses better and concentrates a little harder on psychostimulants. Many a well-intentioned practitioner has said, "Well, your son is doing better since being on Ritalin. We're right. He must have had ADD. The change is amazing!" Diagnoses should take time. There is no advantage to rushing a diagnosis. There is certainly no advantage to starting medication sooner rather than later when in most cases a developing boy's brain needs time to sort itself out, grow, and rewire itself naturally. Be patient.

A study done in 2007 by Dr. Philip Shaw and colleagues at the National Institute of Mental Health indicates that many boys do grow out of ADHD symptoms. This is one of the most important studies to date on this issue, in my opinion, because it gets at the heart of how these kids catch up over time in their ability to focus, suppress high activity level, and pull back impulsive behaviors. Researchers used brain imaging to watch changes over time in the brains of both normally developing children and those identified with ADHD. They found that those with ADHD had about a three-year lag in maturity in the areas involving the control of thinking, planning, and attention, but that their brains caught up and developed normally otherwise. Reviewing these results, I have to ask: How can ADHD be a true disorder of the brain in every kid diagnosed? How can it be a medically based lifelong problem if we see normal development catching up and the "symptoms" vanishing in a large number of cases? To be fair, I do see some kids who carry ADHD symptoms into adulthood. But it has been reported that the vast majority of kids—near 90 percent—diagnosed with ADHD no longer meet the criteria for the disorder by the time they reach young adulthood. Those young adults who still have symptoms do well with the right combination of life-changing/coaching skills and in some cases medication, depending on the severity of their symptoms. Again, the key is to take your time diagnosing, and use tests or multiple examiners to be more accurate.

Sadness and Anxiety

I believe the same conservative diagnostic approach should be used with young children who are experiencing sadness or anxiety. As long as they are not debilitated by their emotions, and are not threatening to cause harm to themselves or others, the most prudent course is to watch carefully and give the situation a few days or a week. Most often young boys who are sensitive, shy, or apprehensive to engage in new situations are most affected by what goes on around them. They react to marital stress, moving, parents changing jobs or work schedules, or going to a new school.

I worked with one boy who had developed a school phobia in kindergarten. He refused to speak in school and was very shy. This boy's cousins had similar problems and had been medicated. But his mother refused medication, and with some help, we hammered things out in a few sessions. I told his mother, "This is not a long-term problem. He won't be fifteen and not talking at school. He's also not suffering with undue anxiety or sadness, and he has been observed to be smiling a fair amount during the day. He's just going through a strong but temporary stage of fearing new people and unfamiliar situations." She actually laughed in relief and was on board with trying more behavioral approaches to help her son. We used some rewards in school-like environments outside the home first and giving him practice looking at other people, making a few simple attempts to stay by himself with his mother nearby. Next, we conditioned him to the real world in which he would have to talk at school. I asked his teachers not to give him any attention or extra help unless he started to use his words and participate. Once he did this, he got the hang of it all too well, and he was never quiet again. His brother said to me one day in the waiting area, "Hey, you got him talking. Now can you get him to please shut up?"

What About Placebo Effects?

Although it is tempting to medicate children who show signs of depression and anxiety, you should know that these medications have a strong placebo effect in children. This power of suggestion is strong and works on families and teachers as well. I've come across so many cases in which a child or adolescent has been pocketing his meds instead of taking them (older kids are unusually clever about this), while his parents and teachers, who believed he was taking them, report that the meds have dramatically improved his behavior.

There's no need to dismiss the placebo effect as something "only in our heads" or a phantom gremlin that messes up research and medical trials. In fact, it's about something quite wonderful in human beings. When we believe we are being cared for, that the course we've taken will improve our problems, and there is hope, our minds and bodies miraculously rally and point us in the direction of health. We become better and stronger. Serious research is under way to figure out how this happens. What is going on in our immune systems when we believe we will improve (even without a drop of medication)? If we can harness that effect, we will open the door to greater power in helping with all that ails us.

What the placebo effect teaches us, practically speaking, is to believe in your child and yourself. For now, remember that your positive expectations for your son's happiness and success may be one of the most potent factors in helping him do better as he develops. Be wary of labeling his challenges as problems and insinuating there is something biologically wrong or broken in his young, developing mind. Those negative expectations are dangerous. I'm not saying don't be smart and don't seek help or get second opinions or hide your head in the sand when problems persist. I'm saying to balance medical and psychological diagnoses and interventions with positive expectations.

CHAPTER 13

What Will He Be Like as a Grown Man?

When parents come to me for help with their sons, I know the real question, the real concern, they have even if they don't say it out loud. They worry that their boys are hopelessly behind in development and that this gap will grow over the years. They worry that their boys won't grow up to be happy and accomplished adults.

Compounding their fears is the vast majority of parenting books that view developmental challenges as abnormal and not as opportunities for growth. Most of these books encourage parents to view most troublesome behavior as pathological. Worried parents who look for an explanation of their sons' behavior will find these books filled with lists of behaviors, called symptoms, along with a ready-made diagnosis. These books encourage parents to be vigilant, to look for trouble in their sons' behaviors. They offer up scary stories about kids who have failed in life or suffered terribly because they didn't get help early enough.

I take the opposite approach. As a child psychologist who has worked with kids for more than twenty years, I can happily say that most boys, even those with early struggles, will grow up healthy and well. I want parents to relax. They are surprised when I tell them that they should imagine their sons all grown up and happy and thanking them for all their hard work as a parent. I can tell them this because I have seen the contrasts between the boys that came into my office years ago, some with problems that seemed serious at the time, and the capable young men they have become. Many of my former patients continue to visit me from time to time to check in. Several of them have enthusiastically agreed to be profiled here, to talk openly about what they felt as kids who, whether they had a diagnosis or not, came to me for treatment. They will talk about what it was like to be the troublemaker in the family or at school or the shy guy who stood on the sidelines.

I want parents who read this chapter to make a crucial leap and begin to see the healthy young adult inside their own sons. Every parent should try to look ahead and see his or her son as a happy, healthy grown man. I tell parents to imagine their sons sitting around in their college dorm rooms with friends or going off to a first job, to really imagine a future in which they are well-adjusted adults. Without this visualization, many parents allow their worries to grow and fester. They become hypervigilant and look only for what might be going wrong. Despite good intentions, any parent can interfere too much with a boy's development, in the belief that he needs more help than he does.

The grown boys I interviewed for this book show that a calm, measured, and thoughtful parenting approach works. A boy needs to feel his parents' confidence in him, to know that they don't think he is damaged or disordered. He needs to know he'll be healthy, happy, and successful. Read on and listen to how these parents guided and nurtured their sons from their earliest, most vulnerable days in ways that gave them the best shot at life.

Brett—the Boy in Charge

Brett, at six feet, two inches tall, was dressed in jeans and a sweatshirt bearing the name of the college to which he was just accepted. He came into my office recently, as have many of the grown boys I've seen over the years, to talk through the biggest transition of his life. He had been accepted to a great college, one of his top choices, and had asked to defer enrollment for a semester so he can travel and work for a youth program before starting as a freshman. His face, now a man's, had traces of a beard and a strong jawline, but it retained the softer, younger features that I remembered when we first met.

Brett had his first appointment with me when he was four years old. At that time he was quite a handful at home, constantly in motion, grabbing things, getting hurt as he careened around the house and scaled the furniture. He was so bossy with other kids that he couldn't get through a playdate. His mother was getting calls from his preschool almost every day. The teachers reported that Brett was too grabby and pushy with the other kids, and repeatedly broke safety rules, such as dashing into the street on the trip between the school and the playground each morning. His pediatrician, a seasoned child expert, told me at that time that Brett was surely a candidate for an ADHD diagnosis, but he didn't want to rush medication with such a young boy. This pediatrician asked me to help Brett, and to help his mom teach him to socialize without fighting and to prepare him for the social demands of kindergarten. Brett was very precocious, headstrong, and smart, but because of his developmental immaturity, he was one incident away from being asked to leave preschool.

I asked Brett what he remembers about those early sessions. The answer was, not much. "I remember playing Connect Four," he said. "And the puppets, and playing with the toys on your shelf." He laughed and added, "And running around not listening while my mom and you were talking." Unlike Brett, his mother, Stacey, remembers all the details of those difficult early years. "He was running circles around me, and raising his older sister had been so easy. She would listen to me," she told me. She remembered one visit to the pediatrician's office in particular. Brett was running everywhere, climbing, not listening, and the pediatrician turned to her and said, "You are such a good parent. You did such a good job with your daughter. But Brett, here, he's in charge, not you." What he meant was that Brett had his own personality, all kids do, and his style was that of a bulldozer.

Now that Brett was eighteen, he could look back and think about his early behaviors. "I was such a pain-in-the-butt child to handle," he recalled with a hint of pride in his voice. "For example, when my mom put me on the steps for a time-out, I didn't care. Everything that worked on a normal child didn't work on me. When she put my older sister on the stairs for a time-out, she'd cry and be very upset. Me? I'd run off and laugh. It didn't faze me one bit."

Brett remembered being wild at kindergarten, too. "I was always out of control, but I wasn't always shunned by the other kids because people liked being with someone who is overly energetic and a bit over the top. Working with you helped me figure out when it's okay to be that way and when it's not. But otherwise it's a cool way to be. Other kids like me, the way I am, sometimes in-your-face and confident."

I asked Brett what he thought it was like for his mom to raise him. There were many difficult times for her. Brett's forcefulness and energy were formidable, and she believed he was too pushy, grabby, and headstrong to get along with others, that he wouldn't ever develop a healthy empathy for others. Worse, she worried his behavioral problems would lead him to get bad grades and, later on, to experiment with alcohol and drugs, or to turn into an angry young man who lacks direction. She has a brother like that.

"My uncle," Brett said. "He's a wild man, too wild sometimes, and he never really got his life together. My mom used to be so scared I'd turn out like him. We kind of look alike, too. But we're very different. His parents just punished him and yelled at him. He never got any help. People didn't do that stuff back then. Things were different."

The help that Brett got from his mother, his teachers, and me taught him how to curb his impulses. In my office he worked on sitting quietly for two to three minutes at a time, not hitting when he was upset, not grabbing toys. Often at first, I removed Brett from my office when he flew into a tantrum because he didn't get his way. Now, I found myself sitting in front of a grown young man, listening to his thoughtful, insightful remembrances about his early problems in school. Brett had developed a great sense of personal direction and a real sense of empathy for others, especially his mother and her early struggles with him. "She was probably feeling very defeated back then. She didn't have any ideas left to try with me, so she needed help from an outside person like you," he said, then paused. "I was sometimes punching her or telling her that I hated her, and those were things she never experienced with my older sister. I think it scared her a bit, and maybe she felt lost as a parent with me."

Once Brett got back on track, once he and his mom learned to work with his style rather than against it, he was ready to grow up to be the intelligent and accomplished young man he is now.

What has always amazed me as a child psychologist is watching the transformations take place in these very young boys over the years, from wild and unfocused, or painfully shy and socially challenged, to productive young men who along the way worked out their kinks, upgraded their skills, and, with their parents' hard work, brought out the best aspects in themselves. Brett, like many other boys, admitted to me the importance of how having strong, firm, but fair parenting helped guide him through those earlier years and into the man he is today. He told me, "I needed to learn to control myself. Those time-outs in my room were the only thing that worked." Brett knows that those consistent, strong boundaries helped mold him into a better man. He credits those boundaries for giving him other skills. "I learned ways to just be able to step back and look at a situation in my life and understand its relevance. I also learned to have a better awareness of other people's views and feelings and what those mean."

Just when I thought Brett couldn't possibly show greater self-awareness and deeper sensitivity, he began to talk about his new girlfriend. "I really like being with my girlfriend," he said. "With her, I can be tender and understanding and also silly (not as silly as with some of my guy friends; that can be over the top). I can be a different guy with her."

These words came from the same boy who once threw toys at other kids, pushed them down, and screamed, "I hate you!" to anyone, kid or adult, he felt got in his way.

Brett told me about his summer job and his excitement about this coming semester. Both of these were opportunities he applied for on his own. "I'm taking the first semester off freshman year to do a national outdoor leadership school program," he said, then recounted his reasons for choosing this program. "There are lots of important stuff they stress in this program, like leadership skills and the need for time management. And you learn these things in an outdoor setting, where you can't just fix it later or ignore things. If I can translate that to my schoolwork in college later on, like not blow off a paper, it will be a real big help for me."

Even though I don't work with Brett anymore in a formal way, he still talks to me about his challenges. He's concerned about his tendency to procrastinate with his schoolwork. Many adults I know confess this same problem. But Brett wants to change his behavior, and he is ready to identify his own problems and work on them. Although he hasn't settled on a college major yet, he is already considering several possible career paths, including planning for internships or graduate school. He has really grown up.

Listening to Brett's measured and well thought through ideas, I couldn't help but wonder where the impulsive, live-in-the-moment kid went. I think those parts of him are still inside the grown young man. Rather than impulsive, he has become playful, fun-loving, and willing to grab at things in the world he loves. I would love for parents I work with to see this young man and how much he has changed. I want to tell them that their impulsive little boy who struggles at playdates and climbs the furniture and grabs at everything can mature into the man who grabs at opportunities and sets aggressive goals for himself and draws friends to him with his confidence and charm.

Before Brett left, we agreed that he can e-mail or call me anytime, and that there is no good-bye between us. I told him the best part of my job is watching guys like him leave and come back from time to time to discuss their achievements and struggles, as all young adults have to face: separating from home and parents, getting through college, exploring intimate relationships, learning to have fun but not to overdo it, making informed and intelligent decisions around socializing, making safe decisions about drinking, and finding a professional direction that is attainable and fulfilling.

We knocked knuckles, then shook hands, and Brett reached to give me a hug. Before Brett left, he had a few last words. Sometimes kids share their most profound thoughts and feelings when they are about to head out the door.

"It's good to try new experiences," he said, thinking about the future. "You should keep an open mind—and to stay aware of others around you and how you affect them."

"Growing up is hard," I said to him. "You did a great job! I have no reservations that you have all the tools you need to go forward."

He thought about that and said, "Yeah. You're right. It's not impossible! Growing up is tough, but it worked for me!" He laughed. "It's going to be hard and different sometimes, but very doable."

Kenny—Mr. Inflexible

Kenny, who is eighteen now, had to stretch his memory to recall the very first time he and I met. I told him the year, and he looked surprised. "I can't believe you knew me when I was four! No way," he said. Kenny has grown into a muscular and handsome young man. His parents adopted him from Thailand when he was just a few months old. He has no other siblings, so he was affectionately called the "King of Siam" by his mother, in reference to his take-no-prisoners, grab-at-the-world temperament. When he came to visit me recently, he brought his mom along. She sat next to him on the sofa in my office and readily jumped into the conversation with her memories of that first visit. "You were tearing up the office; you were into everything, opening all Tony's drawers," she told Kenny. She turned to me to say, "I'll never forget what you said to me. You watched him, smiling, and told me you could tell that he is active and smart. You said, 'Watch out. He's going to give you trouble,' which I already knew. But you also told me that he was going to be great at whatever he chooses to do. You said, 'When he does something, he'll do it 100 percent,' which was a big help to hear." Kenny's mother also remembered another thing that I often tell moms to do. I told her to imagine Kenny as a successful grown man, thanking his parents when he wins a major award or reaches a huge milestone. Who knows, maybe the Nobel Prize. Moms look at me like I'm crazy. I can tell they're saying to themselves, "We can't get him to stop hitting other kids, to look us in the eye, to complete a sentence, to get through a whole day in school. Don't talk to me about the Nobel Prize!" But it works, especially on those really tough days when you want to give up. Imagine your son grown and happy and thanking you for doing your best and giving him those pushes when he needed them. "You told us that," Kenny's mother said, "and it was funny to hear at the time, but I thought of that so often, and it really helped me get through difficult times to think of him older, doing well, and knowing we were all going to be happy at some point."

From day one Kenny was a powerful and challenging child. His mother recalled him as an infant, while Kenny, embarrassed, rolled his eyes. "We noticed almost from the time he came to live with us that he would have days when he was in a bad mood, all day, for no apparent reason." She continued, "Nothing seemed to be right for him, even if he had a nap or got to play outside, or later when he was a bit older and could play at the playground. It was like he got up on the wrong side of the bed some days. Then the next day he would be fine."

Kenny was so active and forceful that he always seemed to be getting hurt. When he was very little, he liked to knock things over when he got angry. Before he was two years old he had pulled his solid oak highchair over on top of himself. His mother took him to the emergency room, where Kenny was treated for a big bump on his forehead. "He was racing around the ER for hours while we were waiting to get seen, playing with the other kids and having a ball," she said.

In my office, Kenny protested at this point, insisting that he couldn't have been that bad. His mom smiled at that and remembered: "He had a lot of temper tantrums. And he didn't do time-outs, at least not in the way all the experts tell you to. When I tried to put him into a time-out, he wouldn't sit. Then I had to hold him. Then he'd rock the chair while sitting in it and move it, actually walking the chair across the room. We tried the bottom of the stairs, but I had to hold him there, too." It was a couple of years before Kenny would sit in a time-out without needing to be held in place, and even longer before he could do it without having one of his parents sitting next to him to supervise. "Even then he would entertain himself with shadow puppets on the stairwell wall. It didn't seem to faze him a bit," said his mom.

Given the amount of time he spent misbehaving at home, Kenny's parents were justified in worrying that he wouldn't get along in school, but here he surprised them. He was able to sit and listen to his preschool and kindergarten teachers. At school, his other side came through, the one that was dazzlingly bright, impish, clever, and happy. His teachers called him "Mr. Adorable," which astonished his parents. At home, though, Kenny always felt comfortable and safe enough to release his strong personality. This is a common profile among many stubborn, strong-willed boys. They can hold it together and perform remarkably well in very structured environments, such as school, but in the relaxed environment of their homes, they push back on everything and try to be in charge.

Boys like Kenny need their parents to double up their efforts at discipline and maintain clear, high standards for behavior. They have to use immediate consequences and deliver those consequences whenever their standards are violated. Parents can't argue with these boys, or explain their reasons, or give warnings, because all that will make parents look weak, and it will make the rules seem like points of negotiation when they are not. Strong-willed boys like Kenny love the challenge of getting away with something, and the back-and-forth of arguing. This is not a defect in his character; it's not a sign of a budding master criminal. This is part of his strength as a person. I tell parents that they happen to have a little boy who is going to be exhausting at first. It gets easier. And the man who grows up out of this boy is going to be astonishing. He will be able to access all the attributes of Mr. Adorable, yet he will have an inner strength, an ability to assess situations. He won't be manipulated or pushed around.

In the meantime, simple, nonverbal consequences work best to reinforce your rules. Kenny's mom had a terrible time getting him to go to his room for his Time-Away when he'd done something wrong. He wanted to argue about it; he wanted to convince his parents that they'd misunderstood, that they were being too harsh with him. I told his mother that if he wouldn't go to his room, rather than argue, she and her husband should leave the room themselves. Leave the scene of the argument. To a parent, this often feels like surrender. "How will he know that I'm mad if I can't make him do what he doesn't want to do?" these parents ask. I tell them to try it. Kenny's mom and dad did it one time. "We found ourselves arguing with him in the living room, so we just turned around, went into our room, and closed the door. There was silence for several minutes. I would have loved to see the look on his face. Then we actually heard him leave the living room and go to his room," she said, and the astonishment is still clear in her voice. After that, it was easier to just tell him to go, and he would go to his room.

During many sessions, I worked with Kenny's parents to make sure they were working together, staying on the same page with discipline. This is crucial with a smart and strong-willed boy like Kenny. These boys are adept at splitting their parents, working one against the other. They seem to have a sixth sense about which parent is the weakest in any situation. Parents who aren't attuned to this technique will begin to argue with each other and disagree on rules or punishments. Meanwhile, a guy like Kenny will sail through the cracks unscathed, feeling proud and satisfied that he got his way and that he won, that he is in charge. Solidarity is the only foil for this.

In my office his mother and I talked about these episodes and about Kenny's love of power plays at home right in front of him. He seemed pleased by our descriptions. Then he leaned over and hugged his mom, giving her a great compliment. "She puts up with me and loves me," he said.

Kenny had other developmental issues aside from discipline problems at home. Although he behaved well in school, or tried to, he still had lots of trouble sitting still in class, especially during story time. He was often impatient during lessons, particularly those in which he had to answer questions out loud. He seemed unable to understand instructions in school and acted out when he was confused. A neighbor suggested that he should get tested for ADHD, something that was then generally called ADD, but Kenny's mother resisted. "It was the age of ADD," she said. "Everyone had it, and everyone was getting diagnosed with it. I didn't like the way it was being given out so freely." She got Kenny tested by a reputable neuropsychologist, who found that Kenny was testing below normal levels in his verbal and language comprehension skills, despite the fact that his IQ was very high. Kenny showed ADHD-like behaviors only when asked to listen to instructions and respond by speaking out loud. He stayed focused and could sit and work on art projects or look at books when he wasn't using language in a back-and-forth way. The neuropsychologist also said that Kenny was acting up because he was stressed, because language tasks were a challenge for him. They frustrated him, making him feel that he would look incompetent. Kenny's mom understood Kenny's high activity was about energy and interest, and frustration, but that he was always directed and purposeful. Following the neuropsychologist's recommendations, she took him to an audiologist to get his hearing evaluated. The evaluation showed a measurable hearing loss, and further speech evaluations showed problems processing sounds and words. That led to seeing an ear, nose, and throat specialist, who prescribed a hearing aid and speech therapy to resolve the problem.

"Soon after getting all that straightened out," she said, "we met with the director of special education and the school principal just before Kenny entered the first grade. We gave them all the evaluations and reports and asked for the accommodations the audiologist recommended, namely, a particular type of speaker system for his classroom. This was flatly refused. The special ed director went on to make the stupid remark that any such special accommodation wasn't needed because Kenny wasn't wearing a hearing aid at the moment. He wasn't because he hadn't gotten it yet! Overall, dealing with the school system was frustrating," she said. "Things are better now because that was many years ago. Parents and teachers are better informed of ways to help kids with all sorts of problems."

I worked with Kenny and his parents on and off until he was six years old. After that I didn't see them with much regularity until he turned fourteen. His strong, powerful personality rose up very forcefully as he entered his teens. He had the natural urge all young men feel to be independent and take control of their own lives. In most boys it's a difficult time, with many challenges to authority and pushing limits, but with Kenny, it went much further.

Kenny often threatened to run away if he didn't get his way. I put a plan in place to help the family stay in control and to empower his parents. It sounded drastic at the time, but once I explained my reasoning, they agreed to try it. I coached them to reach out to their local police department and enlist some reasonable support and help. So many officers like to work with good kids in their communities and use their power and authority to keep them safe, and to remind them to respect their parents and teachers, until these strong-willed kids get through all their powerful and confusing adolescent issues.

"I remember when they threatened me with the cops," he said, "I never believed them. It was over something that I didn't think was a big deal. It was all over my video games, because I wouldn't shut them off when I was supposed to. My parents were probably just fed up with me. And then one day an officer actually came to the house. He came up to my room, knocked on the door, and said to me, 'Get up.' I was lying on my bed in my room. Wow! I was fourteen years old. It was a really rough time back then. I just wanted to leave the house and not come back because I thought my parents were too controlling of my life.

"The cop and I talked. He was really a nice guy actually. He said, 'You have to listen to your parents.' It actually helped me a lot. It put me back in my shoes. I was pretty shaken up by it and felt a bit betrayed, but maybe they were worried about me."

Kenny paused, then brought up career possibilities. During his freshman year in high school, he looked into joining the Marines. "But that's serious combat, and I'm not sure I want to take those risks," he said Being a police officer sounds better to him. "I'm interested in guns and upholding the law, trying to push people into doing the right thing," he explained. "The world needs laws and cops. It would be scary out there without them." He wants to study criminal justice in college, then go to the police academy.

I was reminded of conversations I had with Kenny's mom many times in the past, that guys like Kenny are natural-born leaders and will seek out positions of power and authority. That's why they slam their heads against authority figures so strong early on. They want to grab the power early and are trying to identify with what they would like to become as they mature.

Kenny became a natural leader in high school, but he is also a caring guy who likes to work with young kids. He has worked as a counselor at a summer camp. "I get my own table with kids who are about eight and nine years old. Last year, I was working with six- to seven-year-olds who would not listen at all," he said, sounding like a frustrated parent. At this camp, Kenny is responsible for getting a band of rambunctious young kids to and from their activities, their lunch, and their snacks. He encourages them to try new things, keeps them in line, and cleans up after them, and he loves it. Here his charm and strength work well together. "I like them," he told me. "They make me happy. I always wanted to have a kid. Of course, I'll wait to get my life worked out first," he said. Then he added, "I think I'd want a kid to be like me, someone you can teach to have morals and values you believe in."

This was a great opportunity to ask Kenny what advice he would give parents trying to raise a boy like him. "Know that you are in charge and push your kids to listen to you and be behaved, but let them know you are looking out for them and love them," he said. "Rewards are so important. You want to make sure the kids know they are doing something right. My mom used to do that, like give me money as a reward when I shared, was being nice to people, being polite, looking out for people. And try to let kids do things on their own at certain ages. Let them go at the age when they are ready. When I was ready to get my driving permit at sixteen, I pushed, and my parents let me do it. It let me be more independent. A permit is a big responsibility and a privilege, but I was ready and needed my parents to see I was ready for that."

Ben—the Worrier

Ben is a twenty-one-year-old senior away at college who called me recently to talk through some difficulties he was having. Since Ben moved away from home, he checks in with me from time to time, mostly about challenges guys his age typically face, such as keeping up academically, handling roommate problems, and deciding what to do after he graduates from college. This time, however, he was calling about problems with his girlfriend. He thought he was heading for a break-up, and naturally this upset him.

These check-ins are common in my work with grown boys, many of whom I have known since they were four or five years old. When up against an emotional wall or facing a major life decision, they reach out to get an older guy's perspective. They don't like to talk long, and they get right down to business. Most often they are seeking reassurance that what they are experiencing is normal and that they will be okay. They want direct advice, what to do and what to avoid doing, rather than hashing out their feelings or exploring options at length. Being a therapist, however, I don't let them off the hook so easily. I press them to do the work themselves, reminding them they generally have all the knowledge and skills to solve their own problems.

Ben and I discussed some of the problems he had been having in his relationship, mostly taking care of his girlfriend too much and not spending enough time apart from her. He has historically had a very hard time being alone, something he's struggled with since middle school years. After a few minutes of talking, he came to the conclusion that maybe he doesn't need to do anything drastic. Maybe he can take a wait-and-see approach with his girlfriend. I concurred, happy he had arrived at what I also think is the best course of action, which in this case is no action. Because Ben is a fix-it type guy, everything from squeaky hinges to complicated circuitry panels, he has a hard time letting minor conflicts play out. When he thinks a friendship or relationship is headed in the wrong direction, he tries to fix it, to adjust it. He has never gone with the flow, unlike his older brother, who is affectionately referred to as Mr. Laid Back in his family. Ben likes to range far into the future in his imagination to explore all possible worst-case scenarios in order to prevent them, rather than waiting and seeing how things will turn out. This type of mind makes Ben a high-achieving student, and a brilliant troubleshooter when it comes to computers or anything mechanical, but it also makes him an emotional, overreactive guy who can worry too much.

I think back to our first meeting when Ben was six. At that time his mother wanted Ben to get help adjusting to a recent diagnosis of severe

dyslexia. He had struggled since preschool with recognizing written
letters and learning to read words, as many young boys normally do,
but his struggles didn't go away with practice. After extensive testing,
it was determined that he had a neurologically based problem processing written language. We tried to help Ben understand that his brain
worked differently than those of other kids, but that he was just as
smart as or smarter than anyone else. That turned out to be an understatement. As Ben moved through his early grades at a school that
specialized in learning disabilities, it became apparent he was a gifted
kid. His drive to prove that he was as good as, if not better than, everyone around him pushed his performance up beyond most other kids in
his class. Where many kids with dyslexia, mostly boys, get frustrated
to the point where they give up, and often underachieve, Ben did the
opposite. He doubled and tripled his efforts. This strong drive to be
the best has carried him all the way to becoming a science major with
top grades at a very competitive college.

Ben's childhood had another major turn of events. At age eleven,
he left private grade school and enrolled in public school. His parents
felt that he was ready to return to a regular classroom, surrounded
by his peers. During that first year, Ben went from being a generally happy and well-adjusted youngster to a very worried and socially
shy middle school student. His new classroom was much larger. More
students meant more distractions, and these kids all knew each other
and already had established friendships. Ben struggled to make new
friends and preferred to be alone, playing and working on projects at
home. He had difficulty sleeping at night because he worried about bad
things happening to his parents and feared he'd be left all alone. Despite never having had early separation issues, he suddenly wanted his
mother around almost all the time and wouldn't consider a sleepover,
even at a relative's house.

Ben remembered those struggles in middle school very well: "Socializing was scary back when I was little. It was unfamiliar. It was a
lack of knowing what to do. I was a big fan of logic and science, and
people don't act logically. It was so hard trying to approach social situations like that. I had to learn to read people, and the only way was

through experience, but I was afraid to try. I had to force myself. It didn't improve until I went to college when I was away from my Mom and my family, and they couldn't jump in and make it easy for me, just fix everything."

There were times years ago when Ben was angry at his parents for pushing him to take positive risks when he was young, such as speaking up more in class, advocating for himself with teachers when he had a problem, joining student groups, and learning to go on overnight trips with his classmates. Now Ben sees why the adults pushed him developmentally, to practice being more independent and less afraid when it wasn't warranted.

"I could have stayed there at my old school, but it would have held me back," he told me. "It was time to move on and grow. I needed change, even though change frightened me. I wouldn't be at such a great school now or considering graduate school, maybe even medical school, if I had stayed in that learning disabilities program. As much as you don't want the challenge at the time, in the long run you can look back and realize you need to be challenged. I remember I was crying about it back then, leaving my old school, and even thinking my parents were hurting me. I hated them for what they were forcing me to do at the time. It was hard giving up friends and facing change. But it turns out the challenge was a good thing. It made me grow."

I contrast the eleven-year-old Ben with the young man who later left for college, choosing to attend a school over a thousand miles away. By pushing himself to change and take safe social risks, he faced his worries and fears directly. Along the way, he achieved something that was a long-held dream and earned a pilot's license. The irony wasn't lost on his mom, who once said to me, "He was glued to my side for years; now he flies planes? He used to freak out if I wanted to leave the house, never mind if I wanted to take a weekend trip with his dad, or if I wanted to visit some relatives out of state. He wanted to know that I was always here. I feared he'd never move out, or go to college away from home, let alone have the courage to go up in an airplane and fly it himself."

Ben loves his college. He told me that he has made his best friends there. He said that moving away from home was a great experience for him. It taught him again that change can be good.

Often I tell parents to think of their son years later and realize he will see things differently. They might even wish that their parents had pushed them harder to grow up. Ben said that being unable to read early on threw off his confidence and contributed to his worries about school. "I realize now that when you are young you can't screw your life up. One exam, one grade, it's not a big deal. No one cares how you did on some exam in fourth grade. Back then I wasted so much energy on worries that didn't add up to anything. In the long run it was a waste of energy and time when I did that. If you do one little thing wrong, you should dust yourself off and go on. If something seems a little scary, don't panic. Everything gets easier as time goes on, and everything is a learning opportunity."

This is inspiring, coming from a young man who spent the summer before his senior year at college working an internship at a company that is developing innovative medical products. During this internship, he lived on his own in an apartment in downtown Boston.

When Ben was a little boy, he always told me that he did not want to be a doctor. Ben's father is a doctor who works long hours, and Ben has always been adamant that he didn't want that lifestyle. Now he's not so sure. "I'm thinking about it very seriously, and combining my engineering background with medicine," he told me. "I called my dad up yesterday and talked with him about taking the MCATs and applying to med school. I also want to do something that helps people. I was so sure that I didn't want to become a doctor. And now ten, twelve years later, look at me, I'm probably becoming a doctor. Funny how things work out."

Ronny—Mr. Meltdown

I caught up with Doreen and her son, Ronny, at a coffee shop near their home in a small suburb outside Boston. When they walked in, I didn't recognize Ronny, now nineteen years old. Our first meeting had been when he was five, and I'd met with him on and off for five years.

Ronny had been a very tough young boy to raise and discipline.

He was prone to strong rages when frustrated, very active and impulsive, and struggled in school. Despite this, he was also very sweet, highly emotional, and sensitive. I used to think of him as a sensitive tornado. I've wondered over the years how things turned out for him. And here he was, a tall, stocky young man with a thick beard.

Ronny stepped up to shake my hand, and he smiled. "I remember you, yeah," he said in a deep and confident voice. We huddled around a small cafe table and reminisced. At first, the memories needed some prodding, but soon they started to flow. "I can kind of picture your office now, the toys, the waiting room," he announced to his mom's surprise. "Remember? There were those cool toys with beads on the wires that make different patterns. I got into that. Someone with ADD likes that kind of stuff, to be totally focused on something while doing other things, but it's not like I'm not paying attention to what's important."

Doreen confirmed that over the years Ronny always needed to have a radio or TV sports program on in the background while he was doing homework. "We tried it many different ways," she said, "but he did better with the background noise, as long as it wasn't a playoff game or a TV show that could fully distract him. That was a balancing act, so we had rules about what he could listen to. But there was no way Ronny could do any work in a silent room."

Ronny said he liked going to see me because it was like a playdate. I was surprised to hear that, because many of our meetings weren't fun. They involved Ronny having significant tantrums, after which he would lose the privilege of playing with certain toys or even sit in time-outs while I coached his mom on ways to work with his strong anger. Ronny had to see other professionals during the same time he was coming to my office.

Ronny told me that he remembered one pediatrician who specialized in neurologic disorders. I know the doctor he remembers. He's one of the best. In fact, it was this doctor that recommended that Ronny see someone like me and not solely rely on medications to deal with his ADHD. Yet Ronny's negative memory toward him is not unusual. It echoes what many grown boys have told me over the years, that they didn't like being made to feel that they had a disorder, or that there was something so seriously wrong with them that they needed to miss playdates and see a doctor who gave them pills. Still, Doreen felt that the diagnosis was helpful for her because it was such a relief.

Many parents tell me that a diagnosis does offer them reassurance that something is really wrong, that it's not their failure. That relief feels wonderful, as long as it's not followed by even more tension as the family obsesses over the disorder, assuming that every one of their son's difficult behaviors can be blamed on that one condition. I tell parents to remember that the brain is always developing, always changing. In Doreen's case, the doctor who made the diagnosis reinforced these ideas. He told her that Ronny needed more than a prescription. He needed more structured parenting to help guide him toward more positive behaviors at home and at school. While that meant more hard work for her and her husband, it also ensured that Ronny would learn to cope with his anger and frustration, things the medication wouldn't necessarily improve.

At the time, Doreen struggled most with Ronny's rages and tantrums. They were so bad that her husband often had to hold Ronny in his lap and restrain him from physically destroying the house or hurting himself. Ronny would struggle mightily and calm down only after he had fallen slack with exhaustion. Afterward, Ronny would always feel bad about having a tantrum and apologize. His tantrums were so legendary within the family that none of Doreen's in-laws or siblings would agree to babysit Ronny. "I had no support," she told me. "I would get sick to my stomach before family gatherings. They told me that my son was a brat and that it was my fault." This kind of attitude isolates so many moms who are already in crisis.

Ronny remembered those tantrums, but he saw them in a different light. "I couldn't visualize, couldn't see the effect I was having on my parents, or anyone, when I was in my rage zone," he said. "I was so young, and young kids only care about what they want at that moment. Then, when I got to eleven or twelve years old, I started to see the effect on my mom of getting into a rage like that, and that's when

I started to change on my own, because I now understood what I was doing to her. She was probably under terrible stress." He turned and looked at Doreen and added, "I understand that you went through a lot when I was younger, I drove you crazy, but all turned out well." He shrugged his broad shoulders. It is fairly common for boys to mature in this way when they reach twelve years old, because their brains are now capable of seeing the bigger picture of life. They can think in more abstract terms. They can reflect on what others might be feeling. Until then, they are locked in a much more concrete way of dealing with the world.

Even after he began to control his anger and his tantrums, Ronny continued to struggle in school because he had trouble organizing himself and staying focused in class. He was on an individual education program from his very first year in elementary school. The school pushed Doreen to get him tested and to accept special education services, and she readily agreed, knowing that he could benefit from extra tutoring in class.

Ronny agreed that schoolwork has always been difficult for him, yet he doesn't seem defeated or embarrassed by this admission. "I struggled through every year of school. I'm just a visual guy. I need to do things, and back then I couldn't sit through class," he said. Doreen agreed. "He had bad grades even when he really tried and applied himself, but we always knew that school wasn't the right fit for how he thinks, how he learns," she said. Doreen was one of those parents who worked well with the school system. She learned all about special education services and was a proactive advocate for her son. She never said, "Why me?" or blamed the school or blamed herself or Ronny for the situation. She just dealt with it cheerfully and tirelessly. "I was always kind and respectful when I advocated for my son. Never vinegar. Always honey. If you're not respectful, you can forget it. But if you're nice, school officials will look out for your child," she said. Eventually, she became president of the school's advisory council for special education. "It became clear to me that a parent has to find out how their child learns," she said. "Everyone learns differently."

Although school never became easy for him, and although Ronny struggled with his SAT testing, he told his parents that he wanted to go to college. In fact, he is currently in his sophomore year. Doreen and her husband had a wonderful response to this, given all their struggles with Ronny's schoolwork. "We told him that this is his decision and his life. If he could figure out a way to get into college, we would support him in any way we could. Ultimately, though, it was all up to him," she said. Ronny went to a small local college and set up an interview with someone in administration. He told his whole story and explained his poor grades and test scores, then described his dream of studying criminal justice. "He just blew the guy away in the interview, and the school decided to take a chance on him," said Doreen. Ronny's grades have been great so far. He earned a 3.8 during his first semester at college.

Possibly the most telling anecdote about Ronny concerns several of his friends from junior high. Ronny was always a well-liked kid in school, always a charmer to his teachers, and he had a wide circle of good friends. In junior high, several of those friends made what he calls "bad decisions." They experimented with alcohol and drugs, and a few of them escalated their drug use until they were completely out of control. Ronny never fell into that trap of peer pressure, and he even intervened with some of his friends, telling them that they needed to stop or get help. Eventually, he had to cut off some of these same friends because he didn't want to be influenced by them or to be associated with their behavior. It was a painful decision to make, and it took a lot of courage to stick to this decision. Lately, a few of these same friends have turned their lives around and have approached Ronny to reestablish old friendships because he is known as a solid, stable guy. I think it's wonderful that this same boy, who was once so full of rage and unable to control his impulses, has now grown up to be an anchor to other kids who are struggling to overcome their own problems with impulse control and substance abuse. Despite his past troubles, or perhaps because of them, he has become a model of stability to his peers.

Some Final Thoughts

I wish the parents who come to my office could meet Brett, Kenny, Ben, and Ronny. These four would show them that things turn out well for most young boys. When parents feel confident that their boy is going to grow up to be okay, they can relax a bit and enjoy the fleeting moments of their son's youth. In our hurried and stressful lives, it's easy to lose faith in the natural process of childhood development. Instead of worrying exclusively about what can go wrong in a boy's development, we should be offering a steady hand to guide and support him as he moves along.

Because I have worked with so many boys and parents over the years, I have come to appreciate what good parenting can accomplish in a child's life, especially with boys who are struggling with one or more developmental lags. Parents in my experience are eager to help their sons in any way they can. They are sometimes astonished when I give them the three basic tenets of parenting great boys: clear rules and boundaries; consequences before lectures; rewards for each milestone. But these work, and work well, because boys learn primarily by experience, and because boys remember experiences before words. Young boys can't just be told what to do; they need to beat their own path through boyhood and adolescence. Sure, in many cases, that path is going to look a little uneven. It's going to show some cul-de-sacs and detours. But most boys eventually get to where they're going.

Some boys do need extra help to plow through a difficult time in school or difficult behavioral challenges. These boys might benefit from inventive teaching, extra tutoring, or specific therapies that teach them new behaviors and foster their strengths. They need lots of practice with the skills they are trying to develop. They need opportunities to learn incrementally, the space to make errors and try new approaches. In this way, boys can gradually adjust to the demands around them. It's how they learn to make and keep friends, to get through a difficult homework assignment, to survive a bad school year, and it's what they will need when they face the many future challenges ahead of them.

It's clear that boys like Brett, Kenny, Ben, and Ronny never had a psychiatric disorder even though many adults pushed diagnoses and the use of medications when they were very young. While pills are sometimes helpful for some boys, these boys used them infrequently. Medications might have helped suppress impulses in the short run, but these boys still had to learn better ways to adapt to the demands of the real world without medication.

My real criticism of diagnoses and pills as the sole means for handling the challenge of raising boys in this climate of high expectations is that diagnoses fail to understand, and to celebrate, the individual boys themselves. Every boy I've worked with is a complex little guy, who has unique gifts and who hopes to succeed and to be accepted by friends and family. No diagnosis can fully describe the personalities of these boys. Although pills used judiciously in the short term might help a boy suppress impulses or calm hyperactive behaviors, they do not teach new ways of coping with challenges.

Listening to these boys' stories, it's also clear to me that these young men didn't want their parents to worry about them when they were very young. Worry did them no good. I see this in my practice all the time. I've noticed that when parents are too worried, they jump to conclusions that something serious may be wrong and focus exclusively on problems. They micromanage in hopes of helping, but what they end up doing is accidentally communicating to their sons that they are odd, weak, or, worse, damaged. That's not the best message to help a young boy build his reservoir of self-confidence and resilience.

Finally, unnecessary worry crowds out our ability to see the beautiful moments right in front of our eyes. One mom I know of a seven-year-old boy said it best: "I constantly worried about what would happen to him if I didn't do the right thing. I felt I had to stay on top of him all the time. But when I was able to pull back and just let him be, I started to see things differently. He taught me how to live in the moment. He taught me how to be playful, again, like I was when I was a little girl. He showed me how to stop worrying about all the silly, small things everyone worries about."

Acknowledgments

No idea becomes a manuscript and then a book without the advice and encouragement of many, many people. The authors wish to give thanks to those who helped parent this book.

Many thanks to Eve Bridburg, who first saw this idea as a two-sentence memo, championed it instantly, and would not let it go until it became a proposal. In fact, we're grateful to the whole rollicking gang at Zachary Schuster Harmsworth. Nancy Miller, former executive editor at HarperCollins, offered great enthusiasm for the book and invaluable editorial insights, alongside those about motherhood and boyhood. Additionally, we must thank the whole crew at HarperCollins, including Steve Ross, Margot Schupf, Mary Ellen O'Neill, Jean Marie Kelly, Paul Olsewski, and Molly Lindley.

Tony would like to thank several of his colleagues who lent their professional expertise: April Prewitt, Troy Carr, Melinda Crowley, Lauren Avery, Fred Rothbaum, Michele Millon, Susan Wadsworth, Stuart Goldman, and Brian Baker. Tony would also like to thank his family and close friends who were a great source of support and encouragement. A special thank you to Bill Munger, Scott Estey, Paul Napper, Karen Rao, and Skyeler McCaskill. Michelle would like to thank friend and teacher Jack Falla, who offered encouragement and sage advice and picked up many lunch tabs. Michelle would also like to thank her family: Larry, a wonderful partner and friend, and Garret and Samantha, who provide constant inspiration.

Finally, Tony would like to thank the countless parents, especially moms he has worked with but whom he cannot name. Their stories and insights have taught him a better path to understanding and raising young boys.

References

Most of what is discussed in this book is based on clinical experience and interviews with parents, educators, and mental health professionals. Scientific research was also a very important resource in guiding and informing our views.

Chapter 1: Your Problem Is Spelled B-O-Y

American Psychiatric Association. (2000). *Diagnostic and statistical manual of mental disorders* (4th ed., rev.). Washington, DC: Author.

Aparasu, R., Kemner, H., & Aparasu, A. (2001, June). *Trends in psychiatric illnesses in children in ambulatory settings: 1992–1998.* Poster session presented at the meeting of the Academy for Health Service Research and Health Policy, Atlanta, GA.

Duncan, G., Dowsett, C., Claessens, A., Magnuson, K., Huston, A., Klevanov, P., et al. (2006). School readiness and later achievement. *Developmental Psychology, 43,* 1428–1446.

Elkind, D. (2001). *The hurried child: Growing up too fast too soon* (3rd ed.). Cambridge, MA: Perseus.

Garland, E. J. (2004). Facing the evidence: Antidepressant treatment in children and adolescents. *Canadian Medical Association Journal, 170,* 489–491.

Gilliam, W. (2005). *Prekindergarteners left behind: Expulsion rates in state prekindergarten systems.* New Haven, CT: Yale Child Study Center.

Gimpel, G. A., & Kuhn, B. R. (2000). Maternal report of attention deficit hyperactivity disorder symptoms in preschool children. *Child: Care, Health and Development, 26,* 163–176.

Ginsburg, K. R. (2007). The importance of play in promoting healthy child development and maintaining strong parent–child bonds. *American Academy of Pediatrics, 119,* 182–191.

Hofferth, S. (2008). American children's outdoor and indoor leisure time. In E. Goodenough (Ed.), *A place for play* (pp. 41–44). Ann Arbor: University of Michigan Press.

Jensen, P. S., Arnold, L. E., Swanson, J. M., Vitiello, B., Abikoff, H. B., Greenhill, L. L., et al. (2007). Three-year follow-up of the NIMH MTA study. *Journal of the American Academy of Child and Adolescent Psychiatry, 46,* 989–1002.

Juster, F. T., Ono, H., & Stafford, F. P. (2004, November). *Changing times of American youth: 1981–2003.* Ann Arbor, MI: University of Michigan Institute for Social Research. Retrieved February 12, 2009, from http://www.umich.edu/news/Releases/2004/Nov04/teen_time_report.pdf

Kessler, R. C., Berglund, P., Demler, O., Jin, R., Merikangas, K. R., & Walters, E. E. (2005). Lifetime prevalence and age-of-onset distributions of DSM-IV disorders in the National Comorbidity Survey replication. *Archives of General Psychiatry, 62,* 593–602.

Lakhan, S. E., & Hagger-Johnson, G. E. (2007). The impact of prescribed psychotropics on youth. *Clinical Practice and Epidemiology in Mental Health.* Retrieved March 30, 2009, from http://www.cpementalhealth.com/content/3/1/21; doi: 10.1186/1745-0179-3-21

Moreno, C., Laje, G., Blanco, C., Jiang, H., Schmidt, A. B., & Olfson, M. (2007). National trends in the outpatient diagnosis and treatment of bipolar disorder in youth. *Archives of General Psychiatry, 64,* 1032–1039.

Olfson, M., Blanco, C., Liu, L., Moreno, C., & Laje, G. (2006). National trends in the outpatient treatment of children and adolescents with antipsychotic drugs. *Archives of General Psychiatry, 63,* 679–685.

Olfson, M., Gameroff, M. J., Marcus, S. C., & Jensen, P. S. (2003). National trends in the treatment of attention deficit hyperactivity disorder. *American Journal of Psychiatry, 160,* 1071–1077.

Pelham, W. E., & Fabiano, G. A. (2008). Evidence-based psychosocial treatment for attention deficit/hyperactivity disorder: An update. *Journal of Clinical Child and Adolescent Psychology, 37,* 184–214.

Pergams, O. R. W., & Zaradic, P. A. (2006). Is love of nature in the U.S. becoming love of electronic media? Sixteen-year downtrend in national park visits explained by watching movies, playing video games, Internet use, and oil prices. *Journal of Environmental Management, 80,* 387–393.

Pergams, O. R. W., & Zaradic, P. A. (2008). Evidence for a fundamental and pervasive shift away from nature-based recreation. *Proceedings from the National Academy of Sciences USA, 105,* 2295–2300.

Swanson, J., Greenhill, L., Wigal, T., Kollins, S., Stehli, A., Davies, M., et al. (2006). Stimulant-related reductions of growth rates in the PATS. *Journal of the American Academy of Child and Adolescent Psychiatry, 45,* 1304–1313.

U.S. Department of Education, National Center for Education Statistics. (2007, July). *Demographic and school characteristics of students receiving special education in the elementary grades.* Retrieved February 12, 2009, from http://nces.ed.gov/pubs2007/2007005.pdf

Zaradic, P. A., & Pergams, O. R. W. (2007). Videophilia: Implications for childhood development and conservation. *Journal of Development Processes, 2,* 130–144.

Zimmerman, M., Ruggero, C. J., Chelminski, I., & Young, D. (2008). Is bipolar disorder overdiagnosed? *Journal of Clinical Psychiatry, 69,* 935–940.

Zito, J. M., Derivan, A. T., Kratochvil, C. J., Safer, D. J., Fegert, J. M., & Greenhill, L. L. (2008). Off-label psychopharmacologic prescribing for children: History supports close clinical monitoring. *Child and Adolescent Psychiatry and Mental Health.* Retrieved March 30, 2009, from http://www.capmh.com/content/2/1/24; doi:10.1186/1753-2000-2-24

Zito, J. M., Safer, D. J., de Jong-van den Berg, L. T. W., Janhsen, K., Fegert, J. M., Gardner, J. F., et al. (2008). A three-country comparison of psychotropic medication prevalence in youth. *Child and Adolescent Psychiatry and Mental Health.* Retrieved March 30, 2009, from http://www.capmh.com/content/2/1/26; doi:10.1186/1753-2000-2-26

Zito, J. M., Safer, D. J., dos Reis, S., Gardner, J. F., Boles, M., & Lynch, F. (2000). Trends in the prescribing of psychotropic medications to preschoolers. *JAMA, 283,* 1025–1060.

Zito, J. M., Safer, D. J., dos Reis, S., Gardner, J. F., Magder, L., Soeken, K., et al. (2003). Psychotropic practice patterns for youth: A 10-year perspective. *Archives of Pediatrics and Adolescent Medicine, 157,* 17–25.

Chapter 2: Little Girls Aren't Like This

Baron-Cohen, S. (2005, August 8). Op-ed: The male condition. *New York Times,* p. 15.

Campbell, D. W., & Eaton, W. O. (1999). Sex differences in activity level of infants. *Infant and Child Development, 8,* 1–17.

Carr, M., Jessup, D. L., & Fuller, D. (1999). Gender differences in first-grade mathematics strategy use: Parent and teacher contributions. *Journal for Research in Mathematics Education, 30,* 20–46.

Connellan, J., Baron-Cohen, S., Wheelwright, S., Batki, A., & Ahluwalia, J. (2000). Sex differences in human neonatal social perception. *Infant Behavior and Development, 23,* 113–118.

Eaton, W. O., & Enns, L. R. (1986). Sex difference in human motor activity level. *Psychological Bulletin, 100,* 19–28.

Halpern, D. F., Benbow, C. P., Geary, D. C., Gur, R. C., Hyde, J. S., & Gernsbacher, M. A. (2007). The science of sex differences in science and mathematics. *Psychological Science in the Public Interest, 8,* 1–52.

Kimura, D. (2002, May 13). Sex differences in the brain. *Scientific American, 12,* 32–37.

Kindlon, D., & Thompson, M. (2000). *Raising Cain: Protecting the emotional life of boys.* New York: Ballantine Books.

Levine, S. C., Huttenlocher, J., Taylor, A., & Langrock, A. (1999). Early sex differences in spatial skill. *Developmental Psychology, 35,* 940–949.

Lowry, P. (1993). Privacy in the preschool environment: Gender differences in reaction to crowding. *Children's Environments, 10,* 46–61.

Trost, S. G., Pate, R. R., Sallis, J. F., Freedson, P. S., Taylor, W. C., Dowda, M., et al. (2002). Age amd gender differences in objectively measured physical activity in youth. *Medicine and Science in Sports and Exercise, 34,* 350–355.

Chapter 3: He Doesn't Have Any Friends

Brazelton, T. B., & Sparrow, J. D. (2002). *Touchpoints: Three to six.* Cambridge, MA: Da Capo Press.

Carducci, B. J. (1999). *Shyness: A bold new approach.* New York: HarperCollins.

Chess, S., & Thomas, A. (1996). *Temperament: Theory and practice.* New York: Brunner/Mazel.

Coplan, R. J., Rubin, K. H., & Findlay, L. C. (2006). Social and nonsocial play. In D. P. Fromberg & D. Bergen (Eds.), *Play from birth to twelve: Contexts, perspectives, and meanings* (2nd ed., pp. 75–86). New York: Garland.

Cox, A. J. (2006). *Boys of few words: Raising our sons to communicate and connect.* New York: Guilford Press.

de Rosnay, M., Cooper, P. J., Tsigaras, N., & Murray, L. (2006). Transmission of social anxiety from mother to infant: An experimental study using a social referencing paradigm. *Behaviour Research and Therapy, 44,* 1165–1175.

Hamaguchi, P. M. (2001). *Childhood speech, language, and listening problems* (2nd ed.). New York: John Wiley & Sons.

Hirsh-Pasek, K., & Golinkoff, R. M. (2008). Why play = learning. *Encyclopedia on Early Childhood Development.* Retrieved February 13, 2009, from http://www.ccl-cca.ca/NR/rdonlyres/62DD2BDF-0629-43FF-83BA-86CC5CE9CCB/0/HirshPasekGolinkoffANGxpCSAJE.pdf

Kagan, J., & Snidman, N. (2004). *The long shadow of temperament.* Cambridge, MA: Harvard University Press.

Piaget, J. (1962). *Play, dreams and imitation in childhood.* New York: Norton.

Snowling, M. J., Bishop, D. V. M., Stothard, S. E., Chipchase, B., & Kaplan, C. (2006). Psychosocial outcomes at 15 years of children with a preschool history of speech-language impairment. *Journal of Child Psychology and Psychiatry, 47,* 759–765.

Striano, T., & Rochat, P. (2000). Emergence of selective social referencing in infancy. *Infancy, 1,* 253–264.

Wood, J. J. (2006). Parental intrusiveness and children's separation anxiety in a clinical sample. *Child Psychiatry and Human Development, 37,* 73–87.

Chapter 4: He's a Bully

Arsenio, W. F., & Lemerise, E. A. (2004). Aggression and moral development: Integrating social information processing and moral domain models. *Child Development, 75,* 987–1002.

Bohnert, A. M., Crnic, K. A., & Lim, K. G. (2003). Emotional competence and aggressive behavior in school-age children. *Journal of Abnormal Child Psychology, 31,* 79–91.

Boxer, P., Goldstein, S. E., Musher-Eizenman, D., Dubow, E. F., & Heretick, D. (2005). Developmental issues in school-based aggression prevention from a social-cognitive perspective. *Journal of Primary Prevention, 26,* 383–400.

Cote, S. M., Vaillancourt, T., LeBlanc, J. C., Nagin, D. S., & Tremblay, R. E. (2006). The development of physical aggression from toddlerhood to pre-adolescence: A nationwide longitudinal study of Canadian children. *Journal of Abnormal Child Psychology, 34,* 71–85.

Epley, N., Morewedge, C. K., & Keysar, B. (2004). Perspective taking in children and adults: Equivalent egocentrism but differential correction. *Journal of Experimental Social Psychology, 40,* 760–768.

Espelage, D. L., & Swearer, S. M. (2003). Research on school bullying and victimization: What have we learned and where do we go from here? *School Psychology Review, 32,* 365–385.

Hastings, P. D., Zahn-Waxler, C., Robinson, J., Usher, B., & Bridges, D. (2000). The development of concern for others in children with behavior problems. *Developmental Psychology, 36,* 531–546.

Martinez, C. R., & Forgatch, M. S. (2001). Preventing problems with boys' noncompliance: Effects of a parent training intervention for divorcing mothers. *Journal of Consulting and Clinical Psychology, 69,* 416–428.

Orobio de Castro, B., Bosch, J. D., Veerman, J. W., & Koops, W. (2003). The effects of emotion regulation, attribution, and delay prompts on aggressive boys' social problem solving. *Cognitive Therapy and Research, 27,* 153–166.

Orpinas, P., & Horne, A. M. (2005). *Bullying prevention: Creating a positive school climate and developing social competence.* Washington, DC: American Psychological Association.

Patterson, G. R., Shaw, D. S., Snyder, J. J., & Yoerger, K. (2005). Changes in maternal ratings of children's overt and covert antisocial behavior. *Aggressive Behavior, 31,* 473–484.

Snyder, J., Cramer, A., Afrank, J., & Patterson, G. R. (2005). The contributions of ineffective discipline and parental hostile attributions of child misbehavior to the development of conduct problems at home and school. *Developmental Psychology, 41,* 30–41.

Chapter 5: He Won't Sit Still!

Berman, M. G., Jonides, J., & Kaplan, S. (2008). The cognitive benefits of interacting with nature. *Psychological Science, 19,* 1207–1212.

Cardon, G., Van Cauwenberghe, E., Labarque, V., Haerens, L., & De Bourdeaudhuij, I. (2008). The contribution of preschool playground factors in explaining children's physical activity during recess. *International Journal of Behavioral Nutrition and Physical Activity, 5.* Retrieved March 30, 2009, from http://www.ijbnpa.org/content/5/1/11; doi: 10.1186/1479-5868-5-11

Elkind, D. (2008, Spring). Can we play? *Greater Good Magazine, 4,* 14–17.

Finn, K., Johannsen, N., & Specker, B. (2002). Factors associated with physical activity in preschool children. *Journal of Pediatrics, 140,* 81–85.

Garcia, S. M., & Tor, A. (2008, August). *The N-Effect: More competitors and less competition.* Paper presented at the Academy of Management Conference, Anaheim, CA.

Ginsburg, H. J., Rogerson, K., Voght, E., Walters, J., & Bartels, R. D. (2007). Sex differences in children's physical risk-taking behaviors: Natural observations at the San Antonio Zoological Gardens. *North American Journal of Psychology, 9,* 407–414.

Hedstrom, R., & Gould, D. (2004). *Research in youth sports: Critical issues status.* East Lansing, MI: Michigan State University, Institute for the Study of Youth Sports.

Hofferth, S. L., & Sandberg, J. F. (2001). How American children spend their time. *Journal of Marriage and the Family, 63,* 295–308.

Kuo, F. E., & Taylor, A. F. (2004). A potential natural treatment for attention-deficit/hyperactivity disorder: Evidence from a national study. *American Journal of Public Health, 94,* 1580–1586.

Pellegrini, A. D, & Bohn, C. M. (2005). The role of recess in children's cognitive performance and school adjustment. *Educational Researcher, 34,* 13–19.

Ratey, J. J., & Hagerman, E. (2008). *Spark: The revolutionary new science of exercise and the brain.* New York: Little, Brown.

Tantillo, M., Kesick, C. M., Hynd, G. W., & Dishman, R. K. (2002). The effects of exercise on children with attention-deficit hyperactivity disorder. *Medicine and Science in Sports and Exercise, 34,* 203–212.

Taylor, A. F., & Kuo, F. E. (2009). Children with attention deficits concentrate better after walk in the park. *Journal of Attention Disorders, 12,* 402–409.

Taylor, A. F., Kuo, F. E., & Sullivan, W. C. (2001). Coping with ADD: The surprising connection to green play settings. *Environment and Behavior, 33,* 54–77.

U.S. Department of Education, National Center for Education Statistics. (2005, June). *Rates of computer and Internet use by children in nursery school and students in kindergarten through twelfth grade: 2003.* Retrieved February 12, 2009, from http://nces.ed.gov/pubs2005/2005111.pdf

Chapter 6: He Runs the Household

Ames, L. B. & Ilg, F. (1980). *Your two-year-old: Terrible or tender.* New York: Dell.

Risley, T. (2005). Montrose M. Wolf (1935–2004). *Journal of Applied Behavior Analysis, 38,* 279–287.

Sendak, M. (1988). *Where the wild things are.* New York: HarperCollins.

Staats, A. W. (1968). *Learning, language, and cognition.* New York: Holt, Rinehart & Winston.

Tulve, N. S., Jones, P. A., McCurdy, T., & Croghan, C.W. (2007). A pilot study using an accelerometer to evaluate a caregiver's interpretation of an infant or toddler's activity level as recorded in a time activity diary. *Research Quarterly for Exercise and Sport, 78,* 375–383.

Wolf, M. M., Risley, T., & Mees, H. (1964). Application of operant conditioning procedures to the behavior problems of an autistic child. *Behaviour Research and Therapy, 1,* 305–312.

Chapter 7: He Has to Win, or Else

Benenson, J. F., Antonellis, T. J., Cotton, B. J., Noddin, K. E., & Campbell, K. A. (2008). Sex differences in children's formation of exclusionary alliances under scarce resource conditions. *Animal Behaviour, 76,* 497–505.

Conti, R., Collins, M. A., & Picariello, M. L. (2001). The impact of competition on intrinsic motivation and creativity: Considering gender, gender segregation and gender role orientation. *Personality and Individual Differences, 31,* 1273–1289.

Elkind, D. (2007). *The power of play: Learning what comes naturally.* Cambridge, MA: Da Capo Press.

Morrongiello, B. A., & Rennie, H. (1998). Why do boys engage in more risk taking than girls? The role of attributions, beliefs, and risk appraisals. *Journal of Pediatric Psychology, 23,* 33–43.

Piaget, J. (1965). *The moral judgment of the child.* New York: The Free Press.

San Luis, N. B., & Stein, M. T. (2004). Lying, cheating, and stealing. In S. Parker, B. S. Zuckerman, & M. Augustyn (Eds.), *Developmental and behavioral pediatrics: A handbook for primary care* (2nd ed., pp. 227–230). Philadelphia, PA: Lippincott Williams & Wilkins.

Smith, S. L. (2005). *At what age do children start cheating?* Retrieved February 12, 2009, from http://clearinghouse.missouriwestern.edu/manuscripts/45.asp

Talwar, V., & Lee, K. (2008). Social and cognitive correlates of children's lying behavior. *Child Development, 79,* 866–881.

Chapter 8: He Wants to Be the Bad Guy

Bauer, K. L., & Dettore, E. (1997). Superhero play: What's a teacher to do? *Early Childhood Education Journal, 25,* 17–21.

Bergen, D. (2002). The role of pretend play in children's cognitive development. *Early Childhood Research and Practice, 4.* Retrieved February 12, 2009, from http://ecrp.uiuc.edu/v4n1/bergen.html

Gordon, J., King, N., Gullone, E., Muris, P., & Ollendick, T. H. (2007). Nighttime fears of children and adolescents: Frequency, content, severity, harm expectations, disclosure, and coping behaviours. *Behaviour Research and Therapy, 45,* 2464–2472.

Kirsh, S. J. (2006). *Children, adolescents, and media violence: A critical look at the research.* Thousand Oaks, CA: Sage Publications.

Logue, M. E., & Shelton, H. (2008). The stories bad guys tell: Promoting literacy and social awareness in preschool. *The Constructivist, 19.* Retrieved February 12, 2009, from http://www.odu.edu/educ/act/journal/index.html

Mechling, J. (2008). Gun play. *American Journal of Play, 1,* 192–209.

Merrill C. T., Owens, P .L., & Stocks, C. (2008, May). *Pediatric emergency department visits in community hospitals from selected states, 2005.* HCUP Statistical Brief 52. Agency for Healthcare Research and Quality. Retrieved February 12, 2009, from http://www.hcup-us.ahrq.gov/reports/statbriefs/sb52.jsp

Paley, V. G. (2004). *A child's work: The importance of fantasy play.* Chicago, IL: University of Chicago Press.

Parsons, A., & Howe, N. (2006). Superhero toys and boys' physically active and imaginative play. *Journal of Research in Childhood Education, 20,* 287–300.

Chapter 9: He's Suddenly Fragile

Brooks, R. B. (2005). The power of parenting. In S. Goldstein & R. B. Brooks (Eds.), *Handbook of resilience in children* (pp. 297–314). New York: Kluwer Academic/Plenum Publishers.

Harris, P. L. (2008). Children's understanding of emotions. In M. Lewis, J. M. Haviland-Jones, & L. F. Barrett (Eds.), *Handbook of Emotions* (pp. 320–331). New York: Guilford Press.

Lotan, N., & Yirmiya, N. (2002). Body movement, presence of parents, and the process of falling asleep in toddlers. *International Journal of Behavioral Development, 26,* 81–88.

Masten, A. S., & Gewirtz, A. H. (2006). Resilience in development: The importance of early childhood. In R. E. Tremblay, R. E. Barr, & D. V. Peters (Eds.), *Encyclopedia on Early Childhood Development.* Retrieved February 12, 2009, from http://www.child-encyclopedia.com/documents/Masten-GewirtzANGxp.pdf

McMurtry, C. M., McGrath, P. J., & Chambers, C. T. (2006). Reassurance can hurt: Parental behavior and painful medical procedures. *Journal of Pediatrics, 148,* 560–561.

Rubin, K. H., Cheah, C. S. L., & Fox, N. (2001). Emotion regulation, parenting and display of social reticence in preschoolers. *Early Education and Development, 12,* 97–115.

Seligman, M. (2007). *The optimistic child: A proven program to safeguard children against depression and build lifelong resilience.* New York: Houghton Mifflin Harcourt.

Tronick, E. (2006). The inherent stress of normal daily life and social interaction leads to the development of coping and resilience, and variation in resilience in infants and young children: comments on the papers of Suomi and Klebanov & Brooks-Gunn. *Annals of the New York Academy of Sciences, 1094,* 83–104.

Weinberg, M. K., Tronick, E. Z., Cohn, J. F., & Olsen, K. L. (1999). Gender differences in emotional expressivity and self-regulation during infancy. *Developmental Psychology, 35,* 175–188.

Chapter 10: He Hates School

Crick, N. R., Ostrov, J. M., Burr, J. E., Cullerton-Sen, C., Jansen-Yeh, E., & Ralston, P. (2006). A longitudinal study of relational and physical aggression in preschool. *Journal of Applied Developmental Psychology, 27,* 254–268.

Dee, T. S. (2006). The why chromosome: How a teacher's gender affects boys and girls. *Education Next, 6,* 69–75.

Gurian, M., & Stevens, K. (2007). *The minds of boys: Saving our sons from falling behind in school and life.* New York: John Wiley and Sons.

Holmes-Lonergan, H. A. (2003). Preschool children's collaborative problem-solving interactions: The role of gender, pair type and task. *Sex Roles, 48,* 505–517.

Hyun, E., & Tyler, M. (1999, April). *Examination of preschool teachers' biased perception on gender differences.* Paper presented at the annual conference of the American Educational Research Association, Montreal, Canada.

Nelson, B.G. (2002). *The importance of men teachers and why there are so few.* Minneapolis, MN: Men in Child Care and Elementary Education Project.

Ostrov, J. M., & Keating, C. F. (2004). Gender differences in preschool aggression during free play and structured interactions: An observational study. *Social Development, 13,* 255–277.

Sandberg, A., & Pramling-Samuelsson, I. (2005). An interview study of gender difference in preschool teacher's attitudes toward children's play. *Early Childhood Education Journal, 32,* 297–305.

Sax, L. (2001). Reclaiming kindergarten: Making kindergarten less harmful to boys. *Psychology of Men and Masculinity, 2,* 3–12.

Shannon, D. (1998). *No, David!* New York: Scholastic.

Chapter 11: The Teacher Thinks He Needs Testing

Centers for Disease Control and Prevention. (February, 2007). Prevalence of autism spectrum disorders—Autism and Developmental Disabilities Monitoring Network, 14 sites, United States, 2002. Retrieved February 12, 2009, from http://www.cdc.gov/MMWR/preview/mmwrhtml/ss5601a2.htm

Cleary, M., & English, G. (2005). The small schools movement: Implications for health education. *Journal of School Health, 75,* 243–247.

Coury, D. L., & Nash, P. L. (2003). Epidemiology and etiology of autistic spectrum disorders difficult to determine. *Pediatric Annals, 32,* 696–700.

Families and Advocates Partnership for Education (2001, October). *School accommodations and modification, FAPE-27.* Minneapolis, MN: PACER Center.

Filipek, P. A., Accardo, P. J., Ashwal, S., Baranek, G. T., Cook, E. H., Dawson, G., et al. (2000). Practice parameter: Screening and diagnosis of autism—Report of the Quality Standards Subcommittee of the American Academy of Neurology and the Child Neurology Society. *Neurology, 55,* 468–479.

Fletcher, J. M., Francis, D. J., Morris, R. D., & Lyon, G. R. (2005). Evidence-based assessment of learning disabilities in children and adolescents. *Journal of Clinical Child and Adolescent Psychology, 34,* 506–522.

Ford, L., & Dahinten, V. S. (2005). Use of intelligence tests in the assessment of preschoolers. In D. P. Flanagan & P. Harrison (Eds.) *Contemporary intellectual assessment: Theories, tests, and issues* (pp. 487–503). New York: Guilford Press.

Fuchs, D., & Deshler, D. D. (2007). What we need to know about responsiveness to intervention (and shouldn't be afraid to ask). *Learning Disabilities Research and Practice, 22,* 129–136.

Gardner, H. (1993). *Multiple intelligences: The theory in practice.* New York: Basic Books.

Havey, J. M., Olson, J. M., McCormick, C., & Cates, G. L. (2005). Teachers' perceptions of the incidence and management of attention-deficit hyperactivity disorder. *Applied Neuropsychology, 12,* 120–127.

Hindson, B., Byrne, B., Fielding-Barnsley, R., Newman, C., Hine, D.W., & Shankweiler, D. (2005). Assessment and early instruction of preschool children at risk for reading disability. *Journal of Educational Psychology, 97,* 687–704.

Lyytinen, H., Erskine, J., Tolvanen, A., Torppa, M., Poikkeus, A.-M., & Lyytinen, P. (2006). Trajectories of reading development; a follow-up from birth to school age of children with and without risk for dyslexia. *Merrill-Palmer Quarterly, 52,* 514–546.

Montessori, M. (1964). *The Montessori method.* New York: Schocken Books.

Mosteller, F. (1996). The Tennessee study of class size in the early school grades. *Critical Issues for Children and Youths, 5,* 113–147.

National Association of State Directors of Special Education. (2006, May). *Myths about response to intervention (RtI) implementation.* Retrieved February 12, 2009, from http://www.nasdse.org/Portals/0/Documents/Download%20Publications/Myths%20about%20RtI.pdf

Nye, B., Hedges, L. V., & Konstantopoulos, S. (2000). The effects of small classes on academic achievement: The results of the Tennessee class size experiment. *American Educational Research Journal, 37,* 123–151.

Pritchard, I. (1999). *Reducing class size: What do we know?* Washington, DC: U.S. Department of Education, National Institute on Student Achievement, Curriculum and Assessment, Office of Educational Research and Improvement.

Rutter, M. (2005). Incidence of autism spectrum disorders: Changes over time and their meaning. *Acta Paediatrica, 94,* 2–15.

Rutter, M., Caspi, A., Fergusson, D., Horwood, L. J., Goodman, R., Maughan, B., et al. (2004). Sex differences in developmental reading disability: New findings from 4 epidemiological studies. *JAMA, 291,* 2007–2012.

U.S. Department of Education. (2006). *IDEA regulations: Individualized education program.* Retrieved February 12, 2009, from http://idea.ed.gov/explore/view/p/%2Croot%2Cdynamic%2CTopicalBrief%2C10%2C

Chapter 12: He Has Already Been Labeled

Aboraya, A., Rankin, E., France, C., El-Missiry, A., & John, C. (2006). The reliability of psychiatric diagnosis revisited: The clinician's guide to improve the reliability of psychiatric diagnosis. *Psychiatry, 3,* 41–50.

Baron, I. S. (2004). *Neuropsychological evaluation of the child.* New York: Oxford University Press.

Barsky, A. J., Saintfort, R., Rogers, M. P., & Borus, J. F. (2002). Nonspecific medication side effects and the nocebo phenomenon. *JAMA, 287,* 622–627.

Bolton, D., & Perrin, S. (2007). Evaluation of exposure with response-prevention for obsessive compulsive disorder in childhood and adolescence. *Journal of Behavior Therapy and Experimental Psychiatry, 39,* 11–22.

Bornstein, M. H., Hahn, C. S., Bell, C., Haynes, O. M., Slater, A., Golding, J., et al. (2006). Stability in cognition across early childhood: A developmental cascade. *Psychological Science, 17,* 151–158.

Campbell, S. (2002). *Behavior problems in preschool children: Clinical and developmental issues* (2nd ed.). New York: Guilford Press.

Canivez, G. L., & Watkins, M. W. (1999). Long-term stability of the Wechsler Intelligence Scale for Children–Third Edition among demographic subgroups: Gender, race/ethnicity, and age. *Journal of Psychoeducational Assessment, 17,* 300–313.

Cantwell, D. P., & Baker, L. (1989). Stability and natural history of DSM-III childhood diagnoses. *Journal of the American Academy of Child and Adolescent Psychiatry, 28,* 691–700.

Centers for Disease Control and Prevention. (2005). *Attention-deficit hyperactivity disorder, symptoms of ADHD.* Retrieved February 19, 2009, from http://cdc.gov/NCBDDD/adhd/symptom.htm

Conners, C. K., Sitarenios, G., Parker, J. D., & Epstein, J. N. (1998). The revised Conners' Parent Rating Scale (CPRS-R): Factor structure, reliability, and criterion validity. *Journal of Abnormal Child Psychology, 26,* 257–268.

Conners, C. K., Sitarenios, G., Parker, J. D., & Epstein, J. N. (1998). Revision and restandardization of the Conners' Teacher Rating Scale (CTRS-R): Factor structure, reliability, and criterion validity. *Journal of Abnormal Child Psychology, 26,* 279–291.

Foa, E. B., Liebowitz, M. R., Kozak, M. J., Davies, S., Campeas, R., Franklin, M. E., et al. (2005). Randomized, placebo-controlled trial of exposure and ritual prevention, clomipramine, and their combination in the treatment of obsessive-compulsive disorder. *American Journal of Psychiatry, 162,* 151–161.

Freeman, J. B., Choate-Summers, M. L., Moore, P. S., Garcia, A. M., Sapyta, J. J., Leonard, H. L, & Franklin, M. E. (2007). Cognitive behavioral treatment for young children with obsessive-compulsive disorder. *Biological Psychiatry, 61,* 337–343.

Groopman, J. (2007). *How doctors think.* New York: Houghton Mifflin.

Jensen, A. L., & Weisz, J. R. (2002). Assessing match and mismatch between practitioner-generated and standardized interview-generated diagnoses for clinic-referred children and adolescents. *Journal of Consulting and Clinical Psychology, 70,* 158–168.

Jensen, P. S., Knapp, P., & Mrazek, D. A. (2006). *Toward a new diagnostic system for child psychopathology: Moving beyond DSM.* New York: Guilford Press.

Kim, E. Y., & Miklowitz, D. J. (2002). Childhood mania, attention deficit hyper-activity disorder and conduct disorder: A critical review of diagnostic dilemmas. *Bipolar Disorders, 4,* 215–225.

Lewczyk, C. M., Garland, A. F., Hurlburt, M. S., Gearity, J., & Hough, R. L. (2003). Comparing DISC-IV and clinician diagnoses among youths receiving public mental health services. *Journal of the American Academy of Child and Adolescent Psychiatry, 42,* 349–356.

Mannuzza, S., & Klein, R. G. (2000). Long-term prognosis in attention-deficit/hyperactivity disorder. *Child and Adolescent Psychiatric Clinics of North America, 9,* 711–726.

March, J. S., Silva, S., Petrycki, S., Curry, J., Wells, K., Fairbank, J., et al. (2007). The Treatment for Adolescents with Depression Study (TADS): Long-term effectiveness and safety outcomes. *Archives of General Psychiatry, 64,* 1132–1143.

Mayberg, H. S., Silva, J. A., Brannan, S. K., Tekell, J. L., Mahurin, R. K., McGinnis, S., et al. (2002). The functional neuroanatomy of the placebo effect. *American Journal of Psychiatry, 159,* 728–737.

McCabe, S. E., Knight, J. R., Teter, C. J., & Wechsler, H. (2005). Non-medical use of prescription stimulants among U.S. college students: Prevalence and correlates from a national survey. *Addiction, 100,* 96–106.

National Institutes of Mental Health. (2007, November). *Brain matures a few years late in ADHD, but follows normal pattern.* Retrieved February 12, 2009, from http://www.nimh.nih.gov/science-news/2007/brain-matures-a-few-years-late-in-adhd-but-follows-normal-pattern.shtml

Neyens, L. G. J., & Aldenkamp, A. P. (1997). Stability of cognitive measures in children of average ability. *Child Neuropsychology, 3,* 161–170.

Reynolds, C. R., & Kamphaus, R. W. (2004). *The Behavior Assessment System for Children* (2nd ed.). Circle Pines, MN: American Guidance Service Publishing.

Shaw, P., Eckstrand, K., Sharp, W., Blumenthal, J., Lerch, J. P., Greenstein, D., et al. (2007). Attention-deficit/hyperactivity disorder is characterized by a delay in cortical maturation. *Proceedings of the National Academy of Sciences USA, 104,* 19649–19654.

Wakefield, J. C., Schmitz, M. F., First, M. B., & Horwitz, A. V. (2007). Extending the bereavement exclusion for major depression to other losses: Evidence from the National Comorbidity Survey. *Archives of General Psychiatry, 64,* 433–440.

Wakschlag, L. S., Leventhal, B. L., Briggs-Gowan, M. J., Danis, B., Keenan, K., Hill, C., et al. (2005). Defining the "disruptive" in preschool behavior: What diagnostic observation can teach us. *Clinical Child and Family Psychology Review, 8,* 183–201.

Wechsler, D. (2003). *Wechsler Intelligence Scale for Children* (4th ed.). San Antonio, TX: Psychological Corp.

Wechsler, D. (1989). *Wechsler Preschool and Primary Scale of Intelligence–Revised.* San Antonio, TX: Psychological Corp.

Index

accommodations in the classroom, 205, 215–18
  help in the classroom, 216–17
  more time for work, 216
  preferential seating, 216
  resource room, 217
  when to refuse, 217–18
actions and consequences, 96–97, 141, 171–72
activities for fidgeting, 76–77, 79–86
  older boys, 82–86
  younger boys, 80–82
ADD (attention deficit disorder), 208, 239–40, 252
ADHD (attention deficit/hyperactivity disorder), 10–11, 75–77, 197–98
  DSM-IV criteria for, 233–35
  medications, 239–40
  physical activity for, 77, 78–79, 91
  tracking problem behavior, 229–32
age-appropriate games, 109–10
aggressive behaviors (aggression), 49–73

appropriate social skills for young boys, 62–65
  in bad guy play, 131–32, 136–37
  empathy and, 59–61
  gender differences in conflict styles, 128–29, 167
  impulse control, 51–54
  practicing boundaries at home, 54–55
  practicing calm, 71–72
  reading social cues, 56–58
  at school, 65–73
    dealing with bully label, 65–67
    reasons for bullying behaviors, 68–69
  strategies for containing, 70–73
setting reminders, 70–71
sharing and turn taking, 58–59, 60
anger, 154–62
  in competition, 122–24
  headlines for managing, 161–62
  "I hate you," 156–58
  learning self-talk, 159–60
  plan for managing, 160–61

anger (*continued*)
  practicing calm, 71–72
  Time-Aways for controlling,
    102–6
angry area, 160
anniversary feelings, 192
anxiety
  bad guys and, 128, 129–30,
    143–44
  diagnostic approach to, 240–41
  about school, 44–47, 152–53,
    192–93
  separation, 44–47, 152–53
Asperger's syndrome, 19, 197–200
assessment. *See* diagnosis; testing
athletic games, 86–88, 121–22. *See
  also* team sports
attachment and separation, 42–44
attention problems, 75–91
  activities for, 76–77, 79–86
    older boys, 82–86
    younger boys, 80–82
  causes of movement, 91
  DSM-IV criteria, 233–34
  energy to burn, 77–79
  learning to sit still, 88–90
  myth of team sports, 86–88
  outdoor play benefits, 90–91
  signs of lack of enough movement,
    79–80
autism (autism spectrum disorders),
  196–97, 203
availability, with teacher, 184–85

bad guys (bad guy play), 127–45
  appropriate time for, 141–42
  benefits of being bad, 128–30
  consequences for, 141
  crossing the line, 138–40
  curiosity about disasters or scary
    true stories, 132–34

joining in, 134–36
  link between fear and, 143–44
  obsessing about play, 142–43
  role playing, 130–31
  setting limits, 136–38, 143
  violent toys, 131–32
ballroom dancing, 85–86
Barrel of Monkeys, 109
BASC-2 (Behavior Assessment
  System for Children), 233, 235,
  236
battle play. *See* fight play
bedtime fears, 143–44
behavioral adjustments, 171–72, 173
behavioral checklist, 1–3, 233–35
  for autism spectrum disorders, 197
behavioral setbacks, 26–27, 148–50,
  203
Behavioral Solutions, 2
behavioral therapy, 6–8, 12. *See also*
  Time-Aways
Behavior Assessment System for
  Children (BASC-2), 233, 235,
  236
bipolar disorder, 4, 10–11, 223
biting, 25–26
board games, 59–60, 108, 110–14
body language, 19, 32, 119
boundaries, 49–55
  impulse control, 51–54
  setting, 54–55, 70–71
brain development, gender differences in, 12, 18–22
breathing, flower, 71–72
bullying behaviors (bullies), 49–73
  appropriate social skills for young
    boys, 62–65
  defined, 67–68
  empathy and, 59–61
  impulse control, 51–54
  practicing boundaries at home,
    54–55

practicing calm, 71–72
reading social cues, 56–58
at school, 65–73
    dealing with bully label, 65–67
    reasons for, 68–69
    strategies for containing, 70–73
    setting reminders, 70–71
    sharing and turn taking, 58–59, 60
bullying label, 65–68, 71
burning off energy, 77–86
    activities for, 76–77, 79–86
        older boys, 82–86
        younger boys, 80–82
    myth of team sports for, 86–88
    signs of lack of enough movement,
        79–80

calming down
    for bullying behaviors, 71–72
    learning self-talk, 159–60
Candy Land, 112–13
categorization (categorizing infor-
        mation), gender differences in,
        22–24
changing schools, 218–20
cheating, 110, 118–21
    battling against disappointment,
        117–18
    developmental stages, 118–21
    first loss, 114–16
    losing gracefully, 116–17
chess, 119–21
classroom. *See* school
classroom accommodations, 205,
        215–18
    help in the classroom, 216–17
    more time for work, 216
    preferential seating, 216
    resource room, 217
    when to refuse, 217–18
classroom layout, 219

class sizes, 166, 210–17, 213, 220
clinginess, 44–47, 152–53
competition, 107–25
    age-appropriate games, 109–10
    battling against disappointment,
        117–18
    benefits of, 108–9
    cheating as developmental, 118–21
    gender differences in, 24
    keeping it fun, 110–12
    learning about winning and losing,
        112–17
        first loss, 114–16
        losing gracefully, 116–17
    need for mastery, 150–52
    older boys struggling with, 122–25
    team sports for, 86–88, 121–22
compulsive behaviors, 198, 224–26
concentration. *See* attention problems
conflict, role playing of, 130–31
conflict styles
    in the classroom, 167
    gender differences in, 128–29, 167
Conners, Keith, 233
Conners' Rating Scales-Revised
        (CRS-R), 233, 235, 236
consequences, for actions, 96–97,
        141, 171–72
consistency in actions, 96–97, 171–72
contrariness, 41, 189
controlling impulses, 51–54, 58–59,
        89
conversation. *See* talking
cooling down, 140. *See also* calming
        down; Time-Aways
cooperative play, 29–30, 33–34
    encouraging talking, 36–37
    failing to recognize, 39–40
co-teachers, 166, 216–17
crocodile tears, 147, 159
crossing the line, in bad guy play,
        138–40

crowded environments
  classrooms, 202, 216, 218
  gender differences in, 24–26
CRS-R (Conners' Rating Scales-
  Revised), 233, 235, 236

dance classes, 85–86
dancing, for burning off energy, 81,
  85–86
detention, 98–99
developmental setbacks, 26–27,
  148–50, 203
diagnosis, 223–42. *See also* testing
  criteria of symptom, 226–29
  failures of, 238
  ignoring language of, 201–2
  medications, 239–40
  misdiagnosis, 12–13, 230–32
  overdiagnosis, 1–4, 8–13
  quick culture of, 1–4
  rushing the, 237
  sadness and anxiety, 240–41
  second opinions, 238–39
  tracking problem behavior,
    229–32
  use of term, 223
*Diagnostic and Statistical Manual of
  Mental Disorders,* fourth edition
  (DSM-IV), 233–35
differential diagnosing, 233
dinner hour, practicing sitting still
  during, 88–90
disappointments, 108–9, 115–16
  battling against, 117–18
disasters, curiosity about, 132–34
discipline, 93–106. *See also* rule setting; taking objects away; Time-
  Aways; time-outs
  detention, 98–99
discipline fatigue, 97–98
distractions. *See* attention problems

drive-by school, at end of summer,
  193
Driven to Distraction (Ratey), 77
drugs. *See* medications
*DSM-IV (Diagnostic and Statistical
  Manual of Mental Disorders,* fourth
  edition), 233–35
dyslexia, 197

educational advocates, 220–21
educational assessments, 235–36
elementary school. *See* school
e-mail, with teachers, 177
emotional awareness, 38–39
emotional buttons, 23
emotional fragility. *See* fragility
empathy, 59–61
  boys as late bloomers, 60–61
  gender differences in, 22–23
  mothers and, 151–54
  with teachers, 176
empathy check, 153–54
energy to burn. *See* excess energy,
  burning off
esteem. *See* self-esteem
evaluations. *See* testing
exaggerated statements ("I hate
  you"), 156–58
excess energy, burning off, 77–86
  activities for, 76–77, 79–86
  older boys, 82–86
  younger boys, 80–82
  myth of team sports for, 86–88
  signs of lack of enough movement,
    79–80
excessive warnings with no follow-up
  punishment, 98
exercise balls, for fidgeting, 76–77
explosive child syndrome, 209–10
exposure and response prevention,
  225–26

expressive language, 31
eye contact, 32, 53–54
    in the classroom, 163, 165
    gender differences in, 18–20

facial expressions, 19, 32, 139
fairness, 58–59, 60
fairy tales, and violence, 128
fantasy play, 34–35. *See also* fight play
    gender differences in, 128–30
father-and-son bonding events and
    outings, 40
fear, and bad guys, 143–44
feather pillows, 160
feeling words, gender differences in,
    19
fidgeting, 75–91
    activities for, 76–77, 79–86
        older boys, 82–86
        younger boys, 80–82
    causes of, 91
    energy to burn, 77–79
    learning to sit still, 88–90
    myth of team sports, 86–88
    outdoor play benefits, 90–91
    signs of lack of enough movement,
        79–80
    strategies for, 76–77
fight play, 134–36
    appropriate time for, 141–42
    benefits of, 128–30
    consequences for, 141
    crossing the line, 138–40
    obsessing about, 142–43
    role playing, 130–31
    rules for joining, 135–36
    setting limits, 136–38, 143
first loss, in games, 114–16
flexibility, with teachers, 184–85
flower breathing, 71–72
fragility (fragile boys), 147–62

anger plan, 160–61
developmental setbacks, 148–50
empathy check, 153–54
exaggerated statements ("I hate
    you"), 156–58
headlines for managing, 161–62
learning self-talk, 159–60
mini-manipulators, 159
need for mastery, 150–52
separation anxiety, 152–53
withholding urge to mother,
    153–56
free play, 9
friendships. *See* social skills
frustrations, 149–56
    headlines for managing, 161–62
    learning self-talk, 159–60
    need for mastery, 150–52

games. *See also* competition; fight
    play; team sports
    age-appropriate, 109–10
    battling against disappointment,
        117–18
    benefits of, 108–9
    cheating as developmental, 118–21
    first loss, 114–16
    gender differences in, 21
    keeping it fun, 110–12
    learning about winning and losing,
        112–17
    losing gracefully, 116–17
    social interactions as, 21
gender differences, 17–27
    in brain development, 12, 18–22
    in conflict styles, 128–29, 167
    in emotional fragility, 154–56
    in eye contact, 18–20
    in fantasy play, 128–30
    in language acquisition, 20–21
    in physical activity, 21

gender differences (*continued*)
    in school, 164–68
    in socializing, 23–26
    in spatial awareness, 22
    in stress, 24–26
    in systems approach, 22–24
girls. *See* gender differences
good guys/bad guys. *See* bad guys
green advantage, of outdoor play,
    90–91
Groopman, Jerome, 230
gymnastics classes, 85

"Hansel and Gretel," 128, 144
Harry Potter, 143
headlines, 161–62
headstrong boys, in school, 186–89
home–school connection, 176–78,
    180
homework, exercise balls for,
    76–77
hyperactivity
    DSM-IV criteria, 234
    tracking behavior, 229–32
hyperactivity disorder. *See* ADHD

IEPs (individual education pro-
    grams), 5, 200–201, 217
"I hate you," 156–58
impulse control, 51–54, 58–59, 89
impulsivity
    DSM-IV criteria, 234
    tracking behavior, 229–32
inattention. *See* attention problems
individual education programs
    (IEPs), 5, 200–201, 217
Individuals with Disabilities Educa-
    tion Act (IDEA), 200
inflexibility, in the classroom,
    180–82

insecurity, of bullies, 67–68
intervention-style meetings,
    210–13

joining in boy's bad guy play,
    134–36

Kamphaus, Randy, 233
karate dancing, 81

labels. *See also* diagnosis
    for his emotions, 161–62
    at school, 180–82
        bully, 65–67, 71
language skills. *See also* talking
    bullying behaviors and, 69
    in the classroom, 166–67
    diagnosis, 196–97
    gender differences in, 20–21
    "I hate you," 156–58
    learning self-talk, 159–60
    socialization and, 31–32
learning disabilities, 197, 201
limits, in bad guy play, 135, 136–38,
    143
listening and observing, 32, 148
little warriors, 172–73
Lombardi, Vince, 109
loners. *See* shyness
losing, 112–17
    first loss, 114–16
    gracefully, 116–17
lunch programs, 218
lurking, 29, 41–42, 121

magical thinking, 133
male teachers, 9, 165–66
martial arts, 82–85

mastery, need for, 110, 114, 150–52
medications, 6–7, 9–10, 224, 239–40
  placebo effects, 241–42
meetings, 207–8, 210–13
mini-manipulators, 159
mini trampolines, for burning off energy, 81–82
misdiagnosis, 12–13, 230–32

name calling, 98
National Institute of Mental Health, 240
neuropsychological testing, 236–37
nighttime fears, 143–44
"nip it in the bud" theory, 237
No, David! (Shannon), 166
nonfantasy play, 34–35
note taking
  at parent-teacher conferences, 207–8
  tracking problem behavior, 229–32
"no touching" rule, 57–58, 64, 136, 228–29

object permanence, 45
obsessing about bad guy play, 142–43
obsessive-compulsive disorder (OCD), 224–26
oppositional disorders, 68
outdoor play, green advantages of, 90–91
overdiagnosis, 1–4, 8–13

parallel play, 33–34, 37–38
parent-teacher conferences, 185, 207–8

pathological anger, 4
patience, 72–73
  practicing sitting still, 89–90
  waiting in lines, 54, 59, 84
paying attention. *See* attention problems
peer pressure, 122
perfectionism, 159
persistence of behavior, as criteria for diagnosis, 226–27
personal boundaries. *See* boundaries
pharmaceuticals (medications), 6–7, 9–10, 224, 239–40
  placebo effects, 241–42
physical activities, 9. *See also* games
  for fidgeting, 76–77, 79–86
  older boys, 82–86
  younger boys, 80–82
  gender differences in, 21
physical aggression. *See* aggressive behaviors
pillows, feather, 160
placebo effects, and medications, 241–42
play, 33–36. *See also* bad guys (bad guy play); fight play
  actions leading to talking, 36–38
  determining style of, 35–36
  failing to recognize, 39–40
  gender differences in, 21, 128–30
  at school, 40–42
  social skills at, 33–36
playdates, appropriate social skills for, 62–64
practicing calm, for bullying behaviors, 71–72
praise (praising), 52, 90
preferential seating, in the classroom, 216
processing ability, in the classroom, 181–82

punishment, 93–106. *See also* rule
    setting; taking objects away;
    Time-Aways; time-outs
    detention, 98–99

rage. *See* anger
Ratey, John, 77
receptive language, 31
reciprocity, 58–59, 60
record keeping. *See* note taking
red flags, for autism spectrum disor-
    ders, 197
relational aggression, 167
relational styles, in the classroom,
    168
releasing energy, 77–86
    activities for, 76–77, 79–86
        older boys, 82–86
        younger boys, 80–82
repetitive activities, and encouraging
    talking, 37
resource rooms, 217
response to intervention (RTI), 201,
    213
reverse referencing, 56
rewards
    for behavioral adjustments, 89–90,
        169, 171–72, 173
    in the classroom, 169–73, 182–83
Reynolds, Cecil, 233
rhetorical questions vs. dealing with
    the behavior, 98
Ritalin, 240
role playing, 130–31
routine-oriented boys, 182
RTI (response to intervention), 201,
    213
rule setting
    for bad guy play, 135, 136–37, 139,
        140
    impulse control and, 53–54

making home more like school,
    172–73
practicing boundaries at home,
    54–55, 70
reading social cues, 57–58
    in simple games, 110–12

sadness, diagnostic approach to,
    240–41
safety rules, for bad guy play, 135,
    136–38
scary true stories, curiosity about,
    132–34
school, 163–94. *See also* teachers
    anxiety about, 44–47, 152–53,
        192–93
    behavioral adjustments, 171–72
    boosting behavior at, 168–71
    bullying at, 65–73
        dealing with bullying label,
            65–67
        defining bullies, 67–68
        reasons for behavior, 68–69
        strategies for containing, 70–73
    changing, 218–20
    classroom accommodations, 205,
        215–18
        when to refuse, 217–18
    drive-by, at end of summer, 193
    educational advocates, 220–21
    gender differences in, 164–68
    home's connection with, 172–73,
        176–78, 180
    individual education programs,
        200–201, 217
    labels, 180–82
        bully, 65–67
    male teachers at, 9, 165–66
    pressure to "fix" problems, 190–91
    response to intervention, 201, 213
    separation anxiety, 44–47, 152–53

situational problems in, 186–90
socializing in, 40–42
techniques for the classroom,
182–83
why it's not a good fit, 164–68
second opinions on diagnosis,
238–39
self-control, 51–54, 103–4. *See also*
impulse control
self-esteem, 110, 152
of bullies, 67–68
self-talk, 159–60
Sendak, Maurice, 102–3
sensory integration disorder, 231–32
separation anxiety, 44–47, 152–53
separation issues, 42–47
seriousness of behavior, as criteria
for diagnosis, 226
setting boundaries, 54–55, 70–71
setting limits, in bad guy play, 135,
136–38, 143
setting reminders, for bullying behaviors, 70–71
setting rules. *See* rule setting
shame, 93, 102, 139
sharing, 37–38, 58–61
Shaw, Philip, 240
shyness (shy boys), 19, 29–30
attachment and separation, 42,
43–44
at school, 168–71, 174–75, 178, 180
singing, for burning off energy, 81
sitting still, 88–90. *See also* fidgeting
in the classroom, 218
practicing, 89–90
small rewards, for behavioral adjustments, 169, 171–72, 173
soccer, 82, 85, 122–24
social awareness, 31–32, 38–39
social boundaries. *See* boundaries
social cues, 56–58
social referencing, 32–33, 46–47

social skills (socialization), 29–47
actions leading to talking, 36–38
appropriate for young boys,
62–65
attachment and separation,
42–47
empathy, 59–61
encouraging emotional awareness,
38–39
failing to recognize cooperative
play, 39–40
gender differences in, 18, 23–26
impulse control, 51–54
parameters for social success,
31–33
at play, 33–36
practicing boundaries at home,
54–55
reading social cues, 56–58
in school, 40–42
sharing and turn taking, 58–59, 60
solitary play, 33, 35
Sorry (game), 110–11
spatial awareness, 22, 31, 94
special education services, 4–5
sports. *See* team sports
sports camps, 87
Staats, Arthur, 99–100
staged errands, 59
Star Wars (movies), 127–28, 134
sticker charts, 169–70, 172, 173,
182–83
strange behaviors, for burning off
energy, 80–81
stress response, gender differences
in, 24–26
strong emotions ("I hate you"),
156–58
summer recess, end of, 191–93
summer sports camps, 87
super males, 17
swimming, 84–85

symptoms, 233–35
  for autism spectrum disorders,
    197
  criteria for diagnosis, 226–29
  use of term, 225
systems approach, 22–24

taking objects away, 96–98, 140, 141,
    156
talking (conversation), 31–32
  actions leading to, 36–38
  encouraging emotional awareness,
    38–39
  gender differences in, 20–21
  styles of play and, 35–36
  about teacher with your son, 179
teachers, 163–65
  behavioral updates from home for,
    208–9
  conferences with, 185, 207–8
  gender differences and school,
    164–66
  positive relationship with, 174–78,
    183–86
  talking to your son about, 179
  testing recommendations from,
    195–96, 203–4
teacher's aides, 216–17
team sports, 79, 121–22
  alternatives to, 82–86
  myth of, 86–88
teasing, 57, 66–67, 168
testing, 195–221, 232–37
  anxiety style of parents, 206–7
  diagnostic language, 201–2
  individual education programs,
    200–201, 217
  listening even when disagreeing
    with, 204–6
  meeting with school about, 207–8,
    210–13

reaction to need for, 203–6
reminder to parents about, 203–4
response to intervention, 201, 213
teacher recommendation for,
    195–96, 203–6
useful accommodations, 205,
    215–18
when it goes awry, 198–200
when it's helpful, 196–97
when it's not useful, 197–98,
    213–15
thin-skinned boys. *See* fragility
"Three Little Pigs," 128
Time-Aways, 102–6, 160
  boys as Wild Things, 102–3
  for learning self-control, 103–4
  long view on, 105–6
  making child stay put, 101–2
  time-outs vs., 99–101
time-outs, 52–53, 93–95
  disadvantages of, 95
  origins of use, 99–100
  Time-Aways vs., 99–101
Titanic, 133
touch, "no touching" rule for, 57–58,
    64, 136, 228–29
toy guns, 131–32
toys, taking away, as disciplinary
    action, 96–98, 140, 141, 156
tracking problem behavior, 229–32
turn taking, 58–59, 60

verbal aggression, 167
verbal skills. *See also* talking
  bullying behaviors and, 69
  in the classroom, 166–67
  diagnosis, 196–97
  gender differences in, 20–21
  "I hate you," 156–58
  learning self-talk, 159–60
  socialization and, 31–32

violent toys, 131–32
violent true stories, curiosity about,
    132–34

waiting in lines, 54, 59, 84
war games. *See* fight play
warnings with no follow-up punish-
    ment, 98
Wechsler Intelligence Scale for
    Children (WISC), 235–36
Wechsler Preschool and Primary
    Scale of Intelligence (WPPSI),
    235–36
Where the Wild Things Are (Sendak),
    102–3
winning, 107–25

age-appropriate games, 109–10
battling against disappointment,
    117–18
benefits of, 108–9
cheating as developmental,
    118–21
first loss, 114–16
gender differences, 24
keeping it fun, 110–12
learning about, 112–14
older boys struggling with
    competition, 122–25
team sports and, 86–88,
    121–22
WISC (Wechsler Intelligence Scale
    for Children), 235–36
Wolf, Montrose, 99–101